Introducing Charticulator for Power BI

Design Vibrant and Customized Visual Representations of Data

Alison Box

Apress®

Introducing Charticulator for Power BI: Design Vibrant and Customized Visual Representations of Data

Alison Box
Billingshurst, West Sussex, UK

ISBN-13 (pbk): 978-1-4842-8075-1   ISBN-13 (electronic): 978-1-4842-8076-8
https://doi.org/10.1007/978-1-4842-8076-8

Managing Director, Apress Media LLC: Welmoed Spahr
Acquisitions Editor: Joan Murray
Development Editor: Laura Berendson
Coordinating Editor: Jill Balzano

Cover image designed by Freepik (www.freepik.com)

Distributed to the book trade worldwide by Springer Science+Business Media LLC, 1 New York Plaza, Suite 4600, New York, NY 10004. Phone 1-800-SPRINGER, fax (201) 348-4505, e-mail orders-ny@springer-sbm.com, or visit www.springeronline.com. Apress Media, LLC is a California LLC and the sole member (owner) is Springer Science + Business Media Finance Inc (SSBM Finance Inc). SSBM Finance Inc is a **Delaware** corporation.

For information on translations, please e-mail booktranslations@springernature.com; for reprint, paperback, or audio rights, please e-mail bookpermissions@springernature.com.

Apress titles may be purchased in bulk for academic, corporate, or promotional use. eBook versions and licenses are also available for most titles. For more information, reference our Print and eBook Bulk Sales web page at http://www.apress.com/bulk-sales.

Any source code or other supplementary material referenced by the author in this book is available to readers on GitHub at https://github.com/Apress/introducing-charticulator-for-power-bi.

Printed on acid-free paper

To Stuart

Table of Contents

About the Author

 **Alison Box** is director of Burningsuit Ltd and an IT trainer and consultant with over 30 years of experience of delivering computer applications training to all skill levels, from basic users to advanced technical experts. Currently, she specializes in delivering training in Microsoft Power BI Service and Desktop, Data Modeling, DAX (Data Analysis Expressions), and Excel. Alison also works with organizations as a DAX and Data Analysis consultant. Part of her job role entails promoting Burningsuit as a knowledge base for Power BI and includes writing regular blog posts on all aspects of Power BI that are published on her website. When Charticulator was incorporated into Power BI in April 2021, she felt there was a need for more detailed documentation that takes the learner from no knowledge to being able to design complex and challenging visuals. With this in mind, she started to write a series of blog posts but soon realized the sheer weight of information regarding Charticulator had outgrown the blog post approach and that writing a book might be more helpful as a means to understanding Charticulator. This book is the result of her own journey of discovery in learning how to use Charticulator.

About the Technical Reviewer

Daniel Marsh-Patrick has been helping drive enterprise-wide solutions through process and software engineering for 20 years in the retail, healthcare, aged care, and environmental industries. He is experienced with the Microsoft data platform and has spent the last eight years specializing in Power BI modeling and development.

Daniel often writes, speaks, and presents on options and tooling for expanding the Power BI visual canvas, including getting the most out of Charticulator. He is an author of several Power BI custom visuals, a Power BI Community Super User, and Microsoft Data Platform MVP.

You can read Daniel's blog at `www.coacervo.co` or follow him on Twitter at @the_d_mp.

Acknowledgments

This book would never have seen the light of day if it hadn't been for my husband and colleague, Stuart Box. It was his idea that I might be interested in finding out about Charticulator. What he wasn't to know at that stage was that in doing so he would lose me to Charticulator for the next nine months, and so I am eternally indebted to him for his patience, understanding and support over this time. Many grateful thanks also go to my son and colleague, Alan Harman-Box, who took over many of my business and training commitments and so freed up my time to dedicate to writing this book.

I would also like to thank Daniel Marsh-Patrick, my technical reviewer, for his invaluable comments, suggestions, and contributions. Without his help, I would have felt that writing this book was truly a lone mission, but with his expert knowledge of Charticulator and his extensive technical expertise, he has provided additional credibility to the publication.

Lastly, I would like to thank both Joan Murray, the Apress Acquisitions Editor, who supported and steered me in the right direction when I first started writing and Jill Balzano, the Apress Development Editor, whose calm and professional approach made the publication process less daunting for me.

Introduction

Introducing Charticulator for Power BI is a comprehensive guide to using Charticulator as a custom visual inside Power BI Desktop. It will take you from zero knowledge to being able to create exciting, challenging, and complex visualizations that are impossible to generate using the default visuals of Power BI. It concentrates on the concepts that underpin the software, taking you through every building block of the chart design, enabling you to combine these constituent parts in limitless ways and so create any visual that best tells the story of your data.

The developers of Charticulator feel that their product should be intuitive and easy to use, but the very fact that you are reading this book proves that this is probably not the case. Charticulator has been called "the DAX of the charting world," implying that Charticulator has a simple interface hiding a complex methodology. However, if you want to understand Charticulator's core concepts, there are very few resources out there at the time of writing. This publication at last fills this dearth of information on Charticulator. I hope you will find it informative and enlightening, fulfilling its objective of enabling you to use Charticulator to its very best advantage.

This book is meant as a step-by-step guide to using Charticulator and assumes no prior knowledge of the product. The only precursor skill is being a competent user of Power BI Desktop. Being acquainted with data analysis precepts such as grouping and aggregating data would be an advantage as would a basic knowledge of Power BI data modeling. However, full explanations are always provided, and no specific knowledge is ever assumed.

The challenge in writing this book was to take you on a learning experience in a structured and logical manner. At first, there appeared to be no clear path through the acquisition of knowledge. This is because every aspect of Charticulator is interwoven with every other aspect, and to separate topics into stand-alone packages of knowledge was nigh impossible. The very nature of the software meant that I needed to include cross-referencing and many features of Charticulator are revisited a number of times, each time within a different context.

Having admitted this challenge to you however, you will find that within each chapter the book builds on the knowledge gained and skills learned. The book has been written on the assumption that you are reading it chapter by chapter, and so assumptions are also made regarding what you already know as we progress through the book. By the final chapters, you will have acquired the necessary knowledge to construct complex, intricate and truly customized visualizations.

In Chapters 1–3, I take you through the software interface and you will learn to build a simple chart using Charticulator. Once you have a useful chart up and running, we can start to explore together important ideas that underlie the software. You will understand how Charticulator differs from conventional chart design in that you don't start by dictating where fields will be placed in the chart, whether on the axis, in the legend, or comprising the values. Instead, you have the freedom to choose the role a field will play in the chart, change your mind and try out different permutations. This is what gives Charticulator its great design flexibility.

Through Chapters 4–7, you will discover the major drivers of the chart design and learn to fashion many different chart types. For instance, in Charticulator there is a major difference between point style and bar style charts, both these visual types requiring a completely different approach in how they are built. In these chapters, you will also learn that the key to designing your customized chart will be managing the chart's layout, whether you want bars, columns, a matrix, or a completely different approach instead such as cloud style or simply randomizing data points. In Chapter 8, we will take a break from designing visuals and learn to tackle Charticulator's expression language, known as "d3-format." This will enable you to have more control over how numerical data is formatted within the chart.

You will probably find that Chapter 9 contains the most challenging content, and it was certainly the most challenging chapter for me to write. Here, we tackle learning how Charticulator's scales work. You may think that a scale defines the magnitude of how numerical data is represented. In Charticulator, the scale has a much wider interpretation and includes controlling colors used to decode data as well as controlling how numerical values are plotted on the chart. I hope that I've done this chapter justice as understanding Charticulator's scales will be a milestone on your journey; at last, the software will start to make sense, and what you thought were bizarre behaviors will no longer seem so strange.

By the time you reach Chapter 11, you are well on the way to being able to generate more challenging visuals that combine "charts within charts" and complex glyphs. From this chapter onward, you will have learned the skills to build many diverse visualizations. Chapter 13, for instance, takes you through the creation of circular charts, known as "polar" charts, and in Chapter 14, you will be able to generate box and whisker, tornado, bullet charts, and many more using Charticulator's data axis. Chapter 15 will find you exploring the makings of co-occurrence, chord, area, and Sankey charts that all use Charticulator's links feature. Towards the end of the book, you will understand how Charticulator visuals can integrate with Power BI and how your consumers can use these visuals seamlessly within your report.

The last chapter looks at taking your newly acquired expert knowledge of Charticulator to a higher level and using it in more inventive and inspirational ways. The types of visuals we look at designing in this chapter have all been recommended as powerful visualizations by Steve Wexler in his book *The Big Picture* (published by McGraw Hill, 2021). You will find that DAX code is used extensively and so having knowledge of DAX would be beneficial when working through this content. However, it's not mandatory to understand the details of the code to benefit from the information contained in the chapter. The objective is to illustrate the potential of using Charticulator in creative ways and not to teach you how to use DAX.

Following this introduction, I've included an index to the various chart types and visualizations that we explore creating in this book, with references to the figures where you'll find them. This index includes only the visuals to which I could put a name! This book will give you the skills to build any variation or combination of these visualizations.

To follow along with the examples presented in this book, you will need very simple generic data. For most of the time, all you need is a numerical field and two categorical fields, for example, I use just the following fields from my data model: "Sales," "Year," and "Salespeople." Where a visual requires specific data, the fields used are shown within a screenshot, but the difference in the data is usually only a matter of the number of numerical or categorical fields rather than any specifics within the data itself.

Charticulator, along with Power BI itself, is an ever-developing platform. Each month, new features and updates come along. However, the core elements of Charticulator that are the focus of the book remain constant, and even though some screenshots shown may vary slightly from your experience, this will not detract from the information therein.

INTRODUCTION

The writing of this book reflects my own personal experience of learning how to use Charticulator. I remember how I felt the first time I opened it up and attempted to work with it. I didn't get very far and was very near to giving up completely. Well, I didn't give up and stuck with it, but I felt pretty much on my own. You don't need to have this same experience because I've done all the hard graft for you. I hope through reading this book, you will learn to appreciate what Charticulator can do for you personally and appreciate that it's all to do with generating visuals that are unique to your requirement. The challenge of learning how to build customized visualizations using Charticulator is well worth the effort because once you've mastered its intricacies, you will only be limited by your imagination. Your visualizations will no longer be an approximation of what you want, a necessary compromise if you like, but will be exactly what you are looking to achieve.

I hope through reading this book, you enjoy your own personal learning journey through Charticulator.

Visual Index to Chart Types

Chart Type	Figure References	Chart Type	Figure References
Column	1-6, 2-3, 2-6, 2-17, 3-9, 3-14	Matrix	3-15, 5-18, 6-12, 7-12
Area	15-7	Nightingale	13-15
Arrow	19-16	Peacock	13-14
Bar	5-11	Pie	13-6
Box and whisker	14-21	Proportion plot	15-13
Bubble	4-8	Radar	13-19
Bullet	14-15, 14-17	Radial	13-16, 13-17
Chord	15-21	Ribbon	16-6, 15-11
Cloud	5-22	Rose	13-13
Clustered column	14-5	Sankey	15-23
Combination	11-4, 11-6, 11-10, 11-12, 15-15, 19-1	Scatter	4-8, 5-23, 12-9
Co-occurrence	15-16	Slope	16-6, 16-8
Custom curve	13-22	Small multiples	6-14, 6-15, 17-9
Donut	13-3	Spiral	13-27
Dumbbell	14-18	Stacked bar	5-13
Flag matrix	3-17	Stacked column	5-12, 5-15, 14-18
Jitter plot	5-24, 19-11	Tornado	14-23
Line	4-7, 5-40, 19-5, 19-9	Waterfall	12-2
Lollipop	2-18		

CHAPTER 1

Introduction to Charticulator

With Charticulator's recent (April 2021) integration into Power BI, you can now build customized charts, graphs, and data visualizations right inside Power BI. In the most fundamental of terms, Charticulator has a simple interface that hides a complex methodology under the hood.

Its greatest value is its immense power to generate a whole host of different visuals and graphics. The challenge is that there is a myriad of settings and options that can be combined in what appears to be limitless confusing combinations, making it intimidating to many. Unlike other custom Power BI visuals, Charticulator runs in a separate application window within Power BI with its own user interface, and therefore it requires a completely different set of interactions and associated knowledge.

In this chapter, we are going to get started with Charticulator. We will begin by importing Charticulator into Power BI; we'll create a simple chart and take a tour of the Charticulator screen. Before we begin however, I want you to forget everything you think you know about creating charts and visuals where you are constrained by the limits of what you can plot on an x- or y-axis or the number of categories that you can use. Instead, think in terms of designing a representation of your data from scratch, where you are no longer restrained by your choice of visual.

Importing Charticulator in Power BI

The first step is to import Charticulator into Power BI as a custom visual. You then need to ensure that it's available in all Power BI reports you generate or edit. To import Charticulator into Power BI, in Power BI Desktop click the ellipsis at the bottom of the Visualizations gallery and click **Get more visuals** as shown in Figure 1-1. This will take you to the Microsoft Power BI Visuals App Store.

© Alison Box 2022
A. Box, *Introducing Charticulator for Power BI*, https://doi.org/10.1007/978-1-4842-8076-8_1

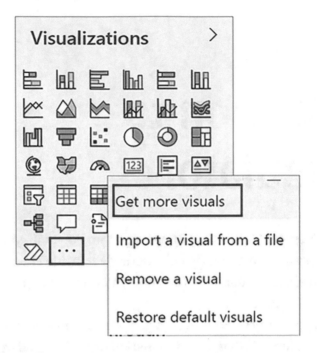

Figure 1-1. *Accessing the App Store*

In the App Store, use the Search box top right of the dialog to search for Charticulator and then click the Charticulator tile as shown in Figure 1-2.

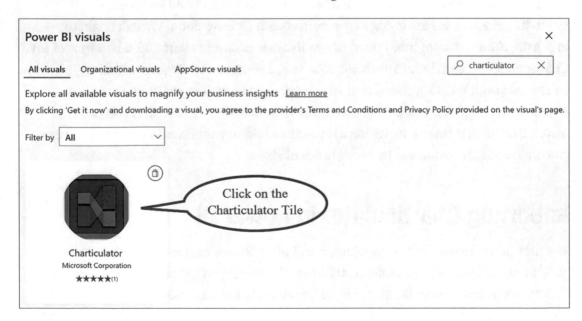

Figure 1-2. *Select the Charticulator custom visual in the App Store*

A window opens detailing the Charticulator custom visual. Click **Get it Now**, and when the visual has been successfully imported into your Power BI Desktop report, you'll see the dialog in Figure 1-3.

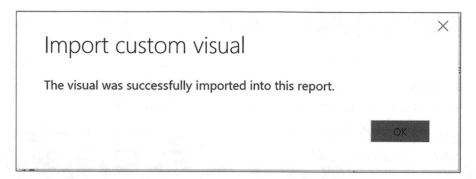

Figure 1-3. *Charticulator has been successfully imported*

To ensure that Charticulator is available in all new reports, right-click on the Charticulator icon in the Visualizations gallery and click **Pin to visualizations pane** as shown in Figure 1-4.

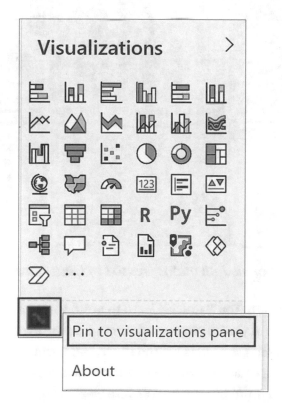

Figure 1-4. *Pinning Charticulator to the Visualizations gallery*

Now that you have successfully imported Charticulator into Power BI, let's move on to create a chart.

Create a Charticulator Chart

With Charticulator safely installed in Power BI, you can now start designing stunning visuals. In Figure 1-5, you can see to what I'm alluding. In the following chapters, these are the varieties of charts and visualizations that you will learn to build.

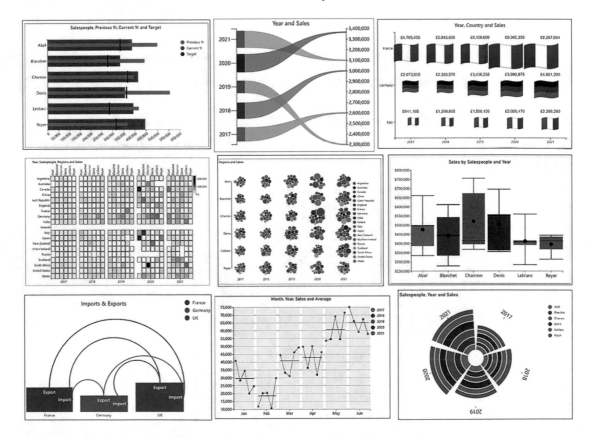

Figure 1-5. *Examples of visualizations created in Charticulator*

But here's the heads-up. You'll quickly learn to build some of these visuals, but as for the others, it won't be until you've progressed through to the final chapters of this book that you'll have discovered the secrets behind those, but it will be well worth the effort. When I first started using Charticulator, I thought it was like trying to rein in a willful child. I would think my commands to the software were clear, but it would be doing the contrary, and I would think, what on earth is going on here? You will see what I mean when you try using Charticulator for yourself. It takes time to understand this wayward piece of software, but it is worth the investment and the return is high. Stick with it and you too will soon be designing innovative visuals.

That's the end of my lecture! It's time to get to work. Let's start out by creating a very simple and unspectacular clustered column chart as shown in Figure 1-6.

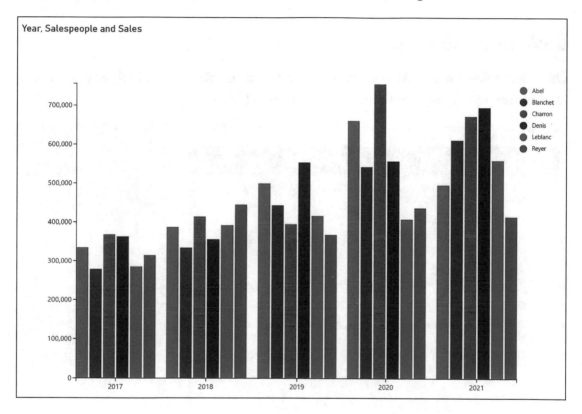

Figure 1-6. *Your first Charticulator chart*

I know you're thinking, but I could easily create this chart in Power BI so why would I want to use Charticulator? I take your point, but remember what we said earlier, that Charticulator has a challenging methodology to get to grips with. However, if you start by creating a chart you can easily produce elsewhere, it'll give you some context on which to hang your hat, and then you'll be ready to move on and explore the more challenging concepts that underpin Charticulator.

If you want to follow along and create a similar chart yourself, all you need are three fields from your data model, two categorical fields and one numerical field, for example, we're using "Year," "Salespeople," and "Sales." The numerical field can be a numerical column or an explicit measure.

Now let's fire up Charticulator! First, click the Charticulator icon in the Visualizations gallery to generate a placeholder for the visual on the Power BI canvas.

Selecting the Data

Drag all the fields you want to use in your chart from the Fields pane in Power BI into the Data bucket of the Visualizations pane as shown in Figure 1-7.

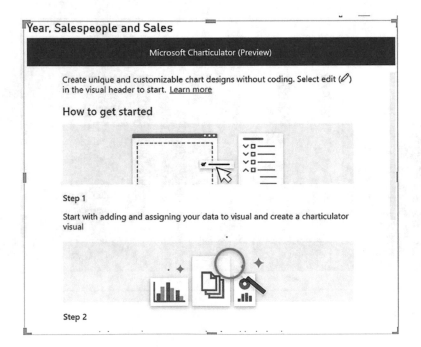

Figure 1-7. *Charticulator placeholder with fields in the Data bucket*

You may feel that putting all your fields into a *single* bucket is a rather odd thing to do, and certainly this got me puzzled too when I was new to Charticulator. In Power BI chart visuals, shouldn't there always be a "Values" bucket for numerical fields alongside buckets such as "Axis" and "Legend" for categorical fields? You can see an example of this in Figure 1-8 that shows the Power BI visual that plots the same data.

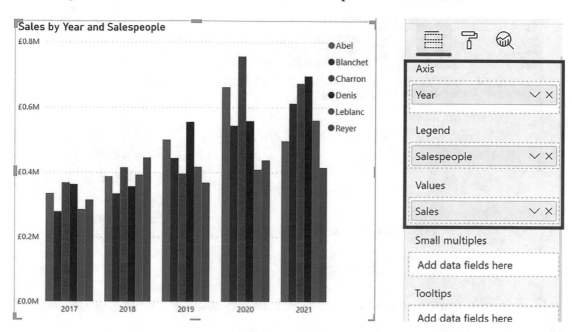

Figure 1-8. *Power BI visual with "categorical" and "values" buckets*

After all, don't all Power BI visuals group and then aggregate data? In Charticulator, there is no concept of constraining fields to behave as a "value" or a "category." However, if this is the case, how does Charticulator know which fields are to be plotted as values and which are to categorize the data? This question will be answered when we look at Charticulator's Fields pane (see the section on "The Fields Pane" below).

Opening Charticulator

Let's get back to creating the chart. In the Charticulator placeholder, click the **More Options** button at the top right of the visual and select **Edit** as shown in Figure 1-9.

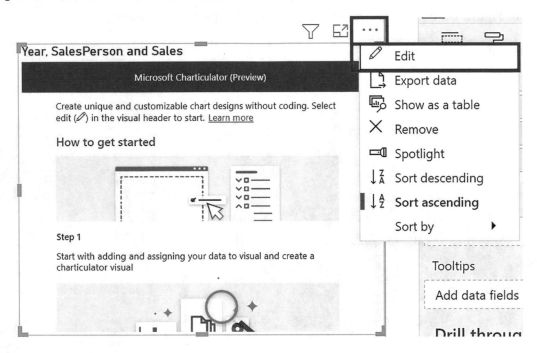

Figure 1-9. *The Edit option on the Options button*

The Charticulator placeholder will expand to fill the Power BI canvas. Click the **Create chart** button, and this will open Charticulator as shown in Figure 1-10.

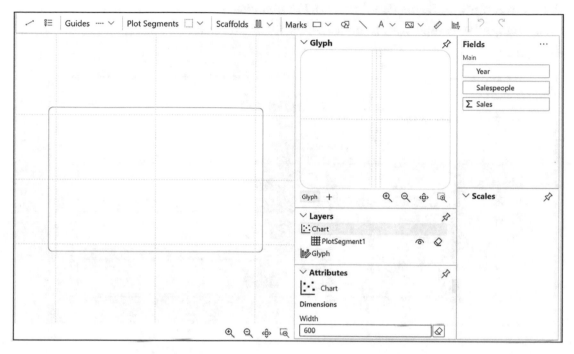

Figure 1-10. *The Charticulator screen*

Designing the Chart

Now that we've got Charticulator open, we can start to construct the chart as shown in Figure 1-6.

Note   The purpose of this exercise is for you to have a Charticulator chart up and running quickly so that we can use it as the basis for the examples that follow. Because your knowledge of Charticulator is as yet limited, I'll be keeping explanations to a minimum, appreciating that at this stage you probably won't understand how it all works. Don't worry, everything will be explained over the next few chapters and beyond.

Before we start piecing the chart together, just ensure the fields that will categorize your data don't have a sigma beside their name in the Fields pane (more on this later, see the section on "The Fields Pane" below). For instance, in our data the "Year" field needs to be changed to categorical. To do this, click the sigma and select categorical, as shown in Figure 1-11.

Figure 1-11. *Changing a numerical field to a categorical field*

The first step in designing any Charticulator chart is rendering the *glyph*. The glyph is the visual representation of your data in the chart. In our chart, the glyph will be a simple rectangle shape that represents the columns of the clustered column chart.

From the toolbar at the top, start by clicking the **Marks** button that shows a rectangle shape. You can then drag and drop the rectangle into the Glyph pane as shown in Figure 1-12. Note how the area into which you can drop the mark is highlighted in orange.

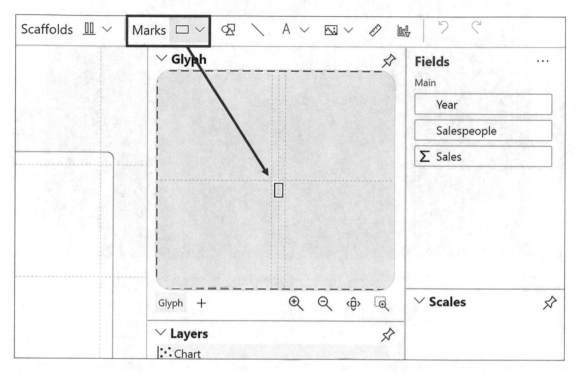

Figure 1-12. *Dragging the mark into the Glyph pane*

On the chart canvas, you will now see a rectangle for every combination of category; see Figure 1-13.

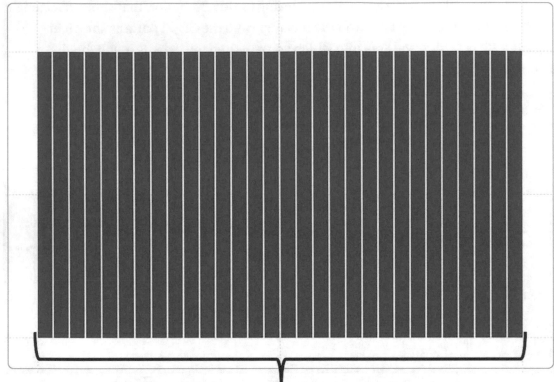

A rectangle for every combination of category
e.g. 5 Years and 6 Salespeople = 30 glyphs

Figure 1-13. *Glyphs are repeated on the chart canvas for every category*

To categorize the rectangles on the x-axis, drag a categorical field from the Fields pane onto the x-axis in the chart canvas. The x-axis will highlight in orange when you're ready to drop the field. For example, we've dragged the "Year" field onto the x-axis, and the rectangles are categorized into years; see Figure 1-14.

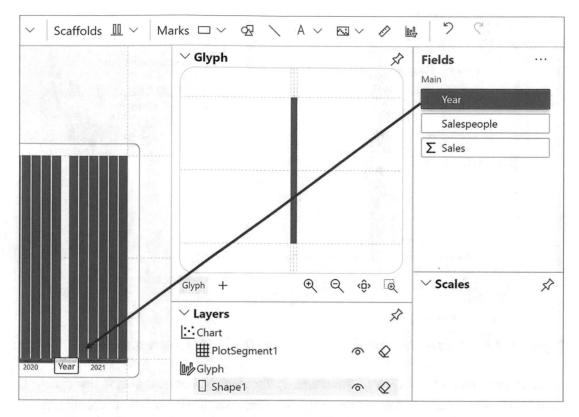

Figure 1-14. *Drag and drop a category onto the x-axis*

At this point, the rectangles on the chart canvas are all the same height, but their heights should reflect the values in the numerical field. Drag your numerical field, for example, the "Sales" field, from the Fields pane onto the rectangle in the Glyph pane, dropping it where it shows the "HEIGHT" line as shown in Figure 1-15. Notice again that the orange highlight indicates where you need to drop the field. The height of the rectangles now reflects the sales values.

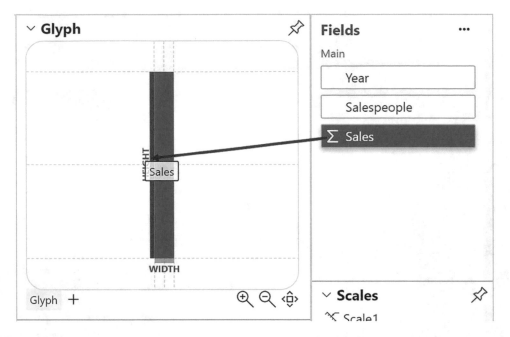

Figure 1-15. *Drag a numerical field onto the HEIGHT of the rectangle*

Each rectangle on the canvas represents a subcategory. For example, in our chart, each rectangle represents a salesperson in each year. We need to color the rectangles accordingly. To do this, make sure you have clicked the rectangle in the Glyph pane. In the Attributes pane at the bottom of the screen, you will find a "Fill" attribute, under the Style group (you may need to scroll down the pane). Drag and drop your category, "Salespeople" in our case, into this attribute; see Figure 1-16.

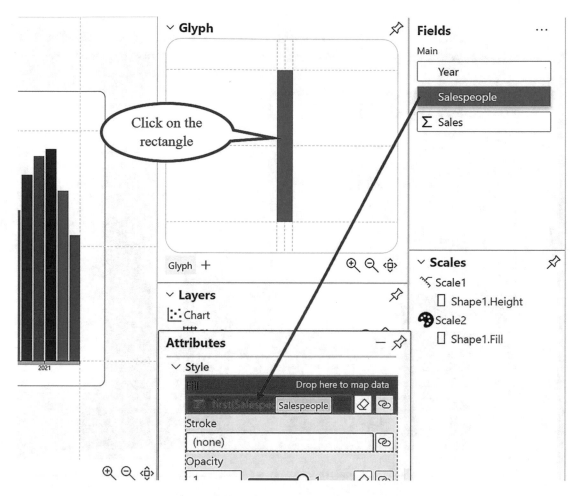

Figure 1-16. *Attributing a color to each rectangle on the chart canvas*

The last step in generating our clustered column chart is to add a "value" axis on the left of the chart so we can understand the numerical values being plotted. To create the y-axis scale, you need to insert a *legend*. I know it sounds bizarre that a numerical y-axis is referred to as a "legend" but just stick with it for now. We'll be exploring Charticulator's legends in more detail in later chapters.

Click the **Legend** button on the top toolbar; select your numerical field, for example, "Sales"; and click **Create Legend** as shown in Figure 1-17. Don't worry if the legend spills off the canvas. We can adjust this when we explore the chart canvas in our tour around the screen (see below).

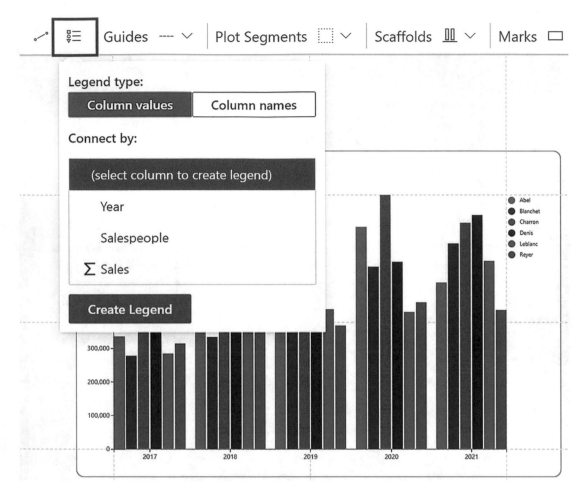

Figure 1-17. *Inserting Charticulator legends*

You can also use this method to create a legend to explain category colors, for example, a legend for the "Salespeople" field, and this will be placed top right of the chart.

Saving the Chart in Power BI

Now click the **Save** button top left of Charticulator's screen and click **Back to Report** at the very top left of the screen.

Congratulations! You have just created your very first Charticulator chart in Power BI. I hope it's very similar to the one shown in Figure 1-18.

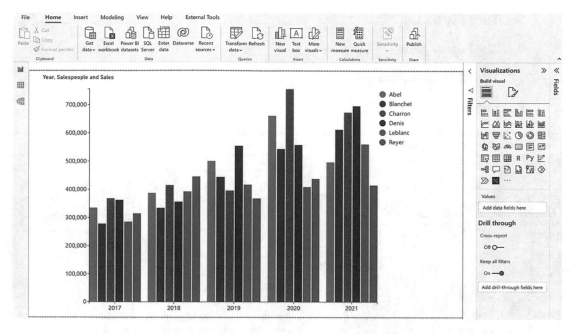

Figure 1-18. *Your first Charticulator chart in Power BI*

Tour of the Charticulator Screen

Now that we have a chart up and running inside Charticulator, we can take a trip around each of the panes of the screen, meeting the components that comprise a Charticulator chart. Please understand, however, that we're only at the very tip of the iceberg of our knowledge. Many of the elements of Charticulator that we encounter now we will revisit in much greater detail in future chapters.

We will start by moving back into Charticulator from Power BI. Use the **More Options** button of the visual and click **Edit**.

The Charticulator panes and parts of the screen that we will be exploring are numbered in Figure 1-19 and are as follows:

1. The chart canvas

2. The Fields pane

3. The Glyph pane

4. The Layers pane

5. The Attributes panes

6. The Scales pane

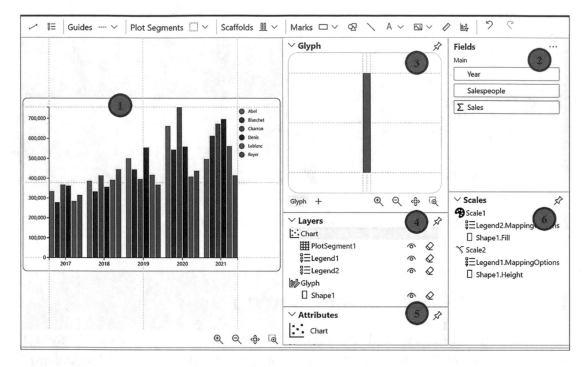

Figure 1-19. *The panes of the Charticulator screen*

You can now work with the panes in the following ways:

- Click the pushpin top right of a pane to undock it, and you can then drag on the top edge of a pane to reposition it.

- Minimize an undocked pane by clicking the minimize button top right. Click again to unminimize.

- Resize an undocked pane by dragging on the bottom-right corner. You will find being able to enlarge the Glyph pane is a great benefit when you are working with many shapes that comprise the glyph.

However, you can't undock the Fields pane.

The Chart Canvas

On the left of the screen is the chart itself sitting on the chart canvas. Notice the faint gray lines, known as *guides,* that define the margin space. We will be looking at using guides in more detail in later chapters, but for now, if you want to change the margin space, drag on one of these guides. Other places where you can drag to manage the canvas are shown in Figure 1-20.

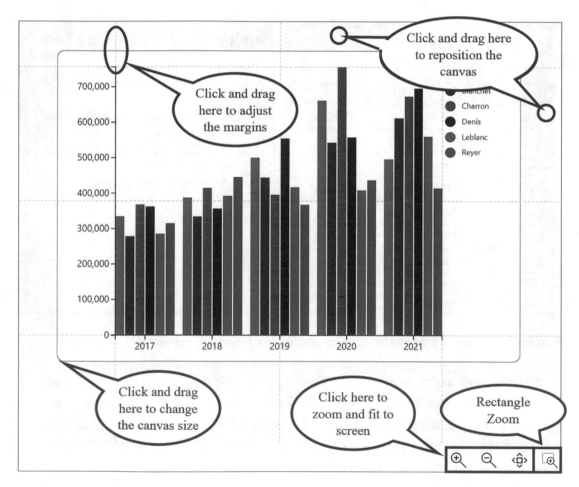

Figure 1-20. *Managing the canvas*

The rectangle zoom button bottom right of the canvas pane can be used as another means to zoom in. To use the rectangle zoom, simply drag over the area of the canvas you want to zoom in on.

You can also use the Attributes pane of the chart to make these adjustments. See the section on "The Attributes Panes" below.

The Fields Pane

This pane lists the fields you are using or want to use in your chart. If you click the ellipsis top right of the pane, a table pops out that shows the data Charticulator will use in the construction of your chart. An example of this table is shown in Figure 1-21, and you can see that it looks very similar to a Table visual in Power BI. In fact, it often helps to imagine that your Charticulator chart is built on top of a Power BI Table visual.

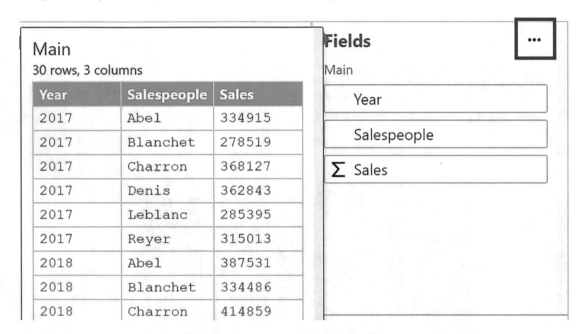

Figure 1-21. *The Fields list showing the table of underlying data*

It's important to understand how Charticulator views the underlying data. Nearly all Power BI chart visuals contain a "Values" bucket where the numerical fields to be aggregated are placed alongside "Axis" and "Legend" buckets that contain fields that group and categorize the data. However, with Charticulator you put all your fields into a *single* Data bucket. You can see this difference in Figure 1-22.

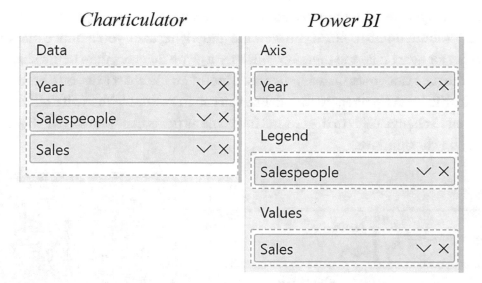

Figure 1-22. *Comparing the buckets in Power BI charts to Charticulator charts*

With this in mind, how is Charticulator going to treat the data? It's not always the case that you want a numerical column to be the "value" and be summarized. For example, you wouldn't want to sum a field that contains peoples' ages or indeed sum the year values of our chart. Charticulator will make assumptions about your data, and you can see this from the symbol that sits beside the field name in the Fields pane. A sigma indicates a numerical field type. This can be either a numerical column in your data model or an explicit measure. These will provide the values that will be associated with numerical "attributes" of the chart and glyph (see the section on "The Attributes Panes" below). Text type fields will usually provide the categories but so do some numerical fields. You may recall that when we were creating our clustered column chart earlier, we needed to change the numerical "Year" field, so it behaved as a category. We did this by clicking the sigma in the Fields list; see Figure 1-11. You may need to make similar changes to your fields.

The thing to note here is that with Charticulator, you don't start by dictating where the field will be placed in the chart, whether it's on the axis, in the legend, or comprises the values. Instead, you assign it a *behavior* through the field type. This means that you have the freedom to choose the role a field will play in the chart, change your mind, and try out different permutations. This is what gives Charticulator its great design flexibility.

There are two more field types: ordinal and temporal. You will meet these if you use a field of a date data type or use a Power BI date hierarchy in the Fields pane. You can see in Figure 1-23 that we have used a date field called "SALEDATE" and that "SALEDATE" is a temporal type field. You can also see that you get the dates categorized by "Year," "Month," "Month number," etc. If you view the underlying data, you'll notice that you have a row for every date and therefore will have a glyph for every date in the chart. You can use the date categories instead, such as "Month" on the chart axes, but there is no ability to drill down from year to month like you can in Power BI. You will find that you don't need to change fields to the ordinal field type as fields like "Month" will be sorted correctly on clicking **Save**.

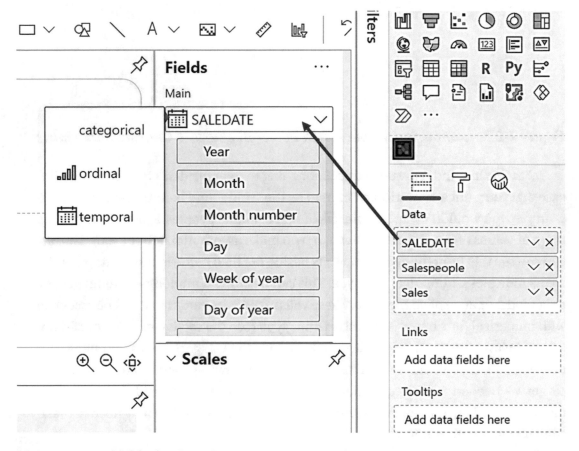

Figure 1-23. *Field of a date data type in the Fields pane*

If you are using a Power BI date hierarchy, all the members of the hierarchy will have a temporal field type which are best changed to categorical field types. Using just the "Year" member from a date hierarchy will be plotted in the same way as the "Year" categorical field in our example data.

One last thing to note regarding the Fields pane is that the order in which the fields are listed in the Fields pane can be important because it determines the categorization of the data. If you don't put a categorical field on the x-axis, the first field is taken as the main category, and subsequent fields are subcategories. This is the effect of Power BI's sort order as shown in the **Options** button top right of the visual. To change the order, you can use the Options button as usual, or you can simply swap the fields in the Data bucket. You can see this difference in Figure 1-24.

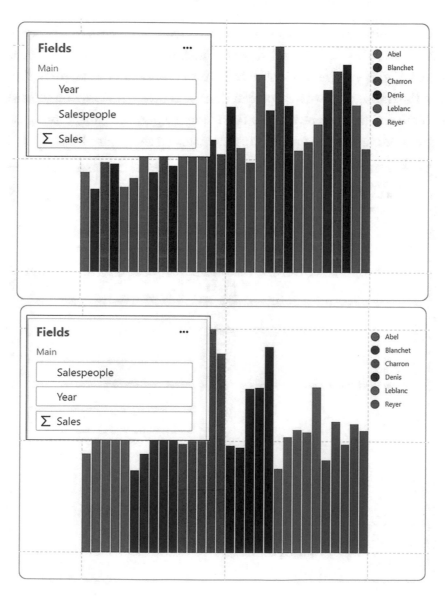

Figure 1-24. *The order of the Fields determines the categorization*

However, once you have selected your sort order in the Options button, rearranging the fields in the Data bucket will have no effect because the sorting is now determined by the selection in the Options button.

Glyphs and the Glyph Pane

Next up is the Glyph pane where you design your glyph. The glyph that we're using in our chart is a rectangle shape. In fact, a glyph can comprise a variety of shapes, symbols, lines, and text marks, and we will look at building a more complex glyph in the next chapter. For the moment however, you can think that the glyph is synonymous with the rectangle shape and that will be fine. You can drag the pane around, zoom in, and use the rectangle zoom just as you can on the chart canvas; see Figure 1-25.

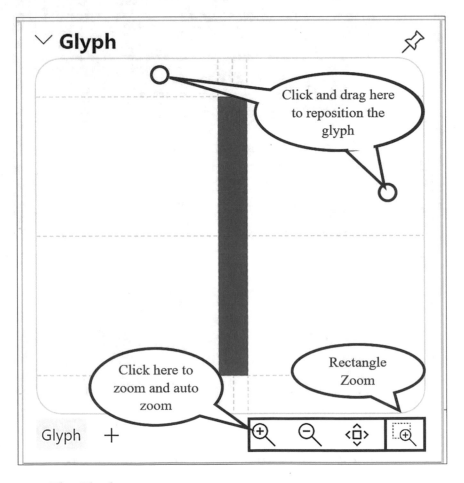

Figure 1-25. *The Glyph pane*

The glyph in the Glyph pane by default represents the values in the first row of the underlying data. In our chart, this would be the sales for salesperson "Abel" in 2017, and so the rectangle mark is colored blue and sized accordingly, as shown in Figure 1-26.

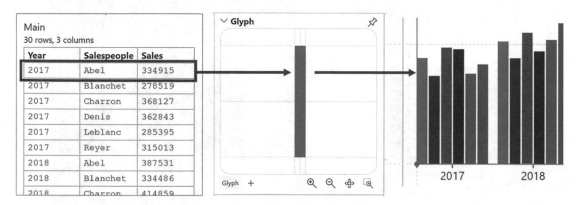

Figure 1-26. *The glyph represents the first row of your data*

Consequently, you need to be vigilant if the first row of your data contains very small values in relation to other values or even contains zero. In this scenario, the glyph in the Glyph pane will be so small; it may not even show.

Note   There is an exception to the glyph representing the first row. If you group a field, the glyph will represent the grouped data. We look at grouping data in a later chapter.

However, clicking a glyph in the chart canvas changes the glyph represented in the Glyph pane. For example, clicking the column for salesperson "Charron" in 2017 would change the glyph in the Glyph pane. See Figure 1-27.

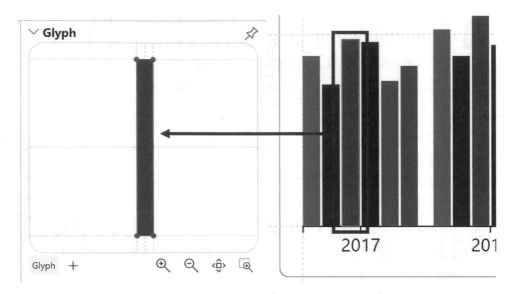

Figure 1-27. *The glyph represented in the Glyph pane can be changed*

On the chart canvas, the glyph is repeated for every row in the underlying data. For example, in our data, we have six salespeople and five years, so we get 30 glyphs in our chart, each representing the sales for each salesperson in each year.

The Layers Pane

The Layers pane lists every element that currently comprises the chart and the glyphs (as we will see, it's possible to have multiple glyphs). It can contain some or all of the elements listed in Table 1-1, and you can have many of each element in both the chart and the glyph.

Table 1-1. *Chart and glyph elements that are listed in the Layers pane*

Chart	Glyph
Plot segment	Shape (i.e., a mark)
Link	Line
Legend	Symbol
Text mark	Guide or guide coordinator
Guide or guide coordinator	Text mark
Shape	Data axis
Symbol	Icon
Line	
Data axis	
Icons	
Images	

You can see an example of elements listed in the Layers pane in Figure 1-28.

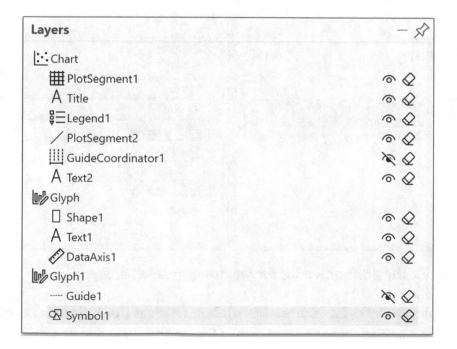

Figure 1-28. *The Layers pane*

You can hide or delete each element by using the "eye" and "eraser" buttons, respectively.

The order of the elements in the pane is important because it determines the stacking or "Z" order of the elements on the canvas or in the Glyph pane. You can change the "Z" order by dragging and dropping an element to change its position in the list. This is synonymous with "send backward" or "bring forward" that you may have met in other applications.

The Attributes Panes

The Attributes panes list all the *attributes* of the currently selected Layer. For example, to show the attributes of the rectangle shape sitting in the Glyph pane, select "Shape1" in the Layers pane, and the Attributes pane will show the attributes for "Shape1," as shown in Figure 1-29. You can also just click on a chart element on the canvas or in the glyph pane to show the attributes for that element.

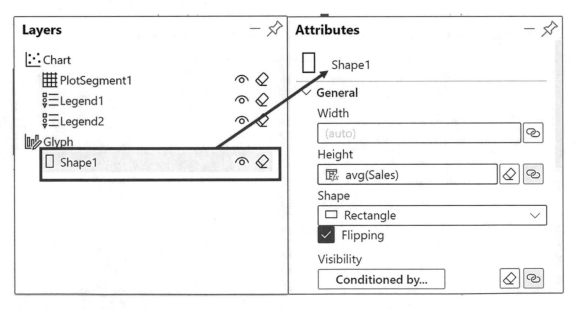

Figure 1-29. *The Attributes pane for the currently selected layer*

The rectangle shape, for instance, has attributes such as Height, Width, Length, and Fill color. The chart has attributes such as Dimensions, Margins, and Background. You populate and edit these attributes to render the specific visual you require. This is why we populated the Fill attribute of "Shape1" with the "Salespeople" field to color the rectangles according to each salesperson. We will be looking more closely at the attributes of each chart and glyph element in succeeding chapters.

It's in the Attributes panes that you can rename elements of the chart listed in the Layers pane. For example, a glyph can comprise multiple marks and symbols with different data associated with each mark or symbol. In this scenario, "Shape1" might be better renamed something like "Rectangle for Sales." In the Attributes pane for "Shape1", you can click into the Name attribute and rename accordingly; see Figure 1-30.

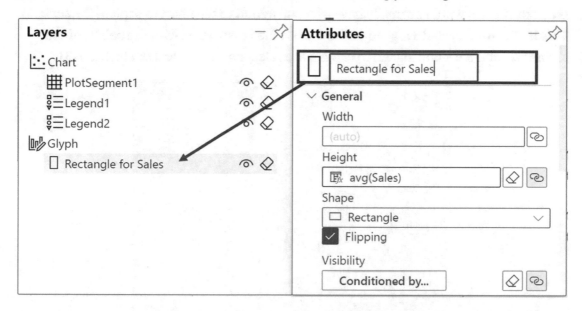

Figure 1-30. *You can rename chart and glyph elements in the Attributes pane*

In fact, you will find that every element of a Charticulator chart can be renamed using the Attributes pane.

The Scales Pane

The Scales pane lists all Charticulator's *scales* used by the chart. Scales are usually created for you, and then if required, you will need to create a legend explaining the scale. Scales in Charticulator can be challenging to understand when you're just starting out, and we will dedicate a whole chapter to learning about them.

The problem is that you may think a scale is something that describes the magnitude of the units being used in a chart. This is not the case with Charticulator's scales which have a much wider interpretation. In Charticulator, a scale is automatically generated when a field is associated with an attribute of a mark, symbol, or line that comprises the glyph. For example, we have associated the "Sales" field with the Height attribute of the rectangle mark, and this has generated "Scale1" with the "Shape1.Height" property in the Scales pane. We have also associated the "Salespeople" field with the Fill color attribute of the rectangle mark, and this has generated "Scale2" with the "Shape1.Fill" property. Scales would normally have a legend added to the chart to explain the scale. This is why we inserted a legend to show the values associated with the height of the rectangles and a second legend to explain the salespeople's colors; see Figure 1-31.

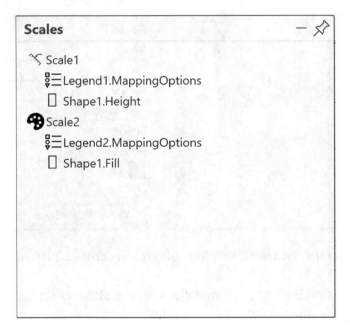

Figure 1-31. *The Scales pane*

We will deep dive into the subject of Charticulator's scales and legends in Chapter 9.

This completes our tour of the Charticulator screen, and hopefully you're now conversant with all the different panes and are comfortable finding your way around the user interface. In this chapter, you also created your first Charticulator chart and learned what a glyph is and how the scales in the Scales pane are generated. In the next chapter, we focus on the glyph and take a detailed look at its composition discovering that a glyph can comprise more than just a simple and predictable rectangle shape.

CHAPTER 2

Marks, Symbols, and Lines

In the previous chapter, you learned that the glyph in the Glyph pane represents the first row of the underlying data, and in the chart itself, the glyph is repeated for each row of the data. However, up to now our glyph has comprised a single rectangle shape, which is somewhat uninspiring as far as designing charts in Charticulator is concerned, especially when you learn that glyphs can be made up of any or all of the following:

- Marks (rectangle, ellipse, or triangle)

- Symbols (circle, square, cross, diamond, etc.)

- Lines

- Text marks

- Icons or images

In this chapter, we're going to look at how we can construct more inspirational glyphs using these different elements. We will start again with the rather lackluster chart in Figure 2-1 and explore ways to liven it up using different shapes, symbols, and lines.

© Alison Box 2022
A. Box, *Introducing Charticulator for Power BI*, https://doi.org/10.1007/978-1-4842-8076-8_2

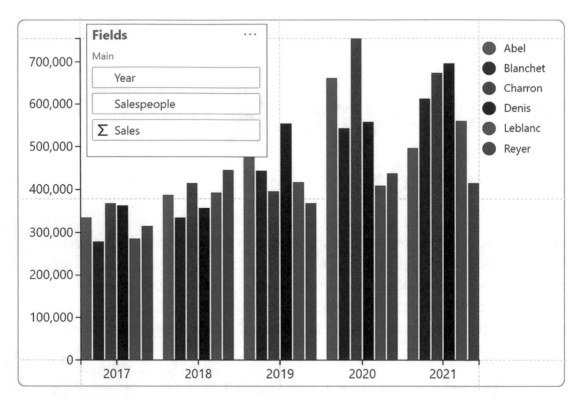

Figure 2-1. *An uninspiring Charticulator chart*

At present, this chart comprises a simple rectangle shape in the Glyph pane.

Marks

A glyph can comprise one or many *marks*. Although in Charticulator, strictly speaking, a mark is either a rectangle, an ellipse, or a triangle, it's often used generically to describe any element of a glyph including lines and symbols. However, here, we will restrict the term mark to refer only to a shape.

Note   Although in this chapter we concentrate on using marks and symbols in the context of building glyphs, they can also be used on the chart canvas as shapes that are not bound to any data. For example, you could use a rectangle mark to place a box around a categorical legend or a text element.

To change the mark from the default rectangle to either a triangle or an ellipse, select the rectangle in the Glyph pane, and in the Attributes pane, change the Shape attribute as shown in Figure 2-2.

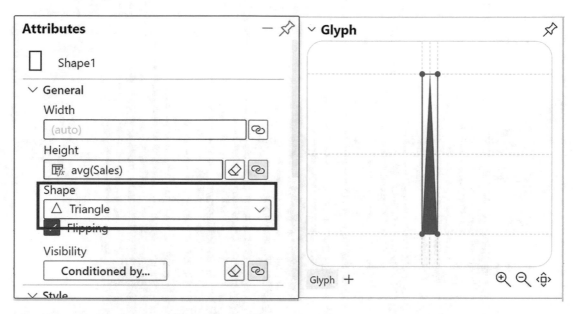

Figure 2-2. *Changing the shape of the mark*

If you have an empty Glyph pane, you can use the dropdown beside the **Mark** button on the toolbar to select a different shape. Then drag and drop the shape into the Glyph pane.

You can see in Figure 2-3 what our chart looks like if we change the shape to a triangle.

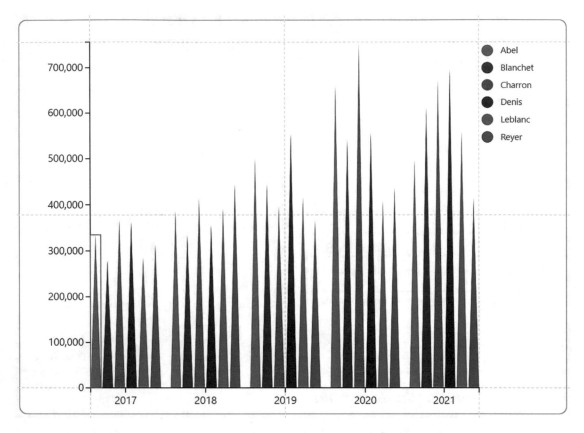

Figure 2-3. *Using a triangle mark in the Glyph pane changes the chart*

Why don't you now alter the look and feel of the chart yet again by changing the glyph to an ellipse shape.

Lines

Instead of using a mark, you could use a *line* in the Glyph pane. Start by deleting "Shape1" by using the eraser button in the Layers pane. Then click the **Line** button on the toolbar and draw the line along a vertical guide in the Glyph pane, ensuring you start and end the line inside the top and bottom horizontal guides; see Figure 2-4.

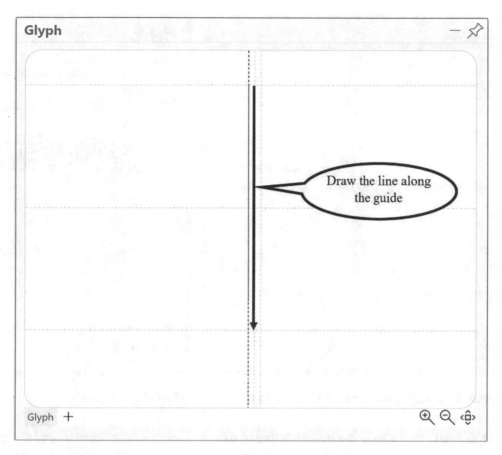

Figure 2-4. *Drawing a line in the Glyph pane*

The line has similar attributes to a shape in that you can drag a numerical field such as "Sales" onto it in the Glyph pane to reflect the numerical value in the height of the line, known as "Y Span"; see Figure 2-5.

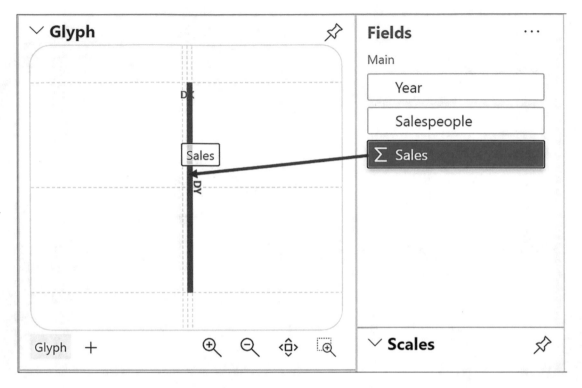

Figure 2-5. *Drag a numerical field onto the line in the Glyph pane*

In the Attributes pane, you can now drag a category such as the "Salespeople" field into the Stroke attribute to change the color accordingly. To change the weight of the line, use the Line Width attribute; see Figure 2-6.

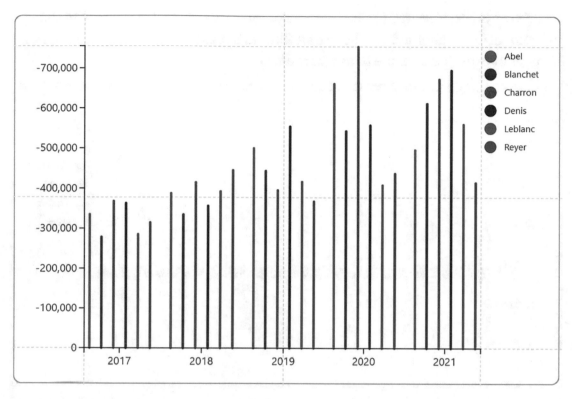

Figure 2-6. *Changing the Line Width and Stroke attributes of the line*

Using a line as your glyph is the starting point for creating the lollipop chart that we will be building in the section on "Using Composite Glyphs" below.

Symbols

Both the mark and the line are used in glyphs where you're designing bar or column type charts. The *symbol*, on the other hand, is used to create a glyph that plots data points such as in line charts or in scatter charts.

To use a symbol in our chart instead of a line or mark, delete the line or rectangle mark from the Glyph pane using the eraser button in the Layers pane.

Select the symbol button on the toolbar and then drag and drop it onto the Glyph pane. Don't worry that the symbols sit stubbornly in the middle of the chart canvas in a long line (Figure 2-7). We will learn in Chapter 4 how to plot the symbol to reflect a value on an x- or y-axis. However, you can now drag a category into the Fill attribute to change the color of the symbol and use the Size attribute to increase its size (you can just type a number into the Size attribute or use the slider).

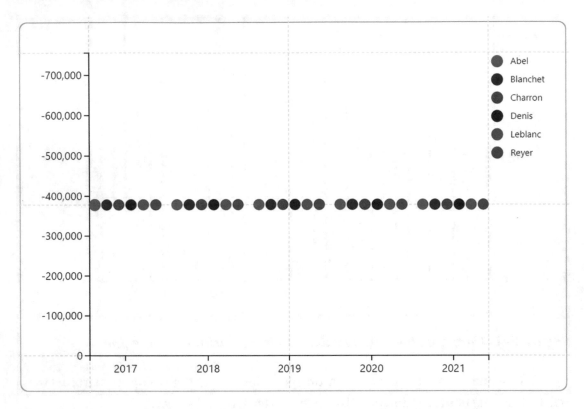

Figure 2-7. *A symbol in the Glyph pane does not get plotted on the chart*

Using the Shape attribute of the symbol, you can change the default circle to a different symbol, for example, a star; see Figure 2-8.

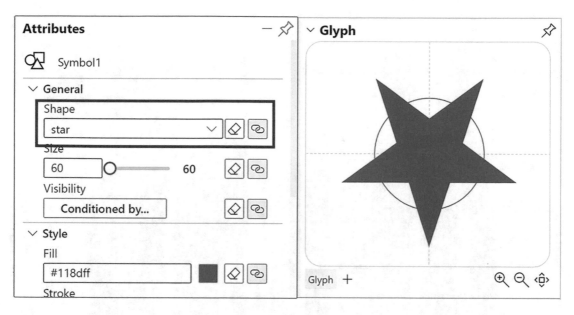

Figure 2-8. *You can change the symbol to a different shape*

By selecting a color in the Stroke attribute, you can give the symbol more definition where required. Just click into the Stroke attribute and select a color (see the section on "The Fill, Color, and Stroke Attributes" below). You are then able to increase the thickness of the stroke by using the Line Width attribute.

Text Marks

You can use the *text mark* in Charticulator to generate what you might refer to as "data labels" in a Power BI visual or an Excel chart.

Note   Just as with marks and symbols, the text mark can also be used on the chart canvas. If you do this, the text mark behaves as a conventional text box and so can be used for chart and axes titles.

You can see the text mark that we will be creating in Figure 2-9. To clarify the sales values for each salesperson in each year, we have labeled each column accordingly.

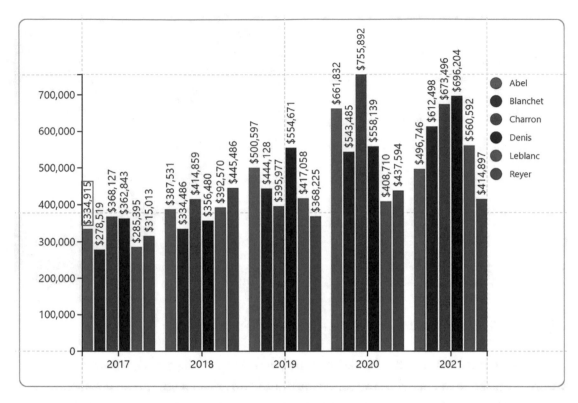

Figure 2-9. *Text marks are used for generating data labels*

To apply these labels to the chart, from the toolbar, drag the Text button onto the rectangle mark in the Glyph pane. Don't worry about where to drop it as it'll be placed in the middle of the rectangle mark by default. To move the text mark to the top of the rectangle, drag the green dot to the top edge; see Figure 2-10.

Tip   Use the zoom buttons bottom right of the Glyph pane to get a closer look at what you're doing. You can also drag in a blank area of the Glyph pane to move the glyph around.

Be careful that the circle remains solid green after dropping it to ensure it's anchored correctly. If the circle goes white, the text mark is not anchored to the top of the rectangle and will sit in odd positions on the canvas.

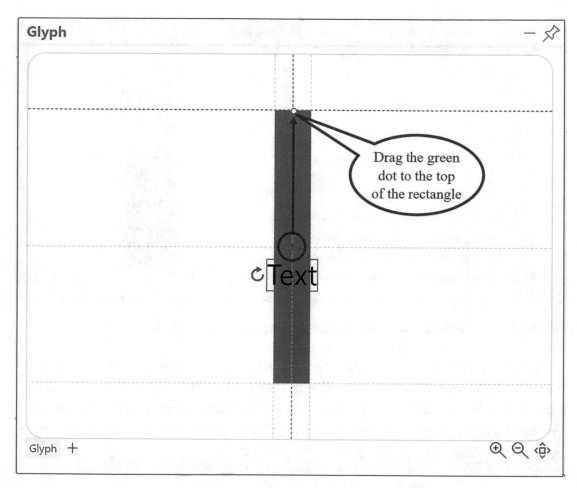

Figure 2-10. *Drag the text mark to the top edge of the shape*

You can then use the rotation handle to rotate the text mark and the Anchor & Rotation attributes to reposition the mark. An example of using these attributes is shown in Figure 2-11.

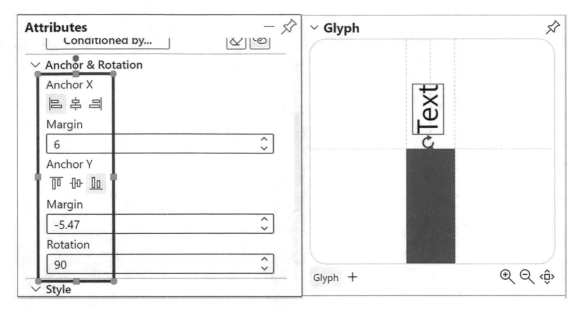

Figure 2-11. *The text mark attributes that reposition the mark*

To show your numerical value in the text mark, drag and drop the numerical field from the Fields pane onto the text mark in the Glyph pane. Irritatingly, the numerical value will be formatted with no comma separator and one decimal place. To format the number correctly, click on the text mark in the Glyph pane, and in the "Text1" Attributes pane, edit the Text attribute as shown in Figure 2-12.

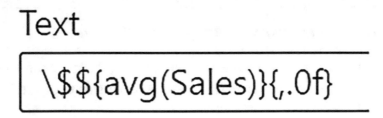

Figure 2-12. *Edit the Text attribute of the text mark*

If you want to add a currency symbol as we've done, type "\$" (backslash, dollar) in front of the dollar sign (for any other currency, just type the currency symbol in front of the dollar sign).

Note   We deep dive into Charticulator's format strings in Chapter 8.

In the Attributes pane, you can also change the font type, the color, and the size of the text as described in the following sections. There is even an Outline attribute with which you can experiment.

Icons

The icon mark allows you to use images as the glyph or as part of the glyph. To do this, drag the icon button from the toolbar into an empty Glyph pane. In the Attributes pane, click the Image attribute and browse for your image; see Figure 2-13.

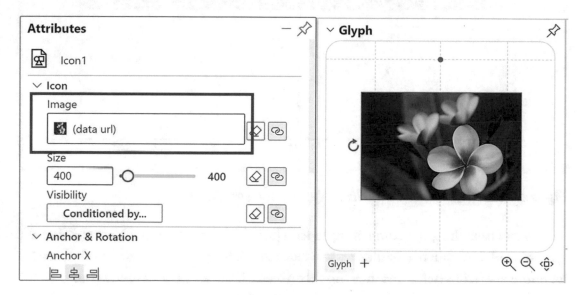

Figure 2-13. *Using an image in the Glyph pane*

The icon behaves like the symbol and sits in one long line on the chart canvas, and because the glyph is repeated 30 times on the canvas, the image in the icon is far too small to see. (Figure 2-14).

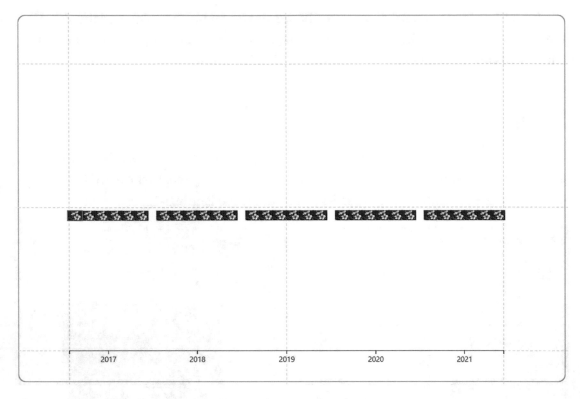

Figure 2-14. *The image in the icon glyph is too small to see*

We can treat the glyph comprising an icon just as we would the glyph comprising a symbol, and as mentioned earlier, we will learn in Chapter 4 how to make symbols and therefore also icons behave as they should on a chart, but for now let's move on.

The Height, Length, and Size Attributes

The Height, Y Span, or Size attributes of the glyph are often populated by numerical fields, and we look more closely at this aspect of the glyph in the next chapter. However, you can just type a value into these attributes instead. This will restrict the height, length, or size accordingly. You can see in Figure 2-15 that we have restricted the height of a rectangle mark to 300.

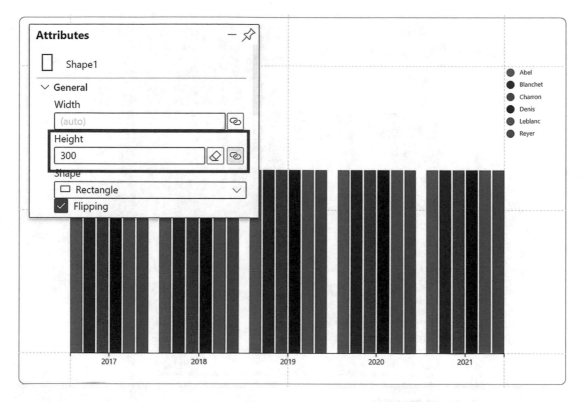

Figure 2-15. *The rectangles are sized according to a specific value*

By entering a value into a numerical attribute, you will constrain the mark, symbol, or line to that value, so, for example, the rectangles will remain the same size irrespective of the size of the canvas.

The Fill, Color, and Stroke Attributes

The Fill, Color, and Stroke attributes are typically associated with a category, for example, the "Salespeople" category in the chart in Figure 2-1. However, you can just select a color to use. Remove any field that is in the attribute by using the eraser. Then click the Fill, Color, or Stroke attribute in the Attributes pane and select your preferred color as shown in Figure 2-16.

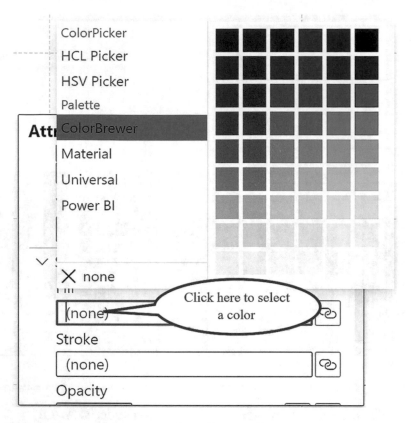

Figure 2-16. *Selecting a color to use in color attributes*

Once you have removed a field from the Fill attribute, there is no default color and you are left with "(none)" which is often another way to hide a mark or symbol.

Using Composite Glyphs

You can mix and match marks, lines, and symbols in the same glyph. For instance, we could liven up the clustered column chart by adding a symbol to sit at the top of the rectangle and a dashed line through the middle. But better still, we could build a lollipop chart where the glyph comprises a line for the "stick" and a symbol for the "lollipop."

Note   If you're using multiple shapes and symbols in the Glyph pane, don't forget that the order in which they appear in the Layers pane determines their stacking order. If you require a shape to sit on top of other shapes, drag the shape further up the list.

Let's now look at building these two examples of glyphs that comprise more than simply a single rectangle shape.

Column Chart with Symbols and Lines

Consider the chart in Figure 2-17 where we have combined a rectangle with a symbol and a line in the Glyph pane.

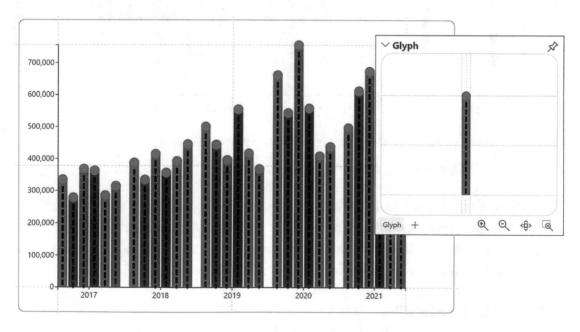

Figure 2-17.   *A column chart comprising a composite glyph*

In this chart, in the Glyph pane, we've drawn a line inside the rectangle mark, increased the Line Width, and changed the Line Style attributes. We then added a symbol, dragging the green dot inside the symbol and anchoring it to the top of the rectangle, as we did for the text mark. We also changed the Fill attribute of the symbol to dark gray.

Lollipop Chart

We will be building the lollipop chart as shown in Figure 2-18. This will be a great way to conclude this chapter because it brings together many skills you have learned so far in building Charticulator charts.

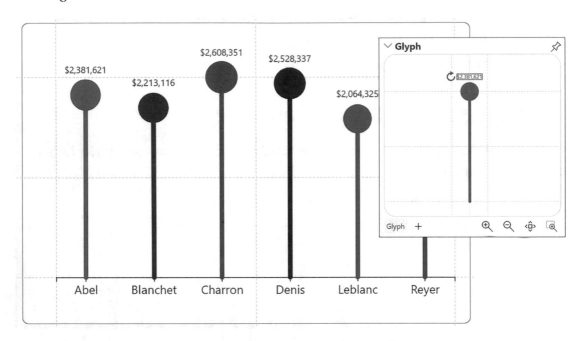

Figure 2-18. *A lollipop chart uses a symbol and a line*

Start over with a new chart. The lollipop chart uses one categorical field and one numerical field. In our example, we're using the "Salespeople" field and the "Sales" field.

To lead you through building the lollipop chart, it's best to look separately at creating the line for the "stick" and then the symbol for the "lollipop."

Creating the "Stick"

We will start with a chart similar to Figure 2-6 where we added a line to the Glyph pane (as shown in Figure 2-4). The "Sales" field was then dragged onto the "Y Span" of the line, and the "Salesperson" field was dragged into the Stroke attribute (see the section on "Lines" above).

Creating the "Lollipop"

Now we are ready to drag and drop a symbol into the Glyph pane. The symbol will be sitting in the middle of the line. Drag the green dot in the middle of the symbol and attach it to the top of the line (you will see orange guide lines when you drop in the correct place). Now, making sure that "Symbol1" is selected in the Layers pane, drag the "Sales" field into the Size attribute and the "Salesperson" field into the Fill attribute.

At this stage, you may think the "lollipop" is a little small. You can remedy this by clicking on "Symbol1.Size" in the Scales pane and increasing the "End" value of the Range attribute; see Figure 2-19.

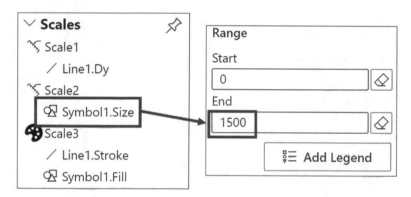

Figure 2-19. *Increasing the size of the "lollipop"*

As the final touch, we added a text mark to the glyph as shown in the section on "Text Marks." The text mark was attached to the top of the lollipop to show the sales value.

In this chapter, we've explored different marks, lines, and symbols that can comprise the glyph, and you've learned how to change their shape, dimensions, and color. You've also learned how to use the text mark to generate data labels and to annotate the glyph.

However, we need to remind ourselves what has been mandatory in generating the successful column and lollipop chart and that has been associating fields in the Fields list with attributes of the glyph and of the chart. For instance, in our column chart, we've associated the "Year" field with the x-axis, the "Sales" field with the height of the rectangle mark, and the "Salespeople" field with its color. Without these associations, the chart would make no sense. In Charticulator, we have a term for making these associations; it's called "binding data." In the following chapter, we will look in closer detail at this important aspect of building your Charticulator chart.

CHAPTER 3

Binding Data

In Chapter 1, we explored the Charticulator screen and learned about the Attributes panes which list the attributes of the currently selected layer. Along the way, you dragged fields into some of these attributes to associate data with the height and color of the glyph and the x-axis of the chart. This enabled you to construct a typical clustered column chart. However, at that time there was no reason for you to understand the implications of what you were doing. Associating fields with attributes in this way is known as *binding data* and is a key concept underpinning the design of Charticulator charts. Binding data entails populating an attribute with a field, generating a scale that drives the behavior or format of that attribute based on the data within the field.

By working through this chapter, you will understand the implications of binding fields to attributes. Specifically, you will learn to identify the attributes to which binding data is possible and how to bind both categorical and numerical data to the attributes of marks and the plot segment's axes. Lastly, you will discover how to bind images to categories that in turn are bound to the icon mark.

In addition to this, you will learn that the binding of data and the creation of the scale are inextricably linked. However, in this chapter we will focus just on the former, looking only briefly at the generation of the scale. This is because managing Charticulator scales is particularly challenging, and we dedicate a whole chapter to this topic later in this book (see Chapter 9). However, because binding categorical data generates color scales that determine the colors used by your chart, you will also learn how to edit these colors right here in this chapter.

How to Bind Data

Any attribute to which you can bind data has a **Bind data** button next to it as shown in Figure 3-1.

© Alison Box 2022
A. Box, *Introducing Charticulator for Power BI*, https://doi.org/10.1007/978-1-4842-8076-8_3

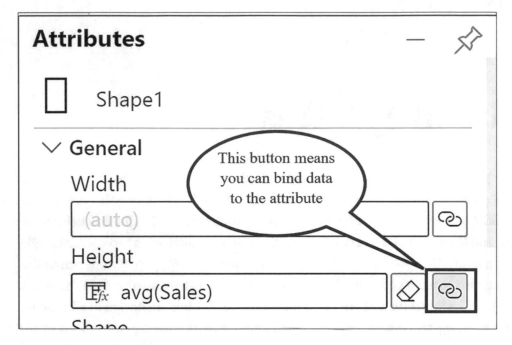

Figure 3-1. *The Bind data button in the Attributes pane*

To bind data to an attribute, you can click the bind data button, or you can drop a field from the Fields pane onto any *dropzone*. There are dropzones in the Attributes panes, in the Glyph pane, and on the chart canvas. The dropzones turn orange when you hover over them and are shown in Figure 3-2.

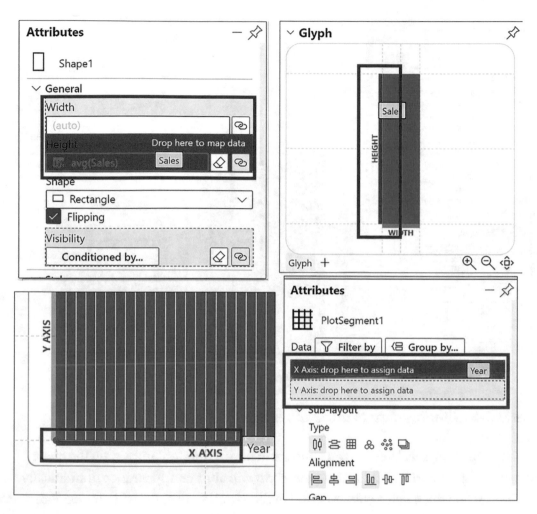

Figure 3-2. *Examples of dropzones*

For example, in Chapter 1 we dragged the "Year" field onto the dropzone on the x-axis of the chart, binding that field to the X Axis attribute of "PlotSegment1." We then dragged the "Sales" field onto the Height dropzone in the Glyph pane to bind this field to the Height attribute of "Shape1." Lastly, we dragged the "Salespeople" field onto the Fill attribute dropzone of "Shape1" to color the rectangles on the chart accordingly. Another instance where we bound data was in Chapter 2, when we bound the "Sales" field to the Text attribute of the text mark. In Figure 3-3, you can see these attributes with the fields bound to them and note how they drive the plotting of the data in the chart.

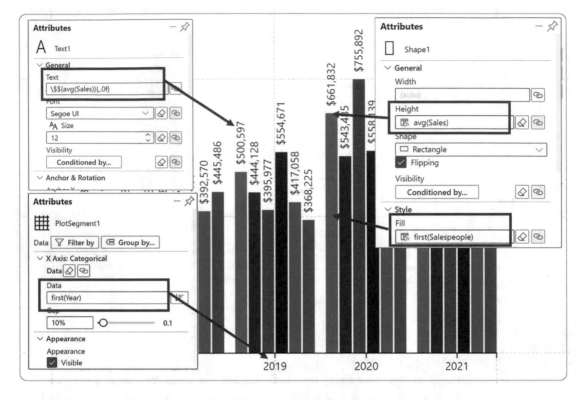

Figure 3-3. *Binding data to attributes drives the plotting of the data*

Binding categorical fields to attributes will have a different impact on the chart than binding numerical fields. Also, your chart will alter its appearance dramatically depending on which fields you've bound to the x- and y-axes. We will now explore these behaviors in detail by using the chart in Figure 3-4 as our example.

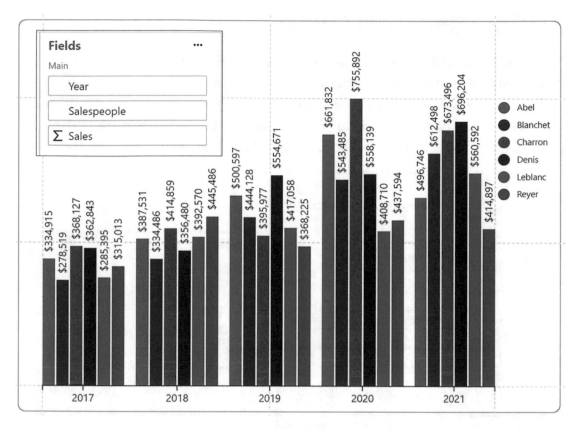

Figure 3-4. *The chart that is used in our examples*

Let's just summarize which fields have currently been bound to which attributes in the column chart in Figure 3-4:

- "Year" to the X Axis of the plot segment

- "Sales" to the Height of the rectangle mark

- "Salespeople" to the Fill color of the rectangle mark

- "Sales" to the Text of the text mark

Also note that in the chart in Figure 3-4, there is no numerical legend on the left as we will add this after we have finished binding data.

Binding Categorical Fields

Binding categorical fields to attributes of a mark, symbol, or line determines the colors you want to use to identify each member of the category and creates a *color scale* in the Scales pane that maps the colors to the categories. In our chart, we bound the "Salespeople" categorical field to the Fill attribute of the rectangle mark, and this generated the "Shape1.Fill" property under the color "Scale2."

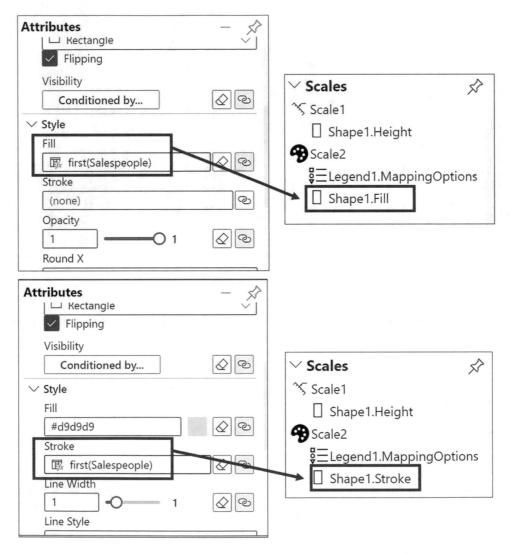

Figure 3-5. *Binding a categorical field to the Fill or Stroke attribute generates a color scale in the Scales pane*

However, we could remove the "Salespeople" field from the Fill attribute of Shape1 (using the eraser) and bind "Salespeople" to the Stroke attribute instead, creating a "Shape1.Stroke" property under "Scale2"; see Figure 3-5. This would color the outline of the rectangle according to each salesperson; see Figure 3-6.

When you remove a field from the Fill attribute, you're left with no color in that attribute, so just click the Fill attribute and reselect a color. We've chosen gray in our example.

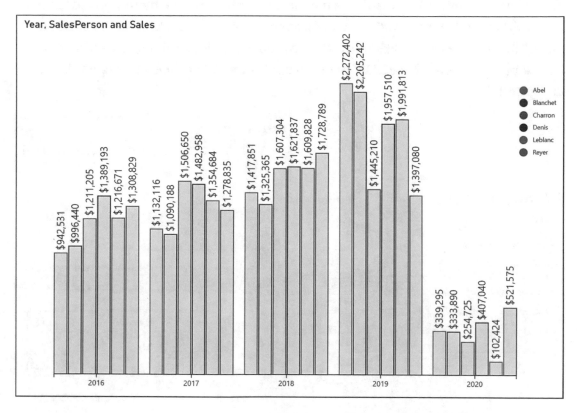

Figure 3-6. *Binding data to the Stroke attribute and changing the Fill color*

You've learned that binding categorical data produces a scale in the Scales pane. However, there is an exception to this and that is when you bind a categorical field to the Text attribute of a text mark. Unlike other attributes, binding categorical data, such as "Salespeople", to the Text attribute of a text mark will not produce a scale in the Scales pane. For instance, in our column chart, we've bound a numerical field to the Text attribute (i.e., the "Sales" field), but instead you could bind a categorical field, thereby generating categorical data labels. You can see an example of this in Figure 3-14 where we have bound the "Salespeople" field to the Text attribute of a text mark, anchored to the bottom of a rectangle shape, and this has labeled the columns accordingly.

Although it may be self-evident, it might be worth noting that you are not able to bind categorical fields to numerical attributes. For example, you can't drag the "Salespeople" field into the Height or Width attribute of a shape.

Editing a Categorical Color Scale

The colors used by the color scale are initially determined by the theme applied to your Power BI report. However, you can edit these colors either by clicking on the attribute in the Attributes pane or by clicking an attribute property under the Scale in the Scales pane, for example, click on "Shape1.Fill" or on "Shape1.Stroke". The dialog that opens is shown in Figure 3-7.

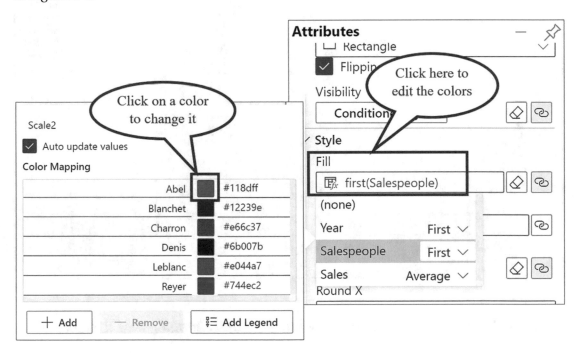

Figure 3-7. *Editing a categorical color scale*

Click the color you want to change. Changing the colors used by the Fill attribute would also change the colors used by the Stroke attribute (or any other attributes that use "Scale2"). This aspect of the scale is covered in detail in Chapter 9.

Binding Numerical Fields

Whereas you can only bind categorical fields to nonnumerical attributes, you can bind numerical fields to both numerical and nonnumerical attributes, and depending on which you choose, this will have a different impact on the chart.

Binding Numerical Fields to Numerical Attributes

You can bind numerical fields to any numerical attribute such as Height, Width, and Size. When you do this, the attribute will reflect the magnitude of the numerical value bound to it and generate the associated *numerical scale* in the Scales pane. For example, in our chart we bound the "Sales" field to the Height attribute of "Shape1," creating the "Shape1.Height" property under the numerical "Scale1" in the Scales pane. This drives the height of the rectangles in the chart to reflect the sales value. However, we could also bind the "Sales" field to the Size attribute of the text mark, to create a third scale, "Scale3," using the "Text1.FontSize" property; see Figure 3-8.

Figure 3-8. *Binding a numerical field to attributes generates a numerical scale in the Scales pane*

You can see now in our chart (Figure 3-9) that the text size in the text mark has been scaled according to the value of the "Sales" field.

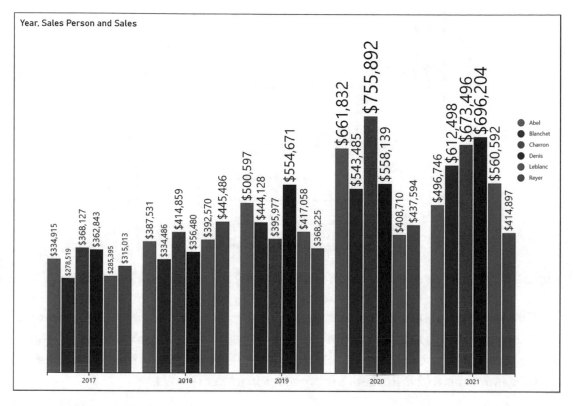

Figure 3-9. *A numerical field bound to the Size attribute of the text mark*

If you want to insert a numerical legend on the left of the chart, ensure that this is done *after* binding the numerical value to the Size attribute of the text mark. This will force "Scale3" to be generated and prevent the "Text1.FontSize" property joining "Scale1" which can result in unexpected behavior.

What is interesting and may also seem a little odd at first is that when you bind numerical data to an attribute, the average function is used on the numerical value; see Figure 3-10.

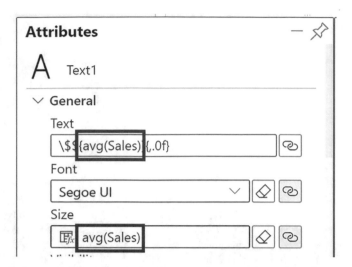

Figure 3-10. *The average function is used by default in numerical attributes*

However, this shouldn't seem strange because remember that the glyph represents a single row in the underlying data, and therefore there is only a single value. The average of a single value is that value. In other words, this is simply the value itself. We will be learning more about Charticulator's expressions in a later chapter.

Binding Numerical Fields to Nonnumerical Attributes

We've already seen that we can bind a numerical field such as "Sales" to the Text attribute of a text mark to show the sales value for each column, effectively adding numerical data labels to the chart.

If a numerical field is bound to attributes that define a color such as Fill, Color, or Stroke, this will create a *gradient* color scale. For example, in our chart we could replace the "Salespeople" categorical field in the Fill attribute of the rectangle mark with the "Sales" numerical field, and this will produce a gradient gray color scale in the rectangles, defining high and low sales values. This will also generate a fourth scale for the Fill attribute of "Shape1"; see Figure 3-11.

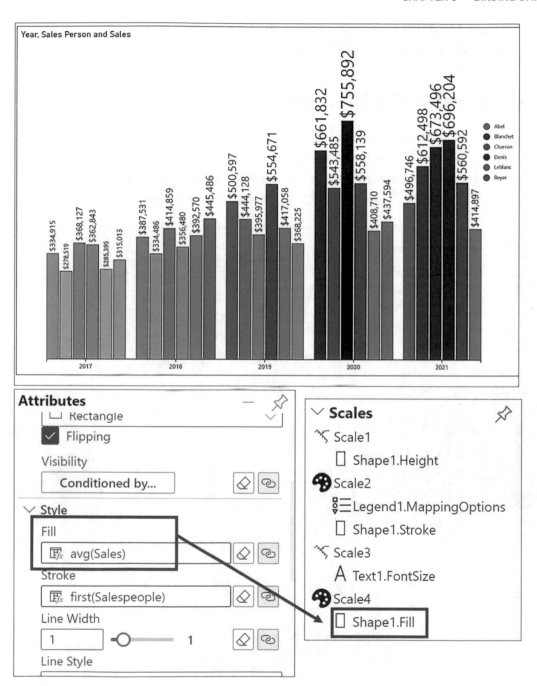

Figure 3-11. *Binding a numerical field to a nonnumerical attribute generates a gradient gray color scale*

It's unfortunate that the default gradient color scale is so dreary! Let's now brighten up the chart by editing the color scale.

Editing a Gradient Color Scale

You may want to edit the gray gradient to something a little more colorful. If you want to change a gradient color scale, just click into the attribute, and you can either select from a variety of preformatted gradient scales or click the custom tab and create your own gradient. We chose the "Spectral" gradient color scale; see Figure 3-12.

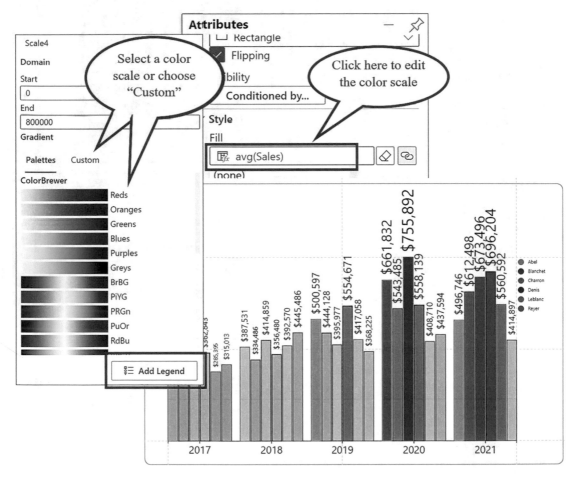

Figure 3-12. *You can edit the gradient color scale and add a legend*

Notice that you have the ability to customize the gradient colors by clicking **Custom** at the top of the color palette.

Adding a Legend for a Gradient Color Scale

You can add a legend for the gradient color scale here too to replace the current legend for the category. Note that you can't use the Legend button on the toolbar because this will insert the default legend for numerical fields which is a numerical legend on the left of the chart. An alternative way to generate specific legends is to use the Scales pane, clicking the property under the scale that requires the legend, in our case "Shape1.Fill" under Scale4, and then clicking the **Add Legend** button; see Figure 3-13.

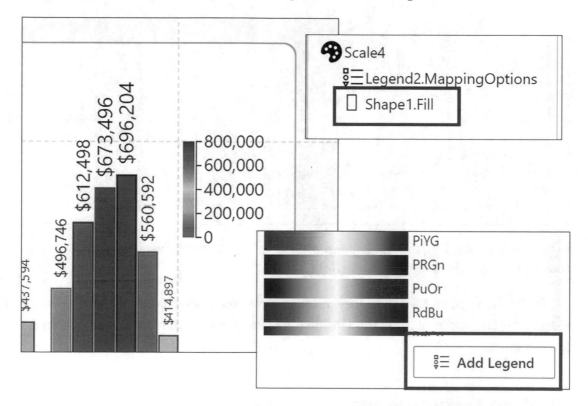

Figure 3-13. *You can add a color scale legend by using the Scales pane*

You can use the attributes of the color scale legend to increase the font size and change the font color of the legend.

The problem is that now you don't know which columns in the chart represent which salesperson. I'll leave it to you to decide how you want to resolve this problem because with Charticulator, there are always a number of options available to you. You can see my resolution in Figure 3-14. I used a text mark and bound the "Salesperson" field to the Text and the Color attributes.

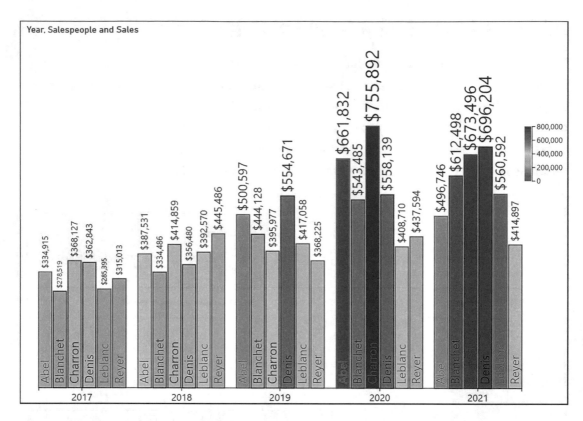

Figure 3-14. *Binding the "Salespeople" field to the Text attribute of a text mark will label the columns accordingly*

In the Glyph pane, the text mark was anchored to the bottom of the rectangle, rotated, and then placed in position inside the rectangle using the Anchor attributes of the text mark.

Binding Data to Axes

It's not just attributes of the glyph that can have data bound to them. In the attributes of "PlotSegment1," you can bind both numerical and categorical data to the X Axis and Y Axis attributes. In the chart in Figure 3-14, we have bound the "Year" categorical field to the X Axis attribute, but we could bind "Year" to the Y Axis attribute instead. In both cases, we are generating categorical axes. You can see that making this simple change in the data binding has totally transformed the design of the chart; see Figure 3-15.

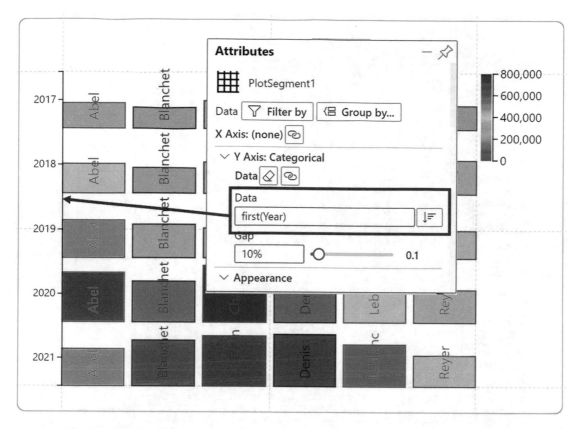

Figure 3-15. *Binding a categorical field to the y-axis*

The height and color of the glyph still represent the numerical value, and we still have the text mark bound to the bottom of the rectangle. However, now each year's data is represented horizontally across the chart.

Note   For clarity, in Figure 3-15, the text mark that showed the sales value has been removed using the eraser.

Having bound a categorical field to the axis, I appreciate that you will now want to know what would happen if we bind a *numerical* field, such as "Sales," to the y-axis. If we do this, it all goes a little awry; see Figure 3-16.

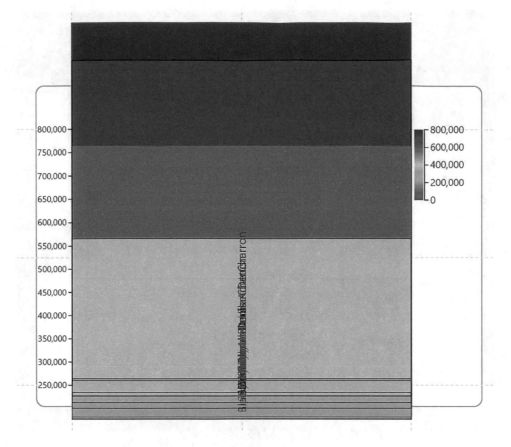

Figure 3-16. *Binding a numerical field to an axis has unexpected results*

Clearly, with Charticulator, generating numerical or value axes will have unexpected results if you don't fully understand how Charticulator plots your data, and looking at the fine mess we've got into, I think it's evident that we still have a lot to learn. Why does the numerical y-axis behave so strangely? To find out, you will need to read the next chapter.

However, there is one more example of binding data that we need to explore before we move on. We have left this to the last section in this chapter because we will need to start over with a new chart and different data. We are going to discover how we can bind images to categories that in turn are bound to an icon mark.

Binding Data to Icons

In the previous chapter, you learned how to add an icon to the Glyph pane and that it can be used for the same purposes for which you might use a symbol, for example, to design point style charts such as line or scatter charts (we look at building these in the next chapter). We saw that we could bind an image to the Image attribute of the icon to generate a single image that showed in the glyph. We could also bind a numerical field to the Size attribute to resize the image according to the numerical value in a similar way we can with a symbol.

However, there is another way that we can use the icon mark, and that is to bind a *category* to the Image attribute and then bind images to each category. You can see the effect of doing this in the flag chart in Figure 3-17 where we have bound an image for each country's flag to the icon.

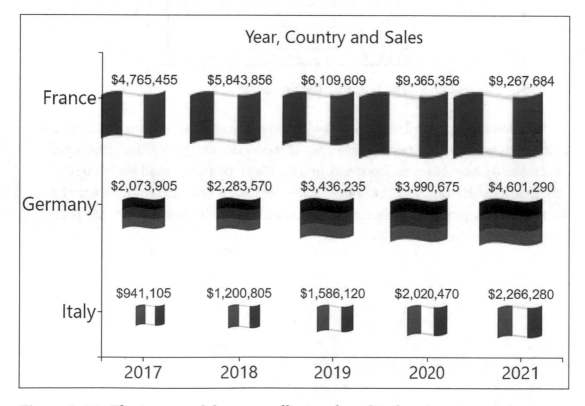

Figure 3-17. *The icon mark becomes effective if you bind an image to each category*

To build this chart, you will need data similar to that shown in Figure 3-18 and some images of flags to bind to the icon.

Main
15 rows, 3 columns

Year	Country	Sales
2017	France	4765455
2017	Germany	2073905
2017	Italy	941105
2018	France	5843856
2018	Germany	2283570
2018	Italy	1200805
2019	France	6109609
2019	Germany	3436235
2019	Italy	1586120
2020	France	9365356

Figure 3-18. *Data used for building the flag chart*

The first step is to bind the "Year" field to the x-axis and the "Country" field to the y-axis. This generates a "matrix" style chart that uses two categorical axes (the topic of Chapter 6). Now, place an icon mark into the Glyph pane and bind the "Country" categorical field to the Image attribute. Doing this means you can now bind each image file to each category. To do this, simply click the Image attribute and then map your image to each category; see Figure 3-19.

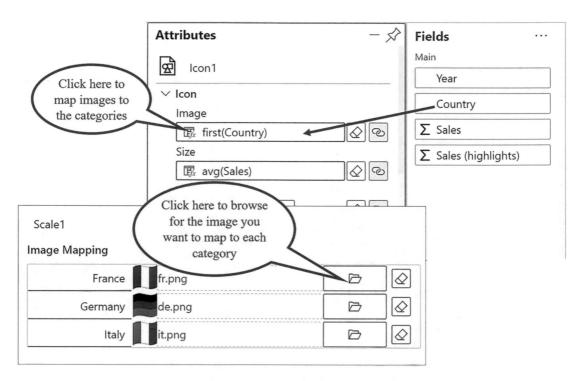

Figure 3-19. *Binding an image to each category rather than to the Image attribute*

In building this chart, just remind yourself that you have only reached Chapter 3, and you're already designing visuals that are not possible to re-create in Power BI. I'm hoping this will encourage and inspire you to read on.

In this chapter, you have learned that it's the binding of data to attributes of the glyph and the plot segment that enables you to plot data successfully using Charticulator and also provides you with a multitude of choices as to how you want to reflect your data. You have seen that with Charticulator the normal process of creating visualizations is reversed whereby you select the data to visualize *first* and then design a chart around that data. In a typical Power BI visual, you select the chart *first* and so are immediately restricted by your choice of visual.

But we still have that pesky visual in Figure 3-16 to sort out where we have bound a numerical field to the y-axis and ended up with a chaotic chart. Let's now see how we can resolve this problem by moving on to the next chapter.

CHAPTER 4

Using Symbols

It may not have escaped your notice that up to now we've always used a rectangle mark in the Glyph pane and only ever created a column style chart. In this chapter, things are about to change because we're going to turn our attention to creating "point" type charts, such as line charts and scatter plots, and learn how to use a symbol in the design of a chart; see Figure 4-1.

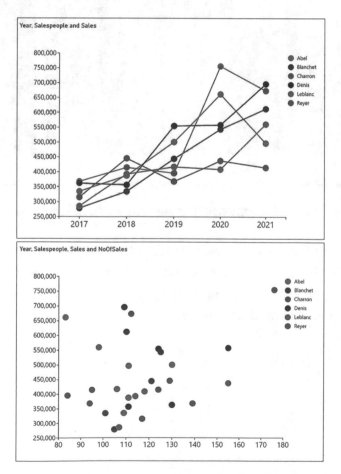

Figure 4-1. *Point style charts using a symbol in the Glyph pane*

© Alison Box 2022

A. Box, *Introducing Charticulator for Power BI*, https://doi.org/10.1007/978-1-4842-8076-8_4

However, although we know how to drag a symbol into the Glyph pane, we still don't know how to plot it successfully onto the chart to produce line and scatter charts. Let's remind ourselves what happens by starting with our default column chart (Figure 4-2).

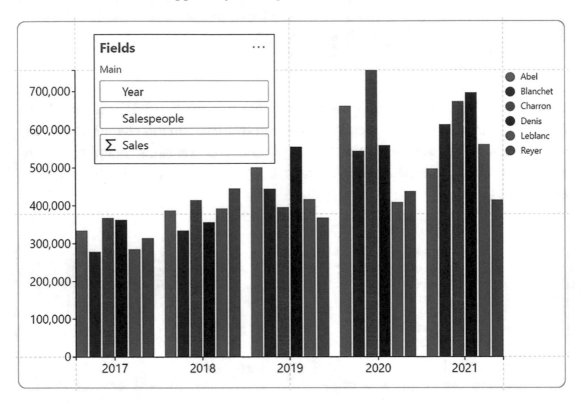

Figure 4-2. *Our default column chart where we have added a numerical legend*

In this chart, we added a numerical legend, but if we replace the rectangle shape with a circle symbol in the Glyph pane, the chart will change as shown in Figure 4-3. What is particularly peculiar about the chart is that the positions of the symbols bear no relation to the numerical legend on the left.

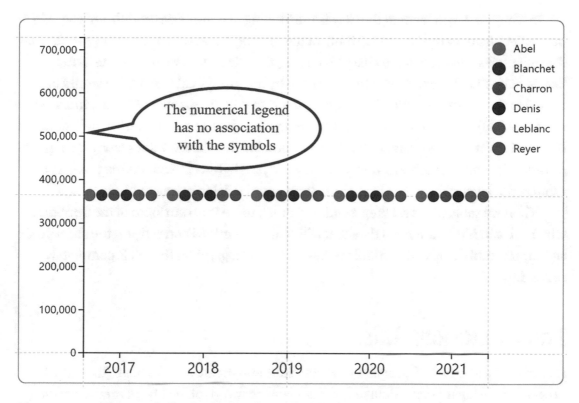

Figure 4-3. *The symbols don't get plotted with the presence of a legend*

What's going on here? To answer that question, you have to understand that in
Charticulator there is a critical difference between using a numerical legend which
we have here and using a numerical axis, which is what we need. They both look the
same when added to a chart, but conceptionally they are completely different elements
and will have a very different impact on the layout of the chart. To throw some light
on the reason why this is, let's compare the numerical legend to the numerical axis in
Charticulator.

The Numerical Legend

In charts generated in Power BI or Excel, whether they are column style charts or point
style charts, the value axis is used to define the magnitude of the numerical fields plotted
on the chart. However, in Charticulator when we created our column chart, we used a
legend for this purpose.

In Chapter 2, you learned that it was the binding of a numerical value, for example, our "Sales" field, to the Height attribute of the rectangle that was responsible for plotting the rectangles correctly in the chart. To do this, Charticulator created a scale in the Scales pane that defined the scale being used by the numerical field which would be from 0 to the maximum value in the field (in our "Sales" field, that is 755,892, rounded up to 800,000). It's the scale that is used to map the values in the numerical field to the height of the rectangles, and, indeed, it's not possible to edit the values along the legend. Adding a legend is purely arbitrary and plays no part in how the data is mapped; if you remove the legend from the chart, the column chart still looks fine.

When we replace the rectangle with a symbol, there is no attribute of the symbol to which we can bind numerical data that will plot the symbols correctly on the chart, and so they sit stubbornly in the middle of the chart. The legend on the left is completely redundant.

The Numerical Axis

However, if we remove the legend from the chart and create a numerical axis, this will now drive the layout of the data in the chart, and so the glyph will be plotted according to the values along the axis. You create a numerical y-axis by binding a numerical value to the Y Axis attribute of the plot segment, or you can drag the field onto the y-axis on the canvas. In our example, we've bound the "Sales" field; see Figure 4-4.

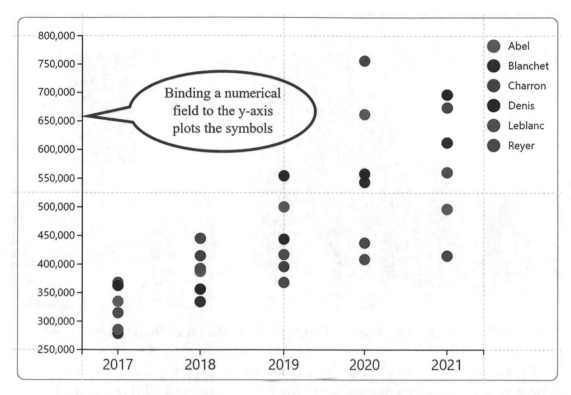

Figure 4-4. *Symbols are plotted according to the field bound to the numerical axis*

What seems odd at first is that the numerical axis impacts on the glyph irrespective of the shape and size of the glyph. When we use a symbol, all seems well, but when we use a two-dimensional shape such as a rectangle, all looks a little bizarre. To see what I mean by this, drag and drop a rectangle shape on top of the symbol in the Glyph pane. The symbol is now sitting behind the rectangle, so you must move "Shape1" in the Layers pane above "Symbol1." Lastly, bind a categorical field such as the "Salespeople" field to the Fill attribute of the shape. You should end up with an odd looking chart as shown in Figure 4-5.

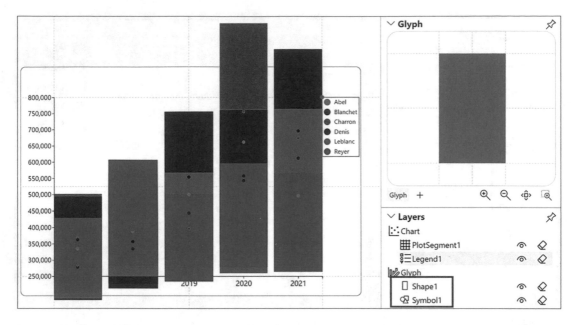

Figure 4-5. *Adding a rectangle to the glyph. Note the order in the Layers pane*

Charticulator is treating the symbol and shape the same; they are both being plotted according to the values on the numerical axis. Because the rectangle is tall and thin, Charticulator takes the midpoint of the rectangle and plots that. It then overlaps the shapes to enable the plotting of the categories on the x-axis. For example, for 2017, all six rectangles that represent the six salespeople are sitting on top of each other. If we reduced the height and width of the rectangle by putting a value in the "Height" and "Width" attributes, for example, 10, essentially creating a data point, the chart would no longer look strange. The rectangles are still sitting on top of the symbols (Figure 4-6).

Warning   Once the glyphs overlap because of the numerical axis, they don't reset themselves if you remove the field bound to the numerical axis. The glyphs will still sit on top of each other, and you will need to reset the sub-layout; see Chapter 5.

If you now look at the glyph in the Glyph pane, you will notice that by reducing the size of the rectangle, this changes the height and width of the entire glyph comprising both the mark and the symbol which are now both constrained inside the guides.

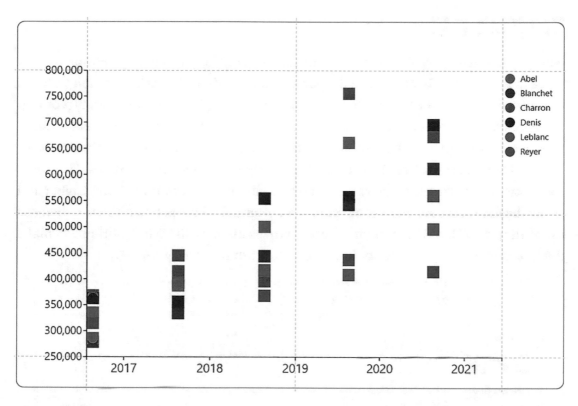

Figure 4-6. Both symbols and marks are plotted correctly on the chart

Notice that binding a numerical field to the Y Axis attribute of the plot segment does not generate a scale in the Scales pane. It's the numerical axis that is responsible for the layout of the glyphs in the chart, and therefore we need no scale to map data onto the glyph.

Note   We've been binding data to attributes of the *plot segment*. If you're wondering what a plot segment is, we will be focusing on plot segments in the next chapter.

With regard to numerical legends vs. numerical axes, it would appear that at the moment it's an "either/or" situation. You can either have a column or bar type chart that uses a legend *or* you can have a point style chart that uses a numerical axis. This is a frustration that we will need to resolve later, but for the moment, you can just understand that you must use symbols if you want to use a numerical axis.

Creating a Line Chart

Now you understand that to plot a symbol onto a chart, you must bind your numerical value to the X or Y Axis attribute of the plot segment. Let's pick up where we left with the chart in Figure 4-4 where we have a symbol in the Glyph pane. It's currently plotting the symbols correctly, but the chart still looks confusing. The symbols represent each salesperson, but because the symbols overlap, it's difficult to see which symbol is which. We need to join each salesperson's symbol with a line. In other words, we need to transform the visual into a line chart. To do this, click the **Link** button on the toolbar and select the field represented by the symbols, for example, "Salespeople." You can then use the attributes of "Link1" to format the line, perhaps increase the Width attribute to make the line thicker, and select Bezier from the Type attribute; see Figure 4-7.

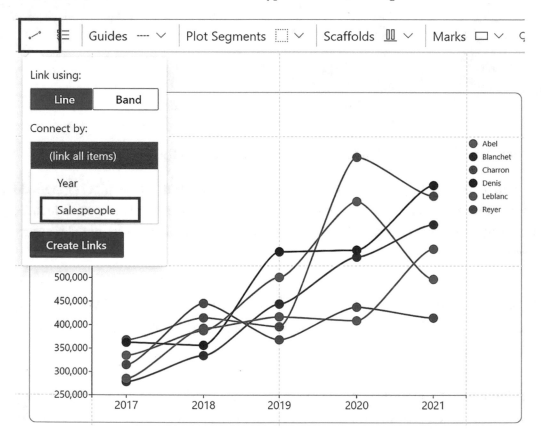

Figure 4-7. *To create a line chart, use the Link option on the toolbar*

The slightly wavy effect on the Bezier line chart is a refreshing alternative to the rather prosaic line chart in Power BI.

Create a Scatter or Bubble Chart

To create a scatter or bubble chart, you need three numerical fields. I've added "NoOfSales" and "Qty" to the Fields pane.

You can now remove the categorical field from the x-axis and replace it with your second numerical field. To turn the scatter chart into a bubble chart, bind your third numerical field to the Size attribute of the symbol; see Figure 4-8.

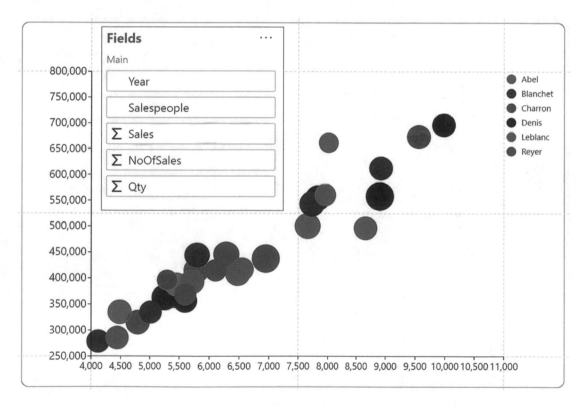

Figure 4-8. *A bubble chart requires two numerical axes*

It's a shame you don't yet know how to insert x- and y-axis titles to show the fields being used on the axes, but all good time. You will learn to do this in Chapter 10. But for the moment, you can just be glad that you now understand why the behavior of Charticulator's numerical axes is totally different from the behavior of the numerical legend. When I was first learning how to use Charticulator, I found this all very bewildering, and it took me some time to get to grips with this fundamental difference. You can consider this is a great leap forward in your knowledge of Charticulator.

For now, let's leave line, scatter, and bubble charts and turn our attention to something we've been frequently alluding, and that is the plot segment. This is the subject of the next chapter, and through reading it, you'll at long last learn how to create bar style charts where the bars sit horizontally rather than vertically, as in the case of the column chart. Who'd have thought that you'd have to work through four chapters on Charticulator until you find out how to build the commonplace bar chart, but when using Charticulator, as you are beginning to realize, very little is plain sailing.

CHAPTER 5

2D Region Plot Segments

In the last chapter, I showed you how to create a line chart using a symbol in the Glyph pane. You also learned something more important, that if you bind a numerical field to the y-axis, glyphs will be plotted against this axis according to their value, regardless of their shape or size.

However, you may be a little perturbed that as yet you don't know how to create this simple clustered bar chart (see Figure 5-1) where the glyphs sit horizontally and the numerical legend is along the x-axis.

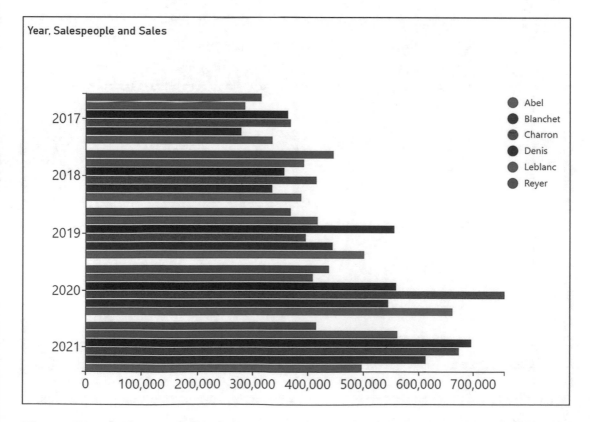

Figure 5-1. *A Charticulator*

A. Box, *Introducing Charticulator for Power BI*, https://doi.org/10.1007/978-1-4842-8076-8_5

The problem is that before you can create this bar chart, you must be aware of a key concept in Charticulator which is that the attributes of the *plot segment* determine the layout of a Charticulator chart. There are two different types of plot segment in Charticulator: 2D region and line. In this chapter, we will only be considering the 2D region plot segment (we will take a look at the line plot segment in Chapter 16) and will be taking a guided tour around the attributes of this chart element. In doing so, you will discover that it's the sub-layout of the plot segment that is instrumental in determining the type of visual you will generate, whether it's a column, bar, matrix, cloud, or jitter style of chart. You will also learn how to manage the more pedestrian elements of the chart design: the spacing, sorting, and alignment of the glyphs and also formatting axis labels and tick marks.

You can consider a 2D region plot segment as synonymous with a "plot area" in conventional charts. If you click "PlotSegment1" in the Layers pane, the plot segment will be selected on the chart, with the plot segment toolbar displayed above, as shown in Figure 5-2.

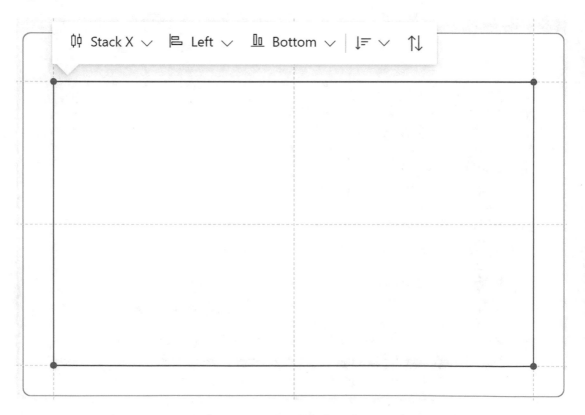

Figure 5-2. *The 2D region plot segment with the plot segment toolbar*

We've already seen the effect of binding fields to the X and Y Axis attributes of the plot segment and how this controls the layout of the glyphs within the chart. For instance, in Chapter 3, we saw that binding a categorical field to the X Axis attribute categorizes the glyphs along the x-axis according to that field. In Chapter 4, we bound a numerical field to the Y Axis attribute, and this generated a value axis that determined the layout of the glyphs on the chart, so much so that rectangle shapes behaved unintuitively and no longer sat neatly along the x-axis; see Figure 4-5.

In fact, the overriding factor in the layout of your chart is the fields you have bound to the x- and y-axes of the plot segment, the *main* layout if you like. Within these constraints, there is additional factor that influences the layout of the glyphs and that is the type of *sub-layout* that has been applied, from which there are six to choose. This is what will decide whether you end up with a column or bar chart, whether they're stacked, clustered, or packed. It's this attribute that will enable you to create the bar chart and indeed a host of alternative chart layouts. Sub-layouts are applied *on top of the layout* determined by the fields currently bound to the x- and y-axes, which always take precedence. This means that sometimes the sub-layout will be negated by the fields bound to the axes. For example, having two categorical axes will result in a grid layout even though the sub-layout is not set to "Grid" but to "Stack X."

It's the impact of axes, sub-layouts, and attributes of the plot segment that results in the final look and feel of your chart, and this is what you'll be discovering in the content of this chapter.

Creating 2D Region Plot Segments

If you delete a plot segment, or you want to create an additional plot segment, you can use the **Plot Segments** button on the toolbar and select **2D Region**. You can then draw your plot segment onto the canvas. Make sure you draw your plot segment within the guides of the canvas; see Figure 5-3. You can double-check you have drawn the plot segment correctly by confirming that each corner of the plot segment has a green dot.

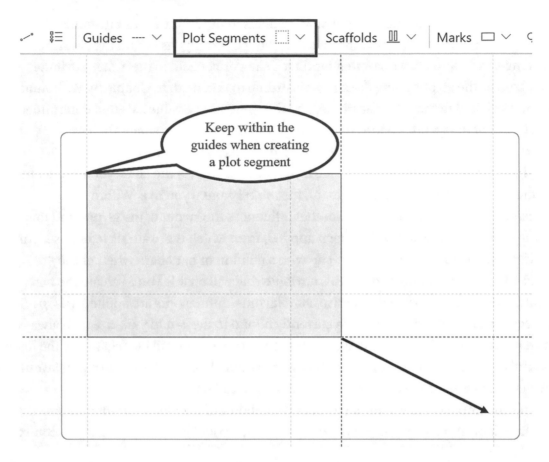

Figure 5-3. *Creating a 2D region plot segment*

Drawing the plot segment will generate a plot segment layer within the Chart layers in the Layers pane.

Using Plot Segment Sub-layouts

You can understand that if the layout of the chart is determined firstly by fields bound to the axes, either categorical or numerical, and then further influenced by a specific sub-layout that has been applied, the combination of these factors can quickly become overwhelming, and it's easy to lose sight of where you need to head to achieve your desired chart. As we explore how sub-layouts impact on our chart, therefore, we will start with a very simple chart where there are no fields bound to the axes and a glyph that comprises a single rectangle shape. Then we can start to look at the combined effect of adding categorical fields bound to the axes and selecting different types of sub-layout. Later, we can explore sub-layouts using symbols with numerical axes.

The chart I will be using in my examples is shown in Figure 5-4 where I have also bound the categorical "Salespeople" field to the Fill attribute of a rectangle mark so we can distinguish between the glyphs as we change the layout.

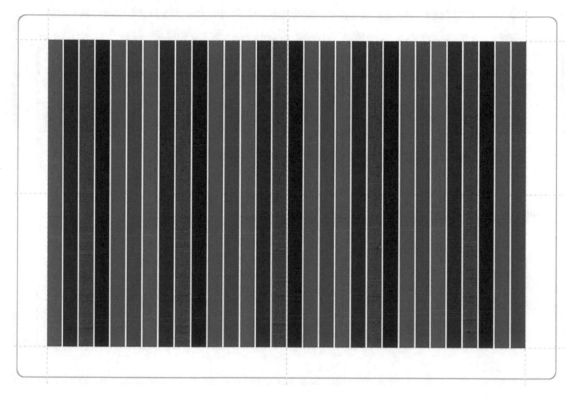

Figure 5-4. *A simple chart with no fields bound to axes*

To find the sub-layouts of a plot segment, ensure you have "PlotSegment1" selected in the Layers pane, and then you can either use the Sub-layout attribute in the Attributes pane or the **Stack X** dropdown button on the plot segment toolbar; see Figure 5-5.

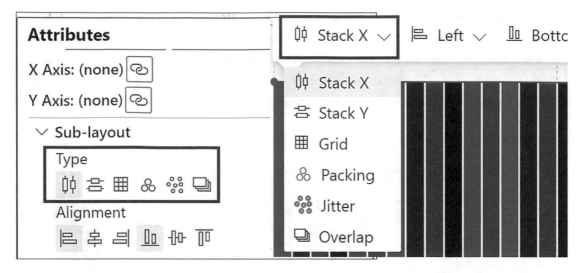

Figure 5-5. *The sub-layouts of a Charticulator chart*

The default sub-layout is Stack X, but you can choose one of five other sub-layouts:

- Stack X (the default)

- Stack Y

- Grid

- Packing

- Jitter

- Overlap

Let's now explore each of these sub-layouts in turn.

Stack X

With this sub-layout, the glyphs are stacked vertically along the x-axis, ordered by the values in the first field of the underlying data or by how you have set the sort order in the Options button top right of the visual header. In our case, we are sorting by the "Year" field because this is the first field in the Fields pane. Notice what happens if we change the order of the fields in the Data bucket of Power BI so that "Salespeople" is now first; see Figure 5-6.

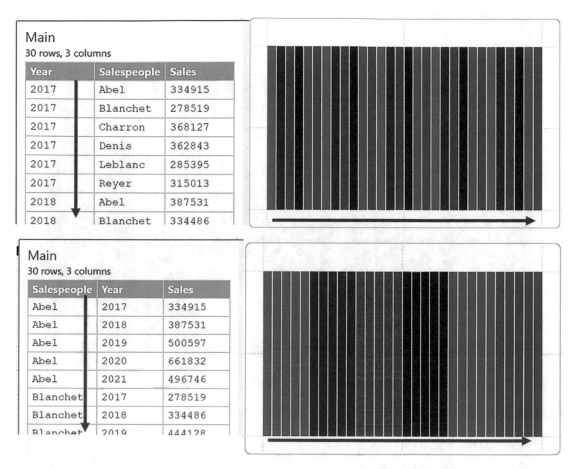

Figure 5-6. *Stack X with no categorical or numerical axes uses the order of the fields to sort the glyphs*

You could change this sorting order again by using the Options button, but nevertheless with no field bound to the x-axis, the sorting of the glyphs is not restrained by any x-axis grouping.

Stack X with a Categorical X-Axis

When we now bind a categorical field such as the "Year" field to the X Axis attribute of the plot segment, the layout changes to group the glyphs accordingly, irrespective of the order of the fields in the Fields pane, because the categorical axis always takes precedence in the layout; see Figure 5-7.

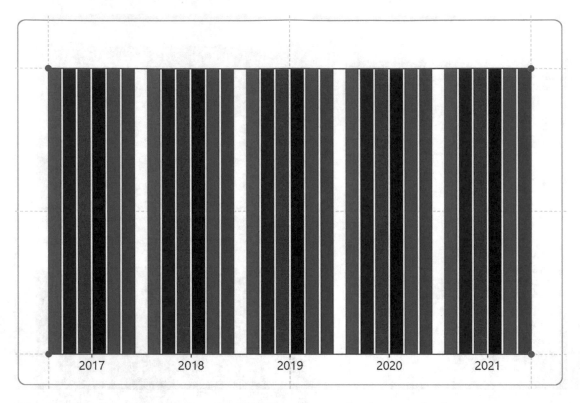

Figure 5-7. *Binding a categorical field to the x-axis changes the layout*

Once you have bound a categorical field to the axis, this will constrain the sorting of the glyphs to within each category.

Stack X with a Categorical Y-Axis

But look what happens if we bind the "Year" field to the Y Axis attribute instead. The glyphs are still stacked side by side for each salesperson but categorized by year down the y-axis; see Figure 5-8.

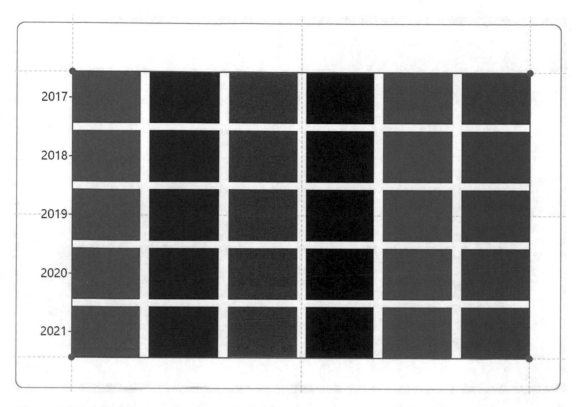

Figure 5-8. *Binding a categorical field to the y-axis changes the layout*

If we put the "Sales" field into the Width attribute (don't forget that you can use the dropzone in the Glyph pane to do this), the chart reveals more insightful data. In fact, what we have created is a stacked bar chart; see Figure 5-9.

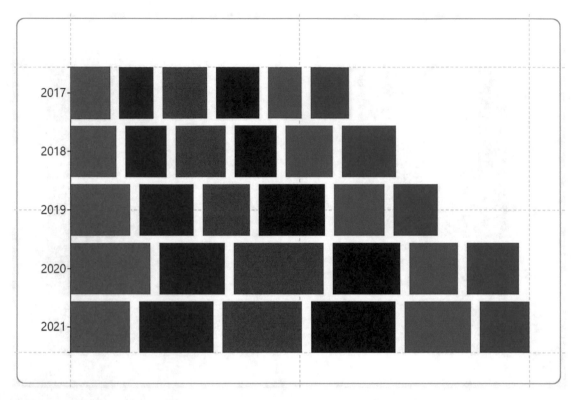

Figure 5-9. *Using Stack X and a categorical y-axis to create a stacked bar chart*

It's worth mentioning here that it's the binding of the data to the Width attribute that is instrumental in plotting the data and arriving at a meaningful visual.

Stack Y

Using the chart in Figure 5-4, where no fields are bound to either axis, and applying this sub-layout, we can see that the glyphs are now stacked horizontally down the y-axis (Figure 5-10).

Figure 5-10. *The Stack Y sub-layout with no categorical axes*

With regard to building our clustered bar chart, the chart in Figure 5-10 is looking promising. At least the glyphs are aligned in the correct direction.

Stack Y with a Categorical Y-Axis

All that's now required to complete the bar chart is to bind a categorical field such as "Year" onto the y-axis. Then if you bind your numerical field to the Width attribute of the rectangle shape instead of the Height attribute, you'll end up with a clustered bar chart. However, there is one thing still missing from our chart; a numerical legend on the x-axis to explain the lengths of the bars, so let's now add in this legend.

Adding an X-Axis Numerical Legend

If you remember when we created our column chart, we generated a legend on the y-axis by using the Legend button on the top toolbar; see Figure 1-17. Clearly, we need to generate a similar legend that will sit along the x-axis. However, you will not be able

93

to use the Legend button on the toolbar because the default numerical legend is only applicable to a y-axis. Instead, you'll must click on "Shape1.Width" in the Scales pane, and in the dialog that pops up, click **Add Legend**; see Figure 5-11.

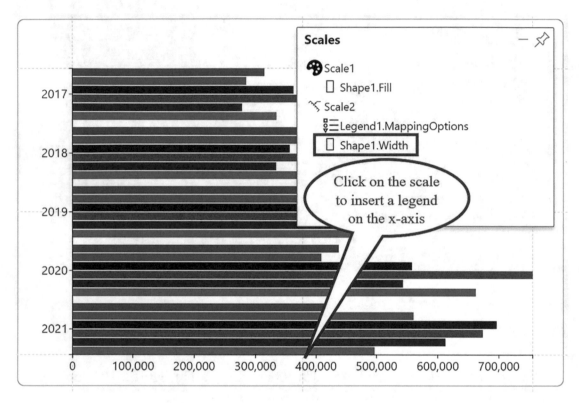

Figure 5-11. *A with a legend on the x-axis*

And that's it. We've finally got there; we've built a clustered bar chart. But great progress as this is, we are still at the tip of the iceberg with regard to what sub-layouts can do for us.

Stack Y with a Categorical X-Axis

For this, let's start again with our default chart as in Figure 5-4. A simple chart with no fields bound to axes. Apply a Stack Y sub-layout and now bind the "Year" field to the x-axis and bind "Sales" to the Height attribute. Because the category bound to the x-axis takes precedence, the glyphs are now categorized for each year along the x-axis, and the glyph for each salesperson is stacked on top, generating a stacked column chart; see Figure 5-12.

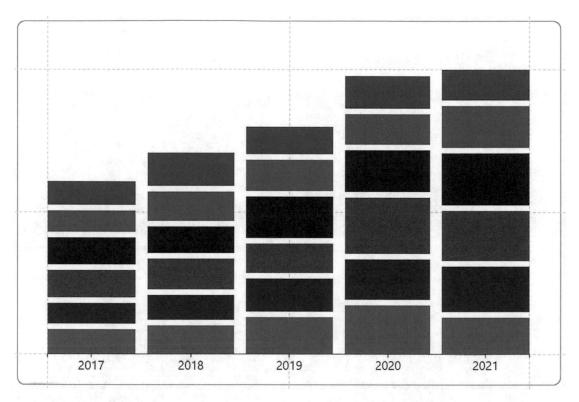

Figure 5-12. *Stack Y with a produces a stacked column chart*

I can appreciate that at this stage, you may be feeling that the different combinations of stacking along the x- and y-axes can be a little confusing. Figure 5-13 may help you understand these different combinations better.

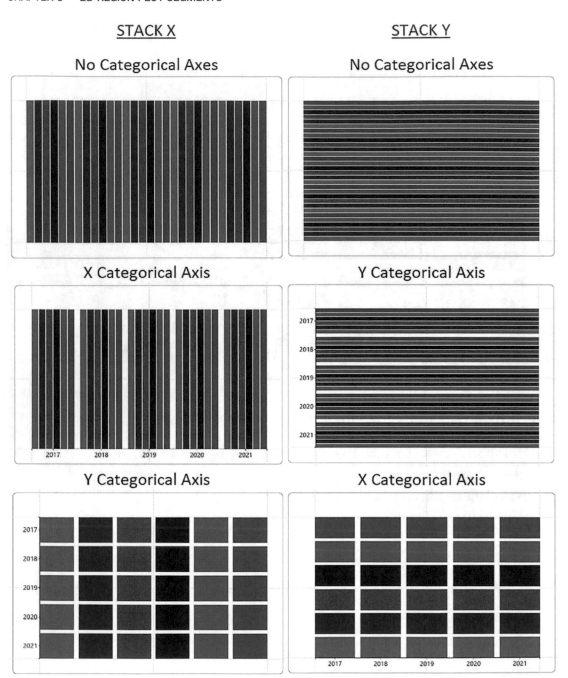

Figure 5-13. *The different combinations of Stack X and Stack Y*

Understanding the stacking sub-layouts has enabled you to generate stacked and clustered bar and column charts. These types of charts are necessary when you are using two categorical fields, such as "Year" and "Salespeople," so that both can be analyzed within the chart. What is particularly interesting about these two sub-layouts is what happens when you only have *one* category to worry about.

Stack X and Stack Y with One Category

In this scenario, we are using just two fields, one categorical and the other numerical, that is, "Salespeople" and "Sales." We've created a chart using a rectangle mark and then bound the "Salespeople" field to the Fill attribute of the shape and the X Axis attribute of the plot segment. The default sub-layout is Stack X. Notice, however, that applying a Stack Y sub-layout has no effect on the layout of the chart (Figure 5-14) because the layout has already been determined by the x-axis field.

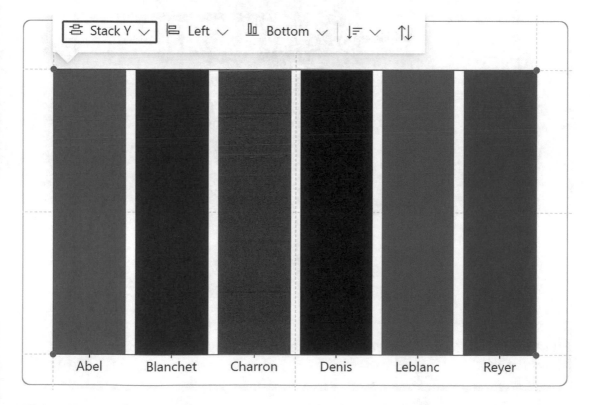

Figure 5-14. *Plotting only one category on the x-axis determines the layout*

Let's consider another example of the impact of binding the categorical field to the axis when you only have one category. Looking at the chart in Figure 5-15, we're analyzing our salespeople's performance by designing a glyph whose height represents their sales value, stacked vertically. In this chart, we have only one category, "Salespeople," but how would you generate this chart? It looks simple, but it hides some important aspects of sub-layouts vs. categorical axes.

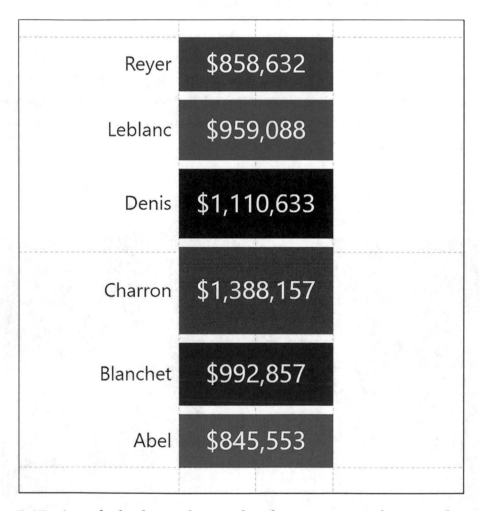

Figure 5-15. *A stacked column chart with only one category, for example,* "Salespeople"

The starting point is easy. You would just create a rectangle mark, bind a numerical field to the Height attribute and a categorical field to the Fill attribute, and then use the Stack Y sub-layout. Increasing the left and right margins of the chart canvas by dragging inwards on the guides will then reduce the width of the chart. The chart looks promising.

But if you now bind a categorical field, for example, "Salespeople," onto the y-axis to label the glyphs, this is not what we want. You can see how the chart has changed in Figure 5-16. Because the axis takes precedence, the glyphs are now plotted along the axis, and the category labels are equally spaced making the spacing of the rectangles look odd.

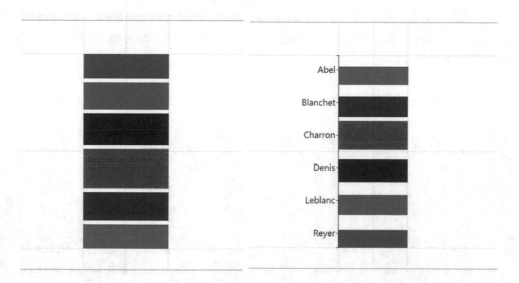

Figure 5-16. *The chart is incorrect when a category is bound to the y-axis (on the right)*

The chart was correct before we bound the y-axis field, so we need to remove this field from the Y Axis attribute. But how do we generate labels for the categories up the left side of the chart? To do this, you can attach a text mark to the left of the rectangle mark in the Glyph pane and bind the category to the Text attribute. The final embellishment is to add another text mark for the numerical value that shows inside the rectangle.

The moral of this story is that in Charticulator, you don't always want to bind categories to axes! Charticulator is quite happy to render a chart with no fields bound to either the x- or y-axis.

Grid

The Grid sub-layout is perhaps the most challenging of the sub-layouts to get to grips with. The reasons for this can be numerous. Like all sub-layouts, its effect will be very different if you have no fields bound to the axes, one categorical axis or two categorical axes, remembering that axes take precedence over sub-layouts. Also, Charticulator uses a default grid size according to the number of glyphs it needs to arrange, and it's not always apparent what this grid size is or how the glyphs have been arranged within it. In addition to these behaviors, the grid layout has attributes for orientation, direction, and count that can be combined in a mind-boggling variety of ways. You will find other aspects of this sub-layout take you by surprise. To explore some of these features of the Grid sub-layout, let's keep it simple, using our original chart, and apply the Grid sub-layout; see Figure 5-17.

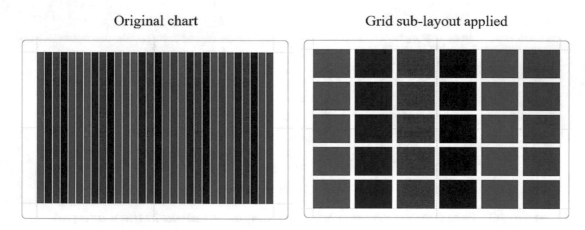

Figure 5-17. *How the Grid sub-layout changes the layout of the*

The Grid sub-layout looks very similar to the layout using Stack X with a categorical y-axis (Figure 5-8). What is the difference? The Grid sub-layout has no fields bound to the axes, and the layout is being driven solely by the sub-layout. This is where this sub-layout can come into its own. Consider the chart in Figure 5-18; you can see that the only factor determining the layout is the Grid sub-layout. In this visual, we've used a gradient color fill and text marks to show the values we want to analyze.

Figure 5-18. *Using the Grid sub-layout removes the need for*

We can now use some of the Grid options on the plot segment toolbar to rearrange the glyphs; see Figure 5-19.

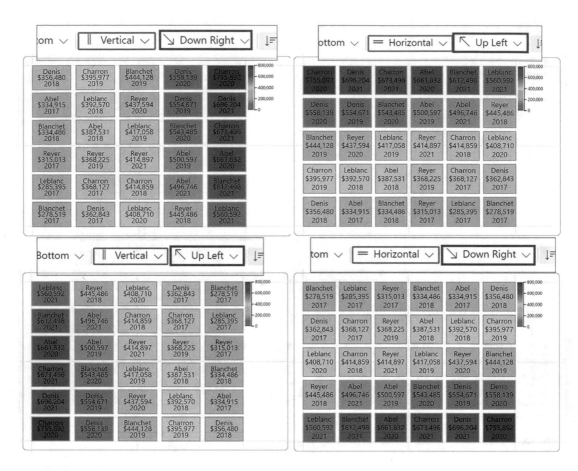

Figure 5-19. *Grid sub-layout options on the*

You can also find these options under the Sub-layout attributes of the plot segment, and you will discover a few more options besides. Take note that there is a Count attribute that controls the number of glyphs in each grid space. I'll let you explore these options yourself and see how you can change the layout of the grid. Why don't you try adding a few more categorical fields to your data and embark on a voyage of self-discovery with Charticulator's Grid sub-layout?

In the meantime, just think on this; in Power BI, the equivalent visual that uses a grid-like structure is the Matrix visual. You can only put numbers (i.e. measures) into the values area of a Matrix, not multiple values, text values, or shapes. Here's a challenge for you; would you be able to reproduce the chart in Figure 5-18 using a Power BI Matrix? You can see my attempt in Figure 5-20 where you can also observe that in Power BI you are restrained by the conventional cartesian layout, and so you must supply both row categories *and* column categories.

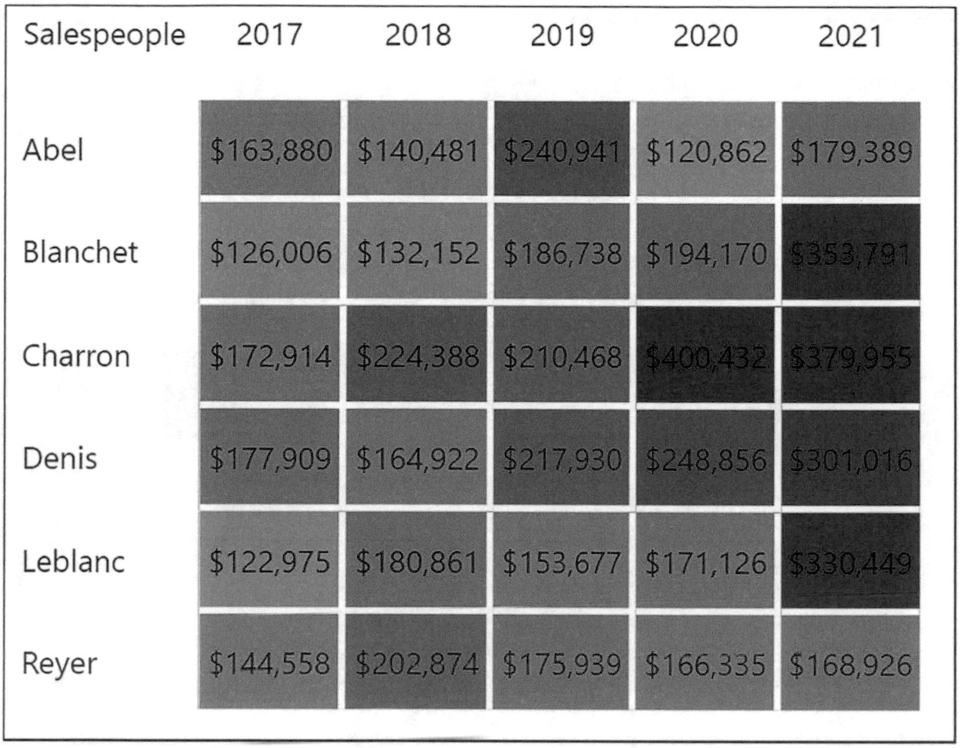

Salespeople	2017	2018	2019	2020	2021
Abel	$163,880	$140,481	$240,941	$120,862	$179,389
Blanchet	$126,006	$132,152	$186,738	$194,170	$353,791
Charron	$172,914	$224,388	$210,468	$400,432	$379,955
Denis	$177,909	$164,922	$217,930	$248,856	$301,016
Leblanc	$122,975	$180,861	$153,677	$171,126	$330,449
Reyer	$144,558	$202,874	$175,939	$166,335	$168,926

Figure 5-20. *The Power BI Matrix visual requires row and column labels*

The Grid sub-layout is great therefore for reproducing matrix style visuals but with many more design options.

Packing

If you have no fields on the x- or y- axis, the Packing sub-layout will pack the glyphs into the center of the canvas. What is important to understand is that the Packing sub-layout uses the existing sub-layout of the plot segment. Therefore, if you start with the chart in Figure 5-4 where you have a rectangle mark as your glyph and Stack X as your sub-layout and you then apply a Packing sub-layout, the chart goes seriously haywire. If, on the other hand, you start with the chart in Figure 5-4 and first apply a Grid sub-layout and *then* apply the Packing sub-layout, things look a little less haphazard particularly if you then bind a numerical field to both the Height and Width of the rectangle mark; see Figure 5-21.

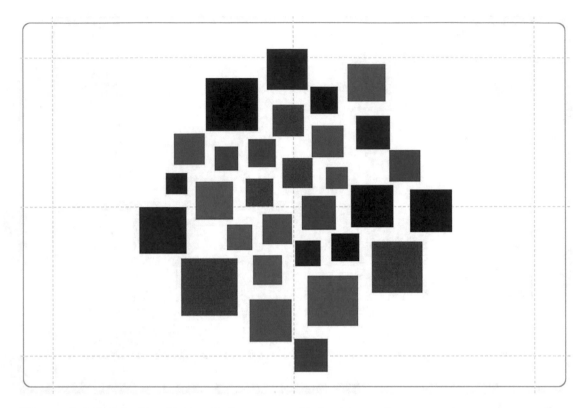

Figure 5-21. *The Packing sub-layout applied on top of a*

On the whole, however, Packing works best with the circle symbol where a numerical field has been populated into the "Size" attribute. Moreover, if you use a symbol, you don't need to apply a grid sub-layout first. This can provide the basis of a "cloud" type chart, or you can bind a categorical field to the x-axis to produce a clustered style of chart; see Figure 5-22.

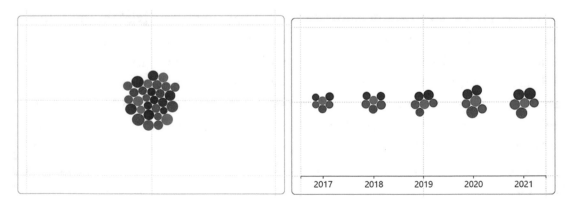

Figure 5-22. *on the Packing sub-layout using a symbol*

The Packing sub-layout also works particularly well with a numerical axis. The default sub-layout when using a numerical axis is the Overlap sub-layout (see the section on "Overlap" below), but you can change this to Packing which gives you a different insight into your data. Consider the visual in Figure 5-23 where I've added a third category to our data, the "Region" field. I've then bound the "Year" field to the x-axis, "Sales" field to the y-axis, and also bound "Sales" to the Size attribute of the symbol.

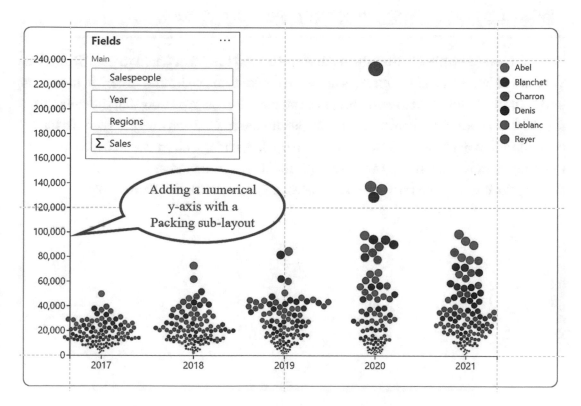

Figure 5-23. *Packing sub-layout with a symbol and a numerical*

What a great visual for spotting outliers. What was salesperson "Charron" doing in 2020 that resulted in such an amazing sales performance?

Jitter

This sub-layout is used to show density of data points and works best when you have many data points to plot and with a symbol in the Glyph pane. To show you how it works, I've started with a new chart that has four categories, "Year," "Month," "Salespeople," and "Regions," and one numerical field, "Sales."

Note   The months should sort correctly when you click **Save**.

I've then used a symbol in the Glyph pane and bound the "Year" field to the Fill attribute. We want to know in which months sales were densest, so I've bound "Year" to the x-axis and "Month" to the y-axis, generating two categorical axes. We know that the axes will dictate the layout of the chart, so with the default Stack X sub-layout, the symbols for each month in each year are all stacked side by side, and the chart does not give us any meaningful information. We can now apply the Jitter sub-layout and can see that in January 2020 sales were not as dense as sales in January 2021; see Figure 5-24.

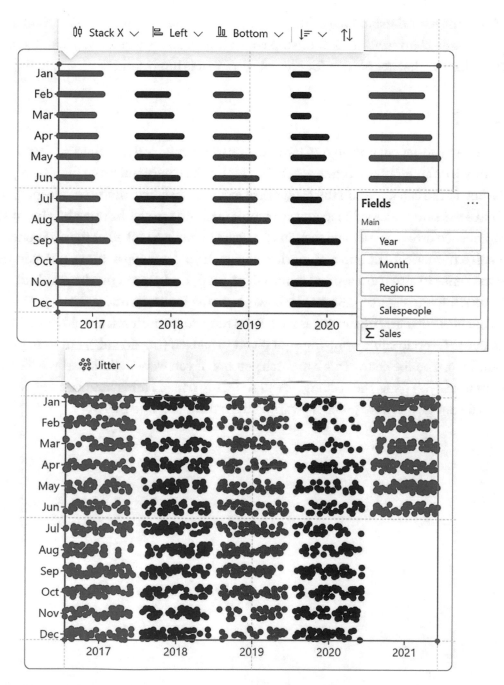

Figure 5-24. *The compared with the Stack X sub-layout*

The thing to understand regarding the Jitter sub-layout is that the positions of the symbols in the chart have no relationship with the data and are randomly arranged; it's just the number that are present for any category that is important.

Overlap

The Overlap sub-layout is used by Charticulator when you bind a numerical field to the x- or y-axis generating a numerical axis. This allows Charticulator to plot the glyphs according to the categories on the categorical axis. For instance, multiple salespeople may have the same sales value in any year, and therefore the glyphs must be able to sit on top of each other. As we have seen in Chapter 4, when we looked at the difference between a numerical axis and a numerical legend, if you're using a numerical axis, then it makes sense to also use a symbol in the Glyph pane, and we can produce a chart that will look similar to Figure 5-25 where you will note the Overlap sub-layout.

What is particularly frustrating is that if you remove the numerical field bound to the axis, the Overlap sub-layout does not revert to Stack X (the default), but remains as the sub-layout on the chart. This can catch you out. If you were to then use a rectangle mark in the Glyph pane, the rectangles will sit on top of each other, and you may wonder where all your glyphs have gone. Be warned. I'm still falling into this trap!

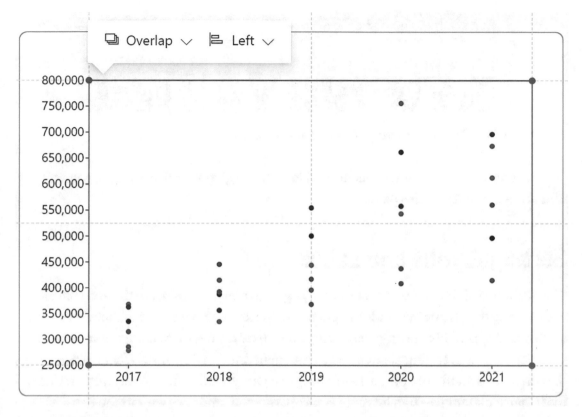

Figure 5-25. *If you use a numerical axis, you get the Overlap sub-layout*

We've now completed our exploration of Charticulator's sub-layouts and from now on will be putting them to good use. I think you can appreciate that with Charticulator, to achieve your design objective, it's all to do with how you combine your x- and y-axis fields with a specific plot segment sub-layout. This has been the most important lesson in understanding plot segments.

Let's move on to look at some of the other attributes of the 2D region plot segment. These allow you to control some of the more mundane matters surrounding plot segments such as sorting axis labels and spacing out the glyphs, among other things. Simple and mundane as these are, what we'll appreciate is that in Charticulator we have many more choices over how and what we can sort, space, and align than we would using a Power BI chart.

We've already explored the sub-layout dropdown button on the plot segment toolbar, and now we can turn our attention to the other buttons on the toolbar which are concerned with aligning (horizontal and vertical) and sorting elements of the chart; see Figure 5-26.

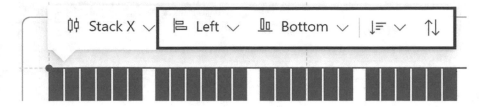

Figure 5-26. *The plot segment toolbar showing the*

With regard to options for spacing and formatting glyphs and axis labels, you will find these in the Attributes pane.

Sorting Glyphs and Labels

The attributes of the plot segment that we're going to explore here are those concerned with sorting the glyphs in the plot segment. To appreciate how Charticulator deals with sorting and to put this into context, it might be a useful exercise to compare sorting in Charticulator with sorting elements in a chart generated in Power BI. What we'll learn is that firstly Charticulator approaches sorting in a completely different way and secondly that Charticulator gives us a lot more control over what and how we sort the data.

Sorting a Power BI Chart

Let's consider the clustered column chart created in Power BI in Figure 5-27. You can see that you are not able to sort the columns.

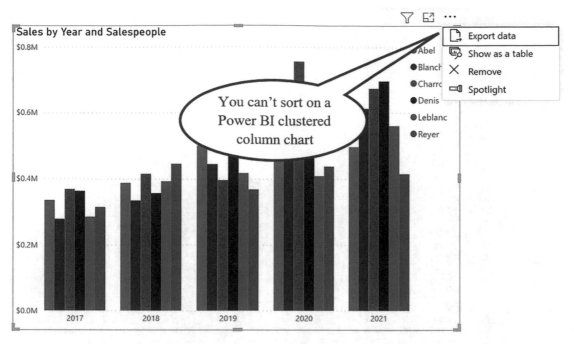

Figure 5-27. *A clustered column chart generated in Power BI showing the absence of sorting options*

You might therefore be tempted to construct the column chart in Power BI by putting all your categorical fields into the Axis bucket and using "Expand all down one level in the hierarchy"; see Figure 5-28.

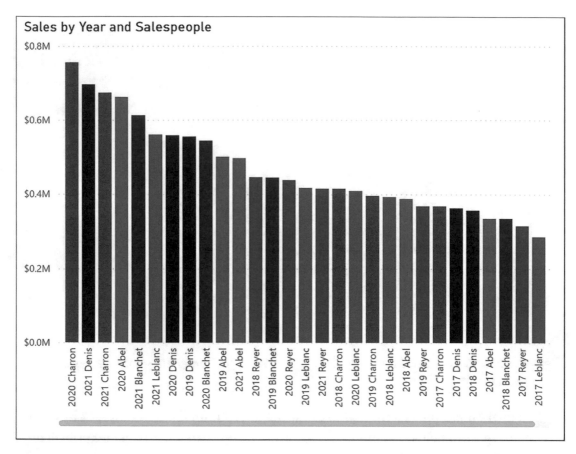

Figure 5-28. *Using a Power BI chart, you can expand into subcategories which allows sorting*

Notice that I've colored the columns by the Salespeople category so we can make a better comparison. What you will note is that like all Power BI visuals, the columns are sorted descending by value. If you want to re-sort the visual using the "More options" button, you will find that the sort order is determined by the order of the fields in the Axis bucket. To change the order of the categories, you need to change the order of the fields in the bucket; see Figure 5-29.

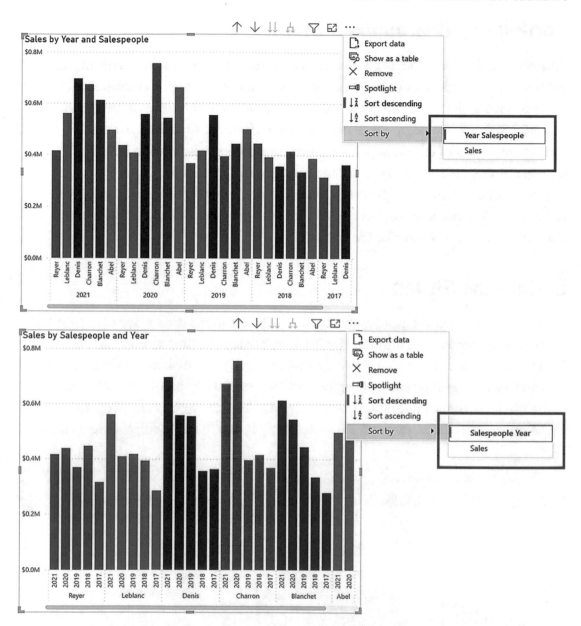

Figure 5-29. *In Power BI, the are sorted in the order they appear*

There are a number of frustrations here. Firstly, in order to sort the columns, you have to use a hierarchical structure and drill down. Secondly, you can't sort by the value within a category. For example, you can't sort salesperson "Reyer's" sales ascending by Sales value, only by Year. Finally, notice that I've used unconcatenated x-axis labels which can be particularly problematic to sort.

Sorting in a Charticulator Chart

I think we're done with looking at Power BI and have concluded that the sorting options are limited. Let's now look at how Charticulator manages sorting. A conventional approach would be to use the "More options" button top right of the Charticulator screen, just as you would for any Power BI visual. However, Charticulator has its own sorting options, and once you start using these, they will override Power BI's sorting options, so it's best to sort using the options inside Charticulator. One of the key differences is that unlike Power BI, where you can only sort either the categories or the value, in Charticulator you can sort both the glyphs and the axis labels in any combination that is allowed by the layout.

Sorting the Glyphs

In the absence of a field bound to the x-axis which constrains the sorting of the glyphs, the default sort order is determined by Power BI's default sorting options as seen on the Options button top right of the visual. To re-sort the glyphs, you can use the sorting and sort direction buttons on the plot segment toolbar, or you can use the "Order" attribute in the Attributes pane under the Sub-layout group. You can sort by any of the fields listed in the dropdown button, for example, descending by the "Sales" field; see Figure 5-30.

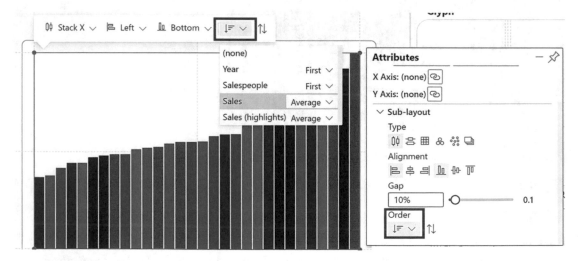

Figure 5-30. *The for the glyphs*

Once you bind a field to the x-axis, the sorting of the glyphs is restrained by that field. For instance, with the "Year" field bound to the x-axis, you can sort ascending or descending by the "Sales" field for each salesperson within each year (this is what we weren't able to do in Power BI); see Figure 5-31.

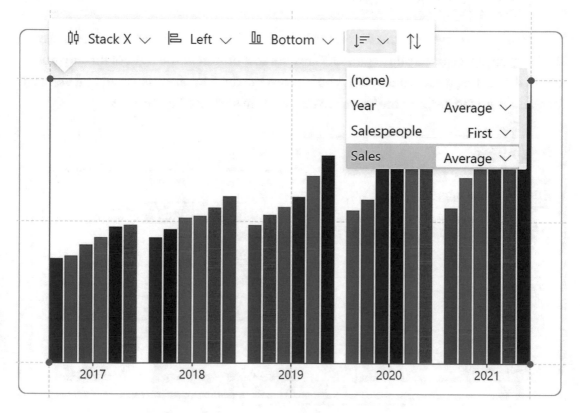

Figure 5-31. *Sorting the glyphs within each*

If you want to sort by the x-axis labels, for example, by "Year" descending, you can't do this from the plot segment toolbar despite the field listed on the sorting button because this only sorts within the x-axis categories. You must use the X Axis attribute in the Attributes pane (see the following section).

Tip If you want to sort an axis by a numerical field, don't bind a category to the axis. Use a text mark instead to label the categories.

The takeaway from this section on sorting glyphs is to remember that binding a categorical field to either an x- or y-axis will restrain the sorting of the glyphs to within the categories.

Sorting the Axis Labels

To sort the labels on the x-axis, for example, by the "Year" field, you will need to use the Order By attribute of the plot segment. Click the sort button to the right of the attribute, and in the sorting dialog that opens, you can reverse the sort, and also note that you can drag and drop the items in the list to create a custom sort; see Figure 5-32.

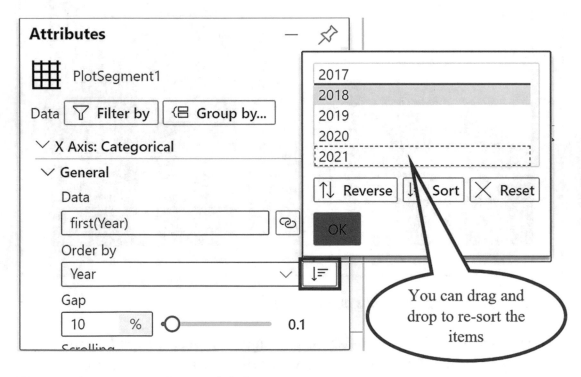

Figure 5-32. *Sorting the axis labels*

To produce custom sorting on x- or y-axes labels in a Power BI chart requires using a "sort column" in the underlying data and therefore, hopefully you're thinking that this is a lot easier.

Spacing Glyphs and Labels

With regard to spacing out elements in your chart, again we can compare the limited choice in Power BI to the richer selection of options in Charticulator.

Spacing in a Power BI Chart

In Power BI, the only option available is the "Inner padding" formatting option on the X Axis formatting card; see Figure 5-33.

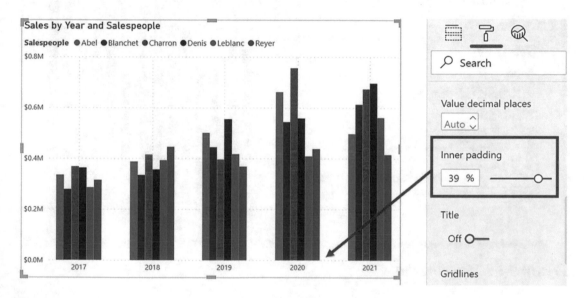

Figure 5-33. *Power BI "Inner padding" option only changes the space between axis labels*

This only allows you to change the spacing between the x-axis labels, not between the columns.

Spacing in a Charticulator Chart

However, in Charticulator, we have a lot more control over the spacing of the elements. The spacing options are similar to the sorting options in that there are two different spaces that you might want to change: the gap between the axis labels and the gap between glyphs.

Spacing the Glyphs

To change the gap between the glyphs, use the "Gap" attribute under the Sub-layout group; see Figure 5-34.

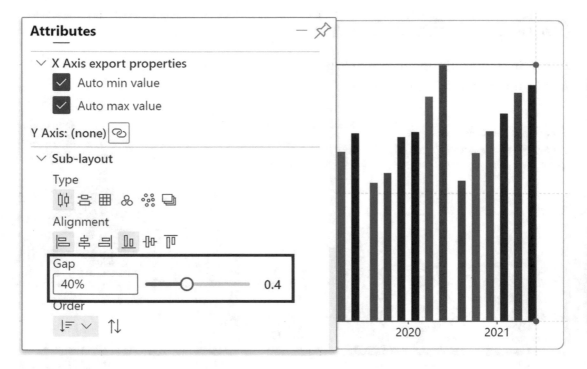

Figure 5-34. *Spacing the*

You can also just drag between glyphs to change the gap.

Spacing the Axis Labels

To do this, use the "Gap" attribute under X Axis: Categorical of the plot segment. Alternatively, you can simply drag between the categories in the chart; see Figure 5-35.

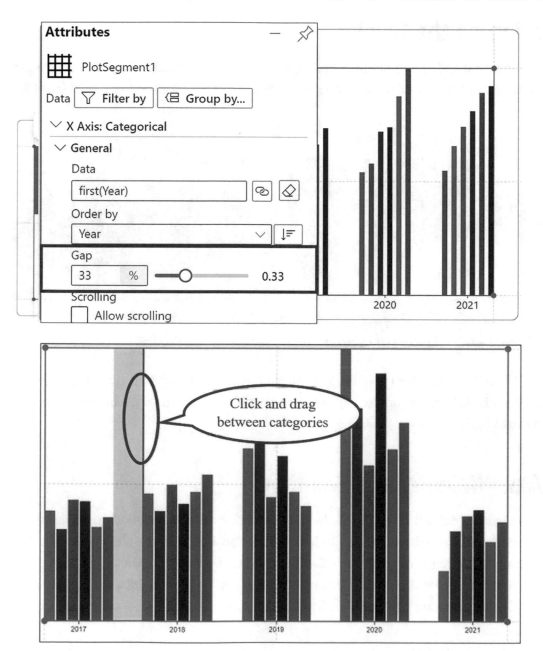

Figure 5-35.   *Spacing the*

We've been concentrating on using these sorting and spacing options with a Stack X sub-layout but they are also applicable to any sub-layout.

Aligning the Glyphs

You can change the alignment of the glyphs by using the alignment options on the plot segment toolbar or under the Sub-layout attributes of the plot segment; see Figure 5-36.

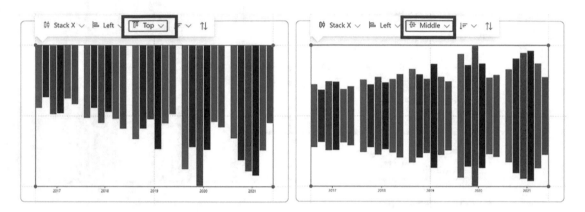

Figure 5-36. *Aligning the glyphs*

However, at the time of writing, if you align your glyphs at the top of the plot segment and you have a legend on the left, you are not able to invert the scale on the legend as you can in Power BI.

Axis Visibility and Position

The Visibility & Position group of attributes permits exciting design alternatives to conventional axis labels. You can hide the axis or position the axis above or on the right of the plot segment. You can also offset the axis labels away from the axis itself. Using a negative number will move the labels inwards. If you do this, the labels may lurk behind the glyphs, so we are given an "On Top" attribute as well.

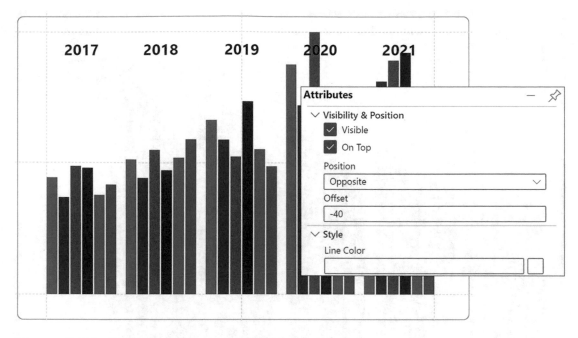

Figure 5-37. *Changing the position of the axis labels*

In Figure 5-37, we have moved the labels to the opposite side and offset the labels by –40. Notice also that the Line Color attribute has been changed to no color (select "none" in the color palette).

Once you have bound data to the X or Y Axis attribute, you can also hide the labels using the Visible attribute. Doing this allows you to control which "labels" show on the axes. For instance, in the example in Figure 5-38, I've bound the "Year" field to the X Axis attribute of the plot segment because I needed to categorize the glyphs accordingly, and I used the Fill attribute to color them by year. I then bound the "Salesperson" field to a text mark and anchored it to the bottom of the glyph. I checked off the Visible attribute to remove the labels for the "Year" field because I only wanted to see the text marks for the salespeople.

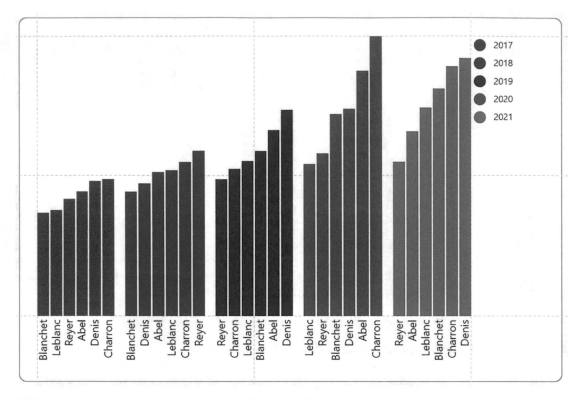

Figure 5-38.   *and using a text mark instead*

Using text marks in this way to label the axis categories gives you great flexibility in how data on the axis is displayed.

Formatting Axis Labels and Tick Lines

This brings us now to look at the formatting attributes of the plot segment.

Note   Formatting options that are specific to a numerical axis will be covered in Chapter 7.

Remember that the formatting of the glyphs depends on the attributes of the mark, symbol, or line that comprises the glyph. The elements that you can format in the plot segment are the axis labels and the tick marks, and you will find these attributes under the Style group of attributes; see Figure 5-39.

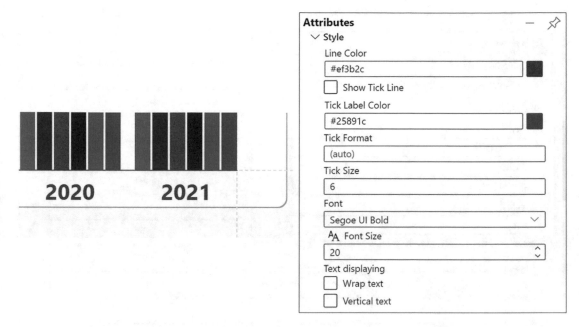

Figure 5-39. *Formatting the axis labels and tick marks*

As an example of how you could format the axis style, I have changed the line color to red, hid Tick Line, changed the label color to green, and increased the Font Size.

Gridlines

Gridlines are often associated with a numerical axis. As we have seen in Chapter 4 when we created a line chart, you need to bind a numerical field to either the X or Y Axis attribute of the plot segment to create a numerical axis and should also use a symbol in the Glyph pane. You can then use the Gridline attributes of either the x- or y-axis as shown in Figure 5-40 where we have added gridlines to the y-axis.

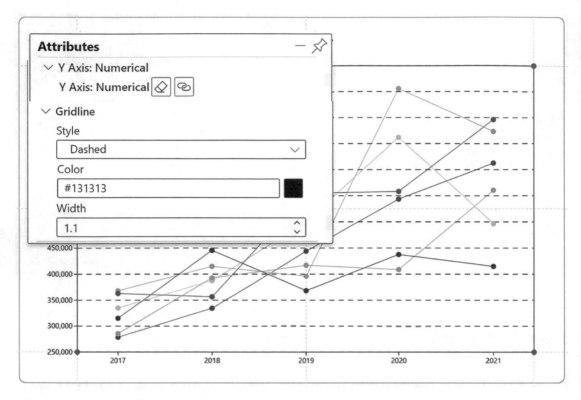

Figure 5-40. *Gridlines on the y-axis*

If you have a numerical x-axis, for example, in a bar type chart, you can also display vertical gridlines which can help clarify the data.

Hands-On with Plot Segment Attributes

Being able to successfully apply the attributes of the plot segment means that you are moving forward in understanding Charticulator and you can now start to reap the benefits of using this software. To prove this is the case, it would be great if you could employ your newly found skills in using Charticulator to build three different charts, some hands-on practice if you like. In Figure 5-41, using your own data, why don't you see if you can build similar charts that all require the use of the plot segment's attributes?

Figure 5-41. *Chart #1*

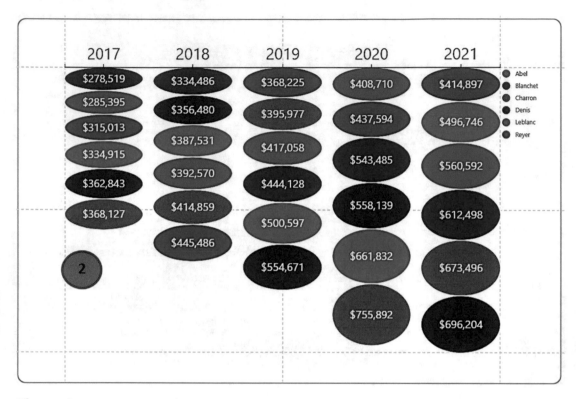

Chart #2

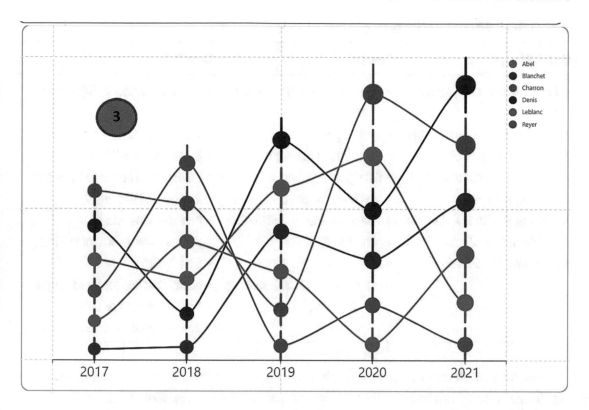

Chart #3

How well did you do? I'm sure your charts are looking great. If not, in Table 5-1, I have listed which attributes were used in each chart using my example data.

Table 5-1. *How the charts in Figure 5-41 were designed*

Chart #1	Chart #2	Chart #3
• Ellipse Shape in Glyph pane	• Ellipse Shape in Glyph pane	• Line and symbol in Glyph pane
• Stack Y	• Stack Y	• Stack Y
• Salespeople bound to Y Axis	• Year bound to X Axis	• Year bound to X Axis
• Sales bound to Width	• Sales bound to Height	• Sales bound to Y Span of Line
• Salespeople bound to Fill	• Salespeople bound to Fill	• Salespeople bound to Stroke of
• Text mark for Year	• Text mark for Sales	line and Fill of symbol
• Text mark Anchor X=Left	• Text mark Anchor Y=Middle	• Increase Line Width
and Anchor Y=Middle	• Align top vertically	• Sales bound to Size of symbol
• Align Middle vertically	• Move Axis to opposite	• Sort by Sales
	• Insert legend for Salespeople	• Insert Link line for Salespeople
		• Format Bezier link line
		• Insert legend for Salespeople

You may think that the preceding charts are eye-catching and buck the trend of traditional charts, but to be quite honest with you, up to now most of our charts have been at best conventional and at worst plain dull, at least as far as Charticulator is concerned. We're still stuck using a *single* categorical axis. What we have yet to explore is one of the great advantages of creating charts in Charticulator, and that is the ability to use *two* categorical axes and no value axis. Like the idea of this? Then you'll need to move on to the next chapter.

CHAPTER 6

Using Two Categorical Axes

At the beginning of this book, I urged you to forget everything you currently know about creating conventional charts, but instead to think in terms of designing a representation of your data, where you're no longer restrained by the number of axes, categories, and values you want to represent. Yet so far, we've been very unambitious in our chart designs.

In the last chapter, we explored how Charticulator gives you more control over the layout of chart elements than you can achieve in charts generated in Power BI. However, all the charts we've produced up to this point have been variations on standard visuals such as bar, column, and line charts. As we have already learned, in Charticulator, the plotting of numerical data can be independent from a value axis and can depend only onto which attributes numerical data is bound. Therefore, the value axis can become redundant, making way for both categorical x- and y-axes. This will be the focus of this chapter: exploring the benefits of designing charts that use two categorical axes. In Figure 6-1, we have two examples of such charts that I'd like you to consider.

© Alison Box 2022
A. Box, *Introducing Charticulator for Power BI*, https://doi.org/10.1007/978-1-4842-8076-8_6

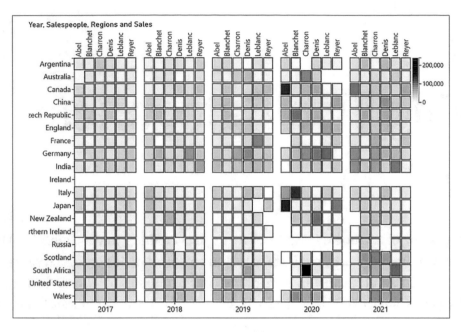

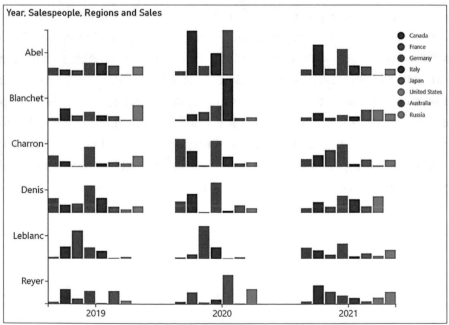

Figure 6-1. *Charts using two categorical axes*

Let me now ask you this. Could you construct these visuals using the default Power BI charts? You might get frustratingly close using a Matrix visual and using "small multiples," respectively, but that's just it; they'll be close but not rendering quite the same detail.

In what follows in this chapter, I'll show you how you can create these charts. We'll explore the possibilities open to us when wanting to plot multiple categories and how in Charticulator, unlike in Power BI, you can use both categorical x- and y-axes in the same chart. You'll also pick up some tips and tricks along the way such as learning how to display only certain elements of the chart, while hiding others.

Before we do this, however, first we need to dismantle the mindset of feeling confined by the conventional cartesian chart layout, that is, a single *categorical* axis with a single *value* axis. In charts generated by Power BI, for instance, because you are constrained by a single categorical axis, if you want to manage multiple categories, you must use one of four methods (shown in Figure 6-2):

1. Clustering

2. Stacking

3. Drill down on a hierarchy

4. Expand all down one level on a hierarchy

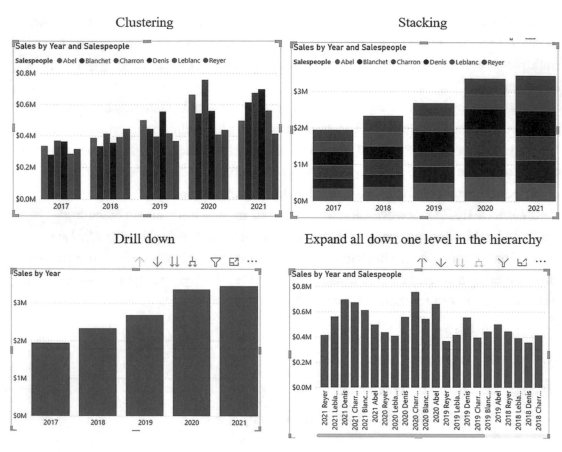

Figure 6-2. *Managing multiple categories in Power BI charts*

In Charticulator, we don't have the same restrictions, and there are almost limitless ways to plot multiple categories. In doing so, there are two approaches you can take. Firstly, you can create a "matrix" style chart where the values being plotted sit at the intersection of the x and y category. Secondly, you can use a type of "small multiples" approach where the sub-layout of the chart produces mini bar or column charts for each combination of x and y category.

Note   To design a visual containing true small multiples, where the same chart is repeated against categorical data, you need to use a nested chart which is the subject of Chapter 17.

Let's take a closer look at both of these options.

Designing "Matrix" Style Charts

We will start with a very simple example using the fields shown in Figure 6-3 with a rectangle mark as our glyph. We can bind the "Year" field to the x-axis and bind the "Salespeople" field to the y-axis to create two categorical axes. Notice how we have a Stack X sub-layout but still get a "grid" layout dictated by the x- and y-axis categories.

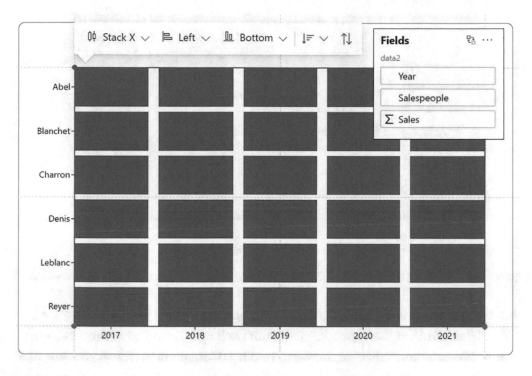

Figure 6-3. *Using two categorical axes creates a "grid" layout*

The chart in Figure 6-3 doesn't tell us much about our sales. What we can do here is bind the "Sales" field to the Fill attribute of the rectangle shape, select the "spectral" gradient color, and insert a legend at the same time. We can now analyze our salespeople's performance and see in Figure 6-4 that the best years were 2020 and 2021. Have you seen this chart before? It's very similar to the chart we created in Chapter 5 when we looked at the Grid sub-layout. What's the difference? In the Grid sub-layout, we had no fields bound to the axes, so the layout was driven by the sub-layout. Here, the categorical axes are responsible for the "grid" style layout.

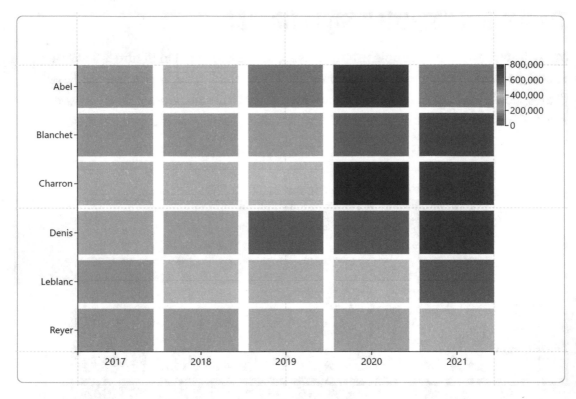

Figure 6-4. *Adding a "spectral" gradient color allows the analysis of the data*

But let's get more ambitious. Up to now, we've always used just two categories, the "Year" field and the "Salespeople" field, but we'll now introduce a third category, "Regions." We can bind "Year" to the x-axis and bind "Regions" to the y-axis. Just like before, notice the "grid" layout even though the sub-layout is Stack X; see Figure 6-5. Each glyph represents sales for each salesperson in each region in each year.

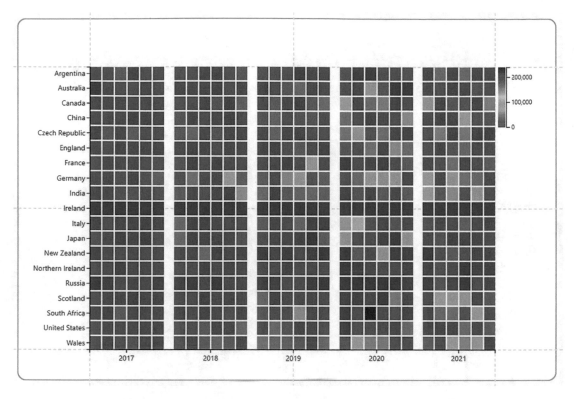

Figure 6-5. *Adding a third category to the chart maintains the grid*

The spectral gradient fill doesn't really work for me. It's difficult to distinguish between the lower sales values. Also, we can't tell which salesperson each glyph represents. What we can do here is edit the gradient color to just grays and bind the "Salespeople" field to the "Stroke" attribute of the rectangle to create a colored border dependent on each salesperson; see Figure 6-6.

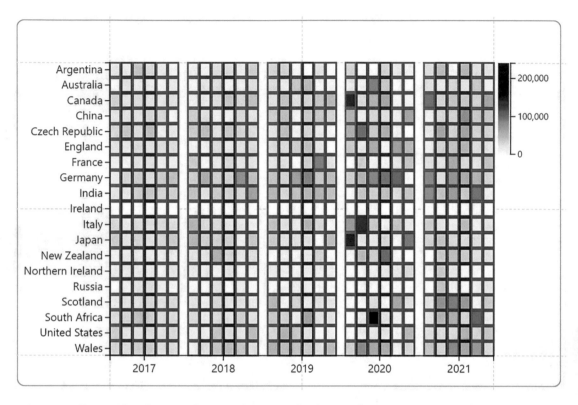

Figure 6-6. *Using the Stroke attribute and editing the gradient color improves the chart*

However, it's still not very clear which salespeople's sales we're looking at particularly as we don't have a legend for the "Salespeople" field. What we want is a secondary x-axis at the top of the chart that labels each "column" of glyphs accordingly. You can see the chart we're heading for in Figure 6-12.

To add the secondary x-axis, we need to add a text mark to the glyph and then follow these steps:

1. Anchor the text mark to the top of the glyph (drag the green dot).

2. Position the text mark above the glyph.

3. Rotate the text mark.

4. Bind the "Salesperson" field to the text and "Color" attributes.

However, we've ended up with a bit of a mess (Figure 6-7).

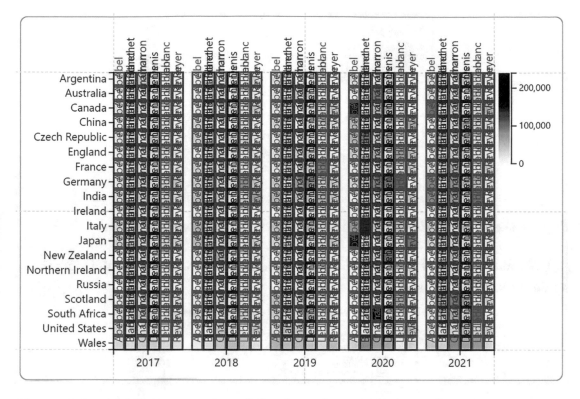

Figure 6-7. *Add the text mark and the chart does not look good*

What's happened of course is that we get a text mark above *every* glyph, not just above the rectangles at the top of the chart. To achieve our desired goal, we need to get to grips with the Visibility attribute of the rectangle shape. Before doing this, however, let's digress a little and remind ourselves how Charticulator controls the visibility of different elements of the chart.

Hiding Elements

We can easily hide any layer in the Layers pane by using the toggle visibility buttons; see Figure 6-8.

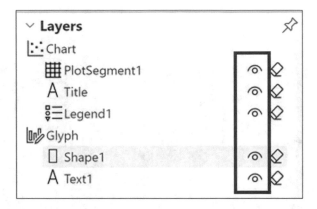

Figure 6-8. *The toggle visibility buttons in the Layers pane*

To hide the x- or y-axis labels, you can use the Visible attribute of the plot segment under Visibility & Position; see Figure 6-9.

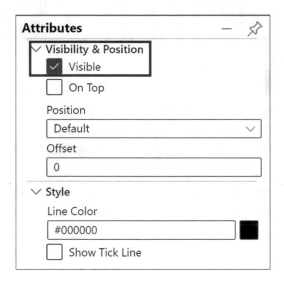

Figure 6-9. *The Visible attribute allows you to hide axis labels*

However, both of these approaches are an "all or nothing" scenario. We want to show only the text marks that lie in the secondary x-axis space at the top of the chart. These are the text marks associated with "Argentina" (the region represented by the top row of glyphs). But if we hide the "Text1" layer, it will hide ***all*** the text marks. So how do we hide some elements but not others?

Conditioned By

Charticulator has provided a way to do this. The attributes of a text mark or a shape include a Visibility attribute that allows you to bind data on which you can filter out specific text marks or shapes. This is the "Conditioned by…" dropzone that you can see under the Visibility attribute. If we bind the "Regions" field to the Visibility attribute by dropping it onto "Conditioned by…", we can then filter on "Argentina" so that only text marks for Argentina show at the top of the chart; see Figure 6-10.

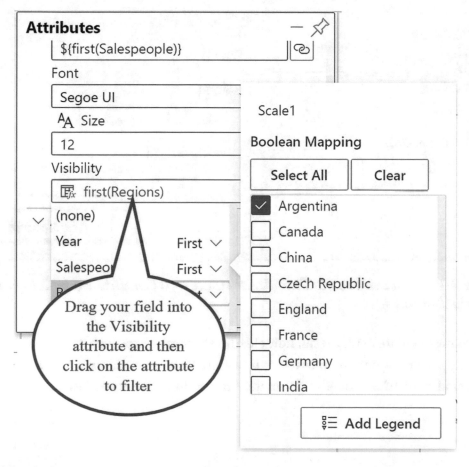

Figure 6-10. *Binding a field to the Visibility attribute and filtering the value to show*

We can do a similar thing to hide a rectangle shape where there are zero sales. Again, using the Visibility attribute of the shape and Conditioned by…, we can bind the "Sales" field and filter sales greater than zero; see Figure 6-11.

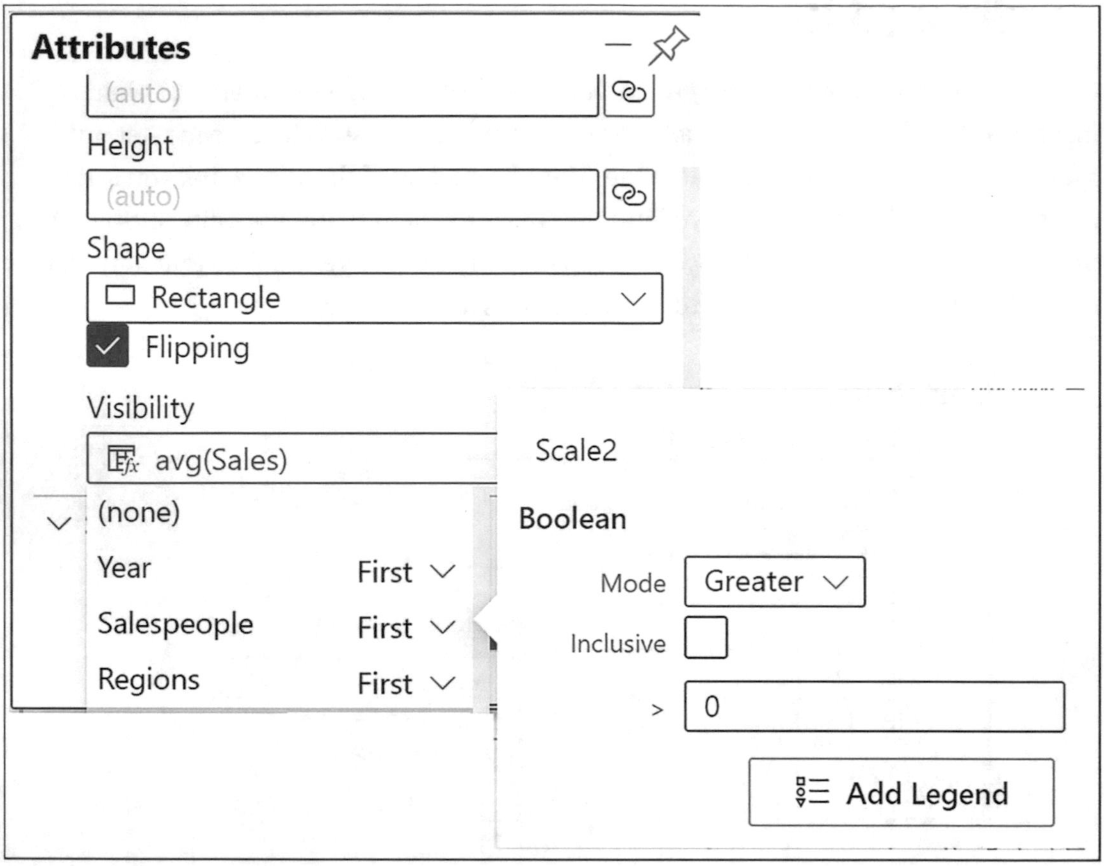

Attributes   — 📌

(auto)   🔗

Height

(auto)   🔗

Shape

▢ Rectangle   ⌄

☑ Flipping

Visibility

🔣 avg(Sales)   │   Scale2

⌄ (none)   │   Boolean

Year   First ⌄   Mode │ Greater ⌄ │

Salespeople   First ⌄   Inclusive ☐

Regions   First ⌄   > │ 0 │

                                        ⦂≡ Add Legend

Figure 6-11. *You can use the Visibility attribute and Conditioned by… to filter on numerical values*

Looking at Figure 6-12, we can now clearly see where there have been no sales. We can easily perform other analyses too. Why was Abel's sales in Canada and Japan so exceptional in 2020? Blanchet's sales in Italy in 2020 look pretty good too.

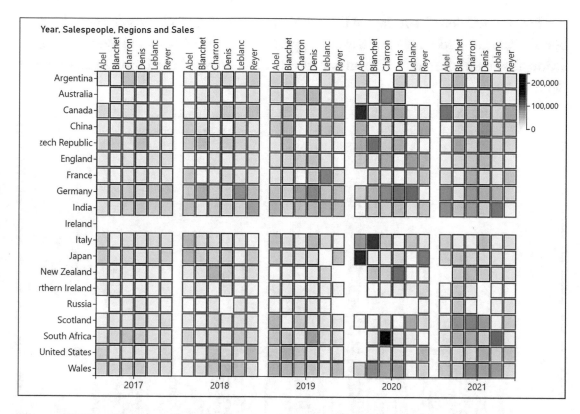

Figure 6-12. *The completed matrix style chart plotting three categories*

Depending on the data you are plotting, this chart would make for a great heat map style visual, using the spectral gradient fill.

Small Multiple Type Charts

An alternative way to plot multiple categories is to use the "small multiples" approach. Let's create a simple column chart using the rectangle mark in the Glyph pane and put the "Regions" into the Fill attribute of the shape and "Sales" into the Height attribute.

Note   For clarity in the chart in Figure 6-14, I have filtered out some of the regions.

Because the default sub-layout is Stack X, at first the chart looks very crowded because there is a rectangle glyph for every year for every salesperson in every region, synonymous with "expand all down one level in the hierarchy" of a Power BI chart; see Figure 6-13.

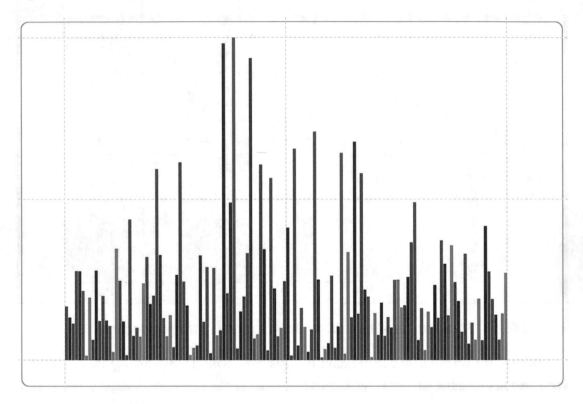

Figure 6-13. *The Stack X sub-layout with multiple categories results in a crowded chart*

But look what happens when we put the "Year" field on the x-axis and the "Salespeople" field on the y-axis. Because we have a Stack X sub-layout, we automatically get mini column charts for each year and each salesperson to show sales in each region; see Figure 6-14. This is equivalent to the "small multiples" option in Power BI.

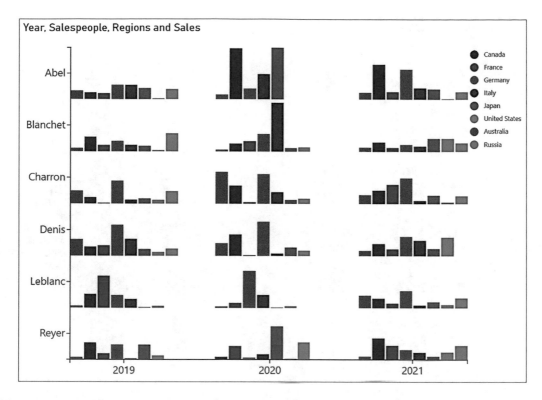

Figure 6-14. *Using a categorical y-axis produces mini column charts*

We could use other sub-layouts to create different "mini" charts. Let's try working with a symbol glyph instead of a rectangle mark and use the Packing sub-layout. In the example in Figure 6-15, I've bound the "Sales" field to the Size attribute of the symbol and the "Region" field to the Fill attribute. Why don't you try out different combinations of axes and sub-layouts when plotting multiple categories?

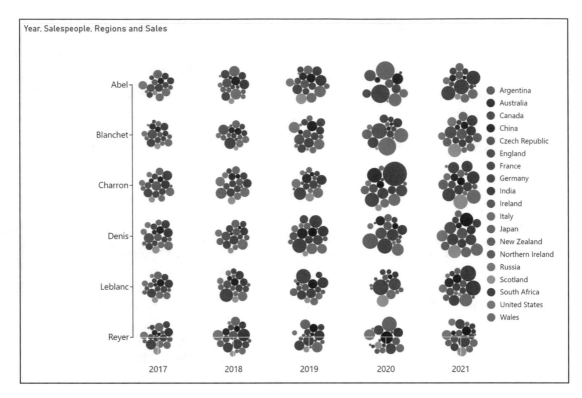

Year, Salespeople, Regions and Sales

Figure 6-15. *Using the Packing sub-layout with two categorical axes*

I hope you've enjoyed our foray into working with Charticulator's categorical axes and appreciate that using two categorical axes allows you to break away from designing standard charts. You've also learned how to limit the visibility of specific values by using the Visibility attribute and assigning a filter through the "Conditioned by…" option.

However, now that you understand Charticulator's categorical axes, this begs the question; what about using Charticulator's numerical axes? We've already had a brief look at using numerical axes when we explored the symbol glyph in Chapter 4. On that occasion, we learned the difference between numerical legends and numerical axes. In the next chapter, we will revisit the numerical axis. We will delve deeper into its attributes looking not only at controlling the scale and numeric formatting but also discovering what Charticulator's "Tick Data" is, the reason for using it and the benefit of doing so.

CHAPTER 7

Using Numerical Axes

In the previous chapter, we explored the possibilities of using two categorical axes, and hopefully this has inspired you to build more adventurous visuals. It would make sense therefore to now focus on how we can use Charticulator's numerical axes to greater effect too. I'm sure you're quite conversant with using value axes in charts you've built in Power BI and other applications, and therefore in this chapter, you would typically expect to learn how to edit the range of values used by the axis and format the labels that are specific to numerical data. Both of these topics we will of course be covering here.

There is however an attribute associated with Charticulator's numerical axis whose behavior is definitely out of the ordinary that can generate a kind of hybrid axis, plotting numerical data but assigning categorical labels to the tick marks on the axis. This is Charticulator's Tick Data, and in this chapter, along with the attributes you would expect to meet, you will also be discovering the benefit of using this more unusual attribute of the numerical axis.

We're going to start by considering the data in Figure 7-1 and exploring a specific scenario. Our salespeople sell a variety of wines, and we've recorded the number of sales of each wine and the price per case in two numerical fields, named accordingly.

© Alison Box 2022
A. Box, *Introducing Charticulator for Power BI*, https://doi.org/10.1007/978-1-4842-8076-8_7

Main 42 rows, 4 columns			
Salespeople	**Wine**	**PricePerCase**	**NoOfSales**
Abel	Bordeaux	75	50
Abel	Champagne	150	54
Abel	Chardonnay	100	41
Abel	Chenin Blanc	50	39
Abel	Malbec	85	49
Abel	Merlot	39	40
Abel	Piesporter	135	34
Blanchet	Bordeaux	75	34
Blanchet	Champagne	150	58
Blanchet	Chardonnay	100	43
Blanchet	Chenin Blanc	50	37
Blanchet	Malbec	85	64

Fields   ...

Main

Salespeople

Wine

Σ PricePerCase

Σ NoOfSales

Figure 7-1. *The data used in the examples that follow*

We want to design a visual to show the number of sales that each salesperson has achieved of *expensive* wines or of *cheap* wines, prices per case ranging from $39 to $150. In Figures 7-2 and 7-3, there are alternative attempts to show this analysis. In Figure 7-2, the "PricePerCase" field has been bound to the y-axis, giving us a conventional numerical axis. The number of sales value is shown in a text mark in the glyph, a symbol in this case. However, we don't know to which wine the prices on the y-axis are referring. In Figure 7-3, however, you can see that the y-axis is now labeled for each wine with the price per case. The y-axis is still a numerical axis despite its appearance.

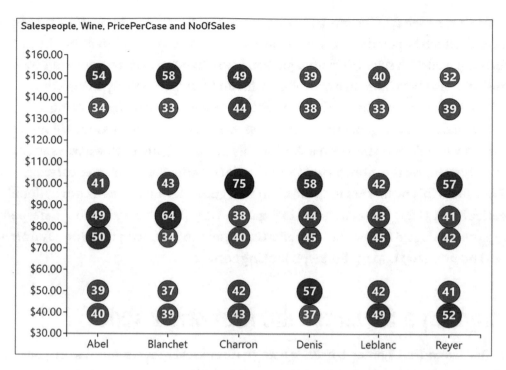

Figure 7-2. *We don't know to which products the prices are referring*

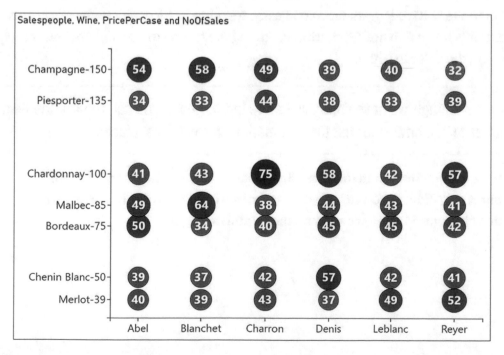

Figure 7-3. *We can see the product name and the price*

We can now see that the most cases have been sold for "Chardonnay" by salesperson "Charron" which is a medium-priced wine. However, salesperson "Abel" has been performing well with sales of Champagne, our most expensive wine, while salesperson "Denis" has also been hard at work selling Chenin Blanc, a relatively cheap wine.

We've been able to arrive at these insights because in Charticulator, using a numerical axis, you can generate text labels associated with specific values along the axis. However, before we move on to look at this intriguing prospect, we will start by learning how to use the more prosaic attributes of Charticulator's numerical axes.

We will do this by first creating the chart in Figure 7-2 which uses a conventional numerical axis. Using the data shown in Figure 7-1, firstly we've bound the "Salespeople" field to the x-axis and bound the "PricePerCase" field to the y-axis, creating a numerical y-axis. The next step is to get the glyph looking correct.

Designing a Glyph for the Numerical Axis

As we discovered in Chapter 4, if we're using a numerical axis, a symbol works best in the Glyph pane, but you could change this to a different shape, such as a square, if preferred. We've then bound the "NoOfSales" field to Size and Fill attributes of the symbol, editing the Fill to the "YlOrRd" gradient color. Lastly, we added a text mark to the glyph and bound "NoOfSales" to the Text attribute, editing the format to zero decimal places and changing the color to white.

Note   Although we have done this before in Chapter 2, you can refer to the next chapter to see how to format the text mark to zero decimal places.

To help align the text in the symbol, you can set the Anchor X and Anchor Y attributes to "Middle." You can see the symbol and text mark attributes that we used in the chart in Figure 7-4. However, our chart is still not right.

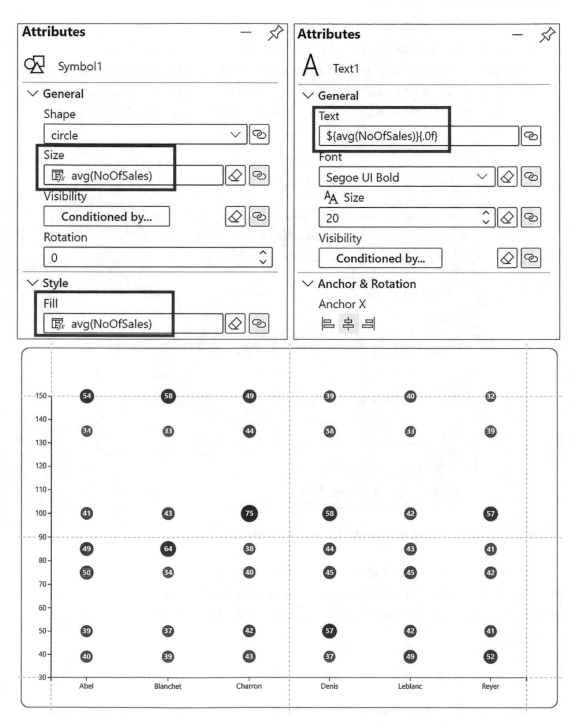

Figure 7-4. *The attributes used to produce the chart*

The symbols do not show a great difference in size from smallest to largest. What we can do here is edit the scale to increase the range of sizes. To do this, click on "Symbol1.Size" under "Scale1" in the Scales pane, and in the dialog that opens, change the End range value (see Figure 7-5). I've increased it to 2500, but you can experiment and see what fits best. We take a closer look at scales and scale ranges in Chapter 9.

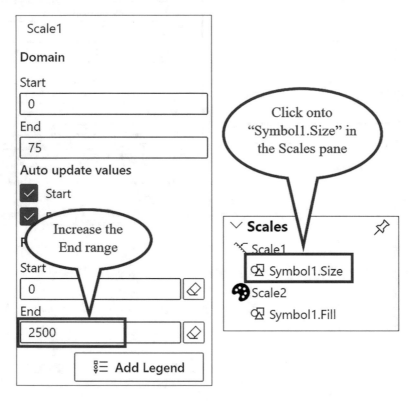

Figure 7-5. *Increasing the range of the Size scale*

Now that we are quite satisfied with the look and feel of the glyph, let's turn our attention to the focus of this chapter, Charticulator's numerical axis attributes. You will find these attributes under "Y Axis: Numerical" in the Attributes pane of the plot segment.

Editing the Range

The Range attribute allows you to increase or decrease the range of numbers displayed on the axis. You can also use the attribute to reverse the direction of the scale from ascending to descending by swapping the start and end values over. In our chart, I've increased the "to" value to 160 in order to extend the axis a little beyond the largest price value of $150; see Figure 7-6. If you change the Range attribute of a numerical axis, ensure that you turn off Charticulator's automatic scaling under the "Y Axis export properties" attribute; otherwise, when you return to Power BI, the range will have reverted.

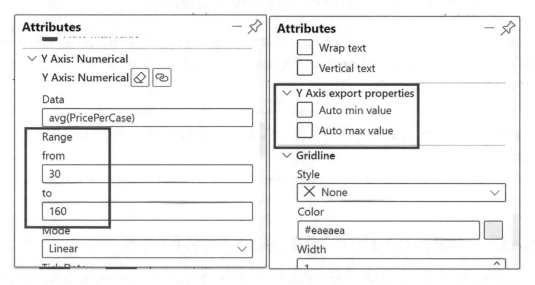

Figure 7-6. *Editing the start and end values on the numerical axis and turning off the export properties*

To move the glyphs away from the x-axis, particularly if they are spilling over the axis, you can decrease the "from" range.

Format the Tick Numbers

To format the numerical axis as currency, you can use the Tick Format attribute and put the format string inside curly braces; see Figure 7-7.

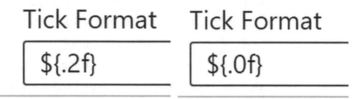

Figure 7-7. *Editing the format string of the numerical axis*

You can see that you simply type your currency symbol outside the braces, and then inside curly braces, type a decimal point followed by the number of decimal places you require and then type an "f".

Note   We will be exploring Charticulator's format string expressions in detail in the next chapter.

Formatting the Tick Font and Tick Lines

Both categorical and numerical axes share the same Style attributes that we have already looked at in Chapter 5, but just to recap here, if you want to change the color or increase the size of the text or tick lines on the numerical axis, you can use the plot segment attributes under the Style group; see Figure 7-8.

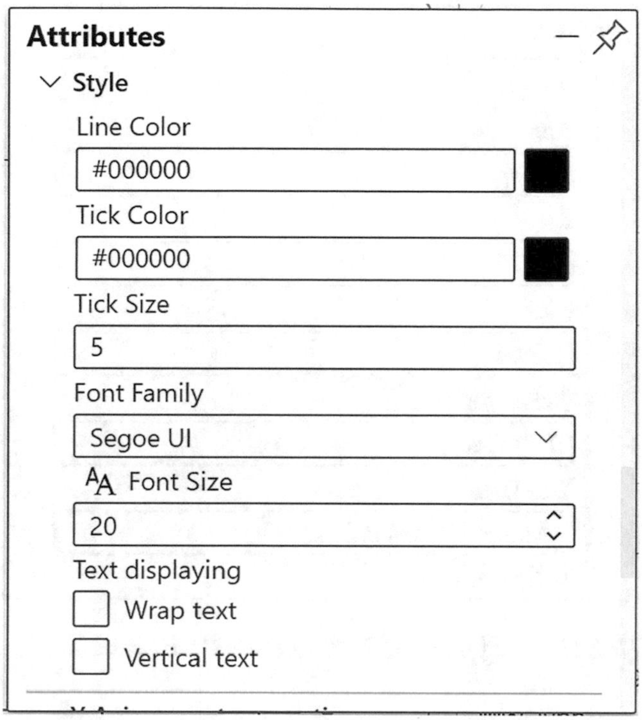

Figure 7-8. *The Style attributes of the numerical axis*

Now that we've completed the design of the glyph and the numerical axis is formatted correctly, we have generated the chart in Figure 7-2.

Tick Data

The problem with the chart we've just built is that you can't tell which wine is being plotted; we only see the prices on the axis. It's here that Charticulator can generate text labels associated with specific values along the numerical axis. To do this, use the Tick Data Type and Tick Data attributes as shown in Figure 7-9.

Attributes   — ⚲

Range

from

30

to

160

Mode

Linear   ⌄

Tick Data Type

Number   ⌄

Tick Data

Wine + - PricePerCase

Tick Format

Figure 7-9. *The Tick Data Type and Tick Data attributes*

You must first set the Tick Data Type attribute before you will see the Tick Data attribute. Our Tick Data will plot the "PricePerCase" field, so the Tick Data Type is "Number." In the Tick Data attribute, simply type the name of the field whose text values you want to use on the numerical axis. In our chart, we are using the "Wine" field that holds the names of the wines. We've also included the "PricePerCase" field, separated with a dash character for clarity of the data; see Figure 7-10.

Tick Data

Wine + - PricePerCase

Figure 7-10. *Editing the Tick Data attribute*

Note the use of the "+" to concatenate the "Wine" and "PricePerCase" fields. Also be careful of the following:

- Charticulator's format strings are case sensitive, so you must type the name of the field in the correct case.

- If you have a space in the name of your field, you must surround the field name with a grave (`) character. You'll find the key for this character at the top-left corner of your keyboard, beside "1" and under "Esc." See Figure 7-11.

Tick Data

Wine + - `Price Per Case`

Figure 7-11. *Use the grave character if your field has spaces in the name*

I've made a couple of additions to the chart, adding a legend for the Fill scale (click on "Symbol1.Fill" in the Scales pane to do this) and a link line for the "Wine" field; see Figure 7-12. Let's now remind ourselves that using the Tick Data attribute in this way has rendered a visual that is simple but insightful and could not have been generated without the help of Charticulator.

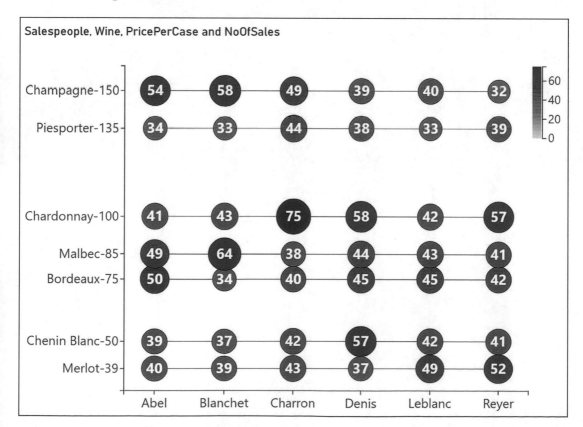

Figure 7-12. *The final chart with the Tick Data*

In this chapter, you have learned to manage the numerical axis and discovered the benefits of displaying Charticulator's Tick Data. So now you're up to speed with using both Charticulator's numerical and categorical axes and can design visuals that reap the benefits of using these to their best advantage.

However, you may have noticed there's one area that we've been consistently passing over and really not explaining at all. This is the expressions that Charticulator uses when binding data, for example, the formulas that begin with a dollar sign and the formatting of data in the text mark. And what's going on with the numeric formatting syntax, that is, the characters inside the curly braces? Apparently, these formatting expressions are known as "d3-format." So, without further ado, let's move on to the next chapter where we'll explore Charticulator numerical expressions and the obscure world of "d3-formats."

CHAPTER 8

Charticulator Expressions

In this chapter, we take a break from designing charts and instead take a detailed look at the expressions used by Charticulator when you bind data to an attribute. You also may have been at a loss as to how Charticulator's rather unusual numeric formatting method works. This is where you edit characters inside the curly braces. It's a syntax known as "d3-format." Have you ever heard of it? No? Well, neither had I nor indeed have any of my more "techie" friends. It doesn't help that Charticulator's documentation doesn't throw much light on how you're meant to use this syntax (it took me some time to find out how to insert a comma separator). Just to fill you in, "d3-format" is used by JavaScript programmers to format numbers, apparently for "human consumption," according to GitHub (`https://github.com/d3/d3-format`), and is based on Python 3's formatting specifications. However, I don't suppose knowing this really helps a lot, so in this chapter I will throw some light on this rarefied syntax language. What we will also discover is that there is an alternative approach to formatting numerical fields using DAX, and we will explore this possibility at the end of this chapter.

All Charticulator's expressions are introduced by the dollar ($) sign if they are in the Text attribute of a text mark or by an "f of x" button if they are in an attribute that defines a scale, such as the Height or Fill attribute. In the latter case, you can click the button to change the function. The major difference between DAX or Excel formulas and those in Charticulator is that in Charticulator part of the expression can include the format specifier. Also, a field is referenced without a qualifying table name because all Power BI visuals, including Charticulator visuals, can only ever see their own underlying data set, not the data model.

Understanding these aspects of the Charticulator expression means that we can focus on these five separate elements:

1. Referencing field names

2. The aggregation of the data

3. The format of the numerical expressions using d3-format

© Alison Box 2022
A. Box, *Introducing Charticulator for Power BI*, https://doi.org/10.1007/978-1-4842-8076-8_8

4. The format of the tick label on the numerical axis using d3-format

5. Using DAX to format numerical fields

Referencing Field Names

When you reference a field name inside a Charticulator expression, you use the field name with no qualifying table name. However, if the field name has spaces in it, you must surround the field name with the grave character (`) which is situated top left of your keyboard, to the left of "1" and under "Esc." You can concatenate field names in a text mark by using the plus (+) symbol and insert a space by using double quotes between the space. In Figure 8-1, you can see how field names are referenced when bound to the Text attribute of the text mark.

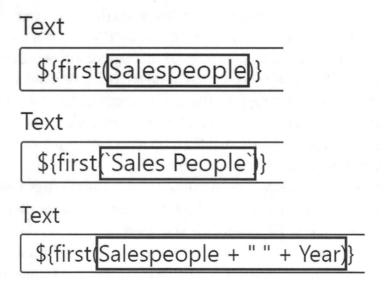

Figure 8-1. *Using field names bound to the Text attribute*

You may remember that in the previous chapter, we looked at using "Tick Data" on a numerical axis where you reference a field name that will label the axis. This is one occasion where there is no field bound to the attribute, and therefore you can just type the field names into the attribute. For instance, in Figure 8-2 we've concatenated the "Wine" field and the "PricePerCase" field, separated by a space. Notice that you don't need an aggregating function (e.g., the function "first") because the aggregation is already being expressed in the "Data" attribute of the plot segment.

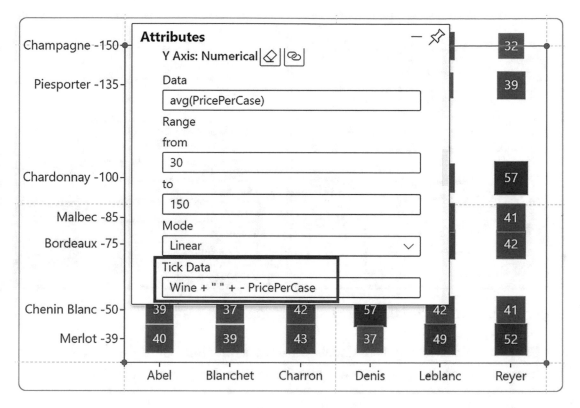

Figure 8-2. *Field names in the Tick Data attribute*

It's interesting to note that although the space character requires double quotes surrounding it, the dash character does not.

Using Charticulator's Aggregate Functions

Just like DAX measures, Charticulator supports functions that return scalar values such as "sum," "avg," "max," "min," "count," "stdev," "variance," "median," "first," and "last."

Expressions Using Categorical Data

Let's start with the text expression that is used when you bind a categorical field to an attribute. For instance, in Figure 8-3, we've added the "Salespeople" field to the Fill attribute of a rectangle mark and the Text attribute of a text mark. When using categorical data, Charticulator uses the "first" function.

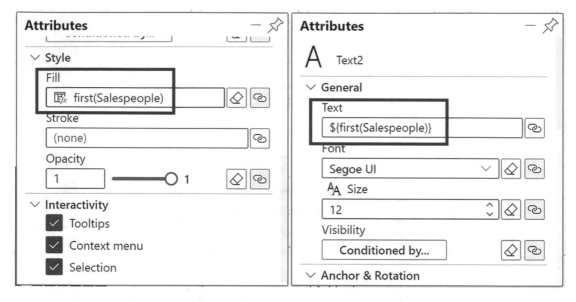

Figure 8-3. *Categorical fields use the "first" function*

Charticulator, as all Power BI visuals, must use a function to retrieve a single value, but because you can't aggregate text values, it uses the "first" function by default.

Expressions Using Numerical Data

When you first bind a numerical field to an attribute, Charticulator will use the "avg" function by default. For instance, in Figure 8-4 we've bound the "Sales" field to the Height attribute of a rectangle shape.

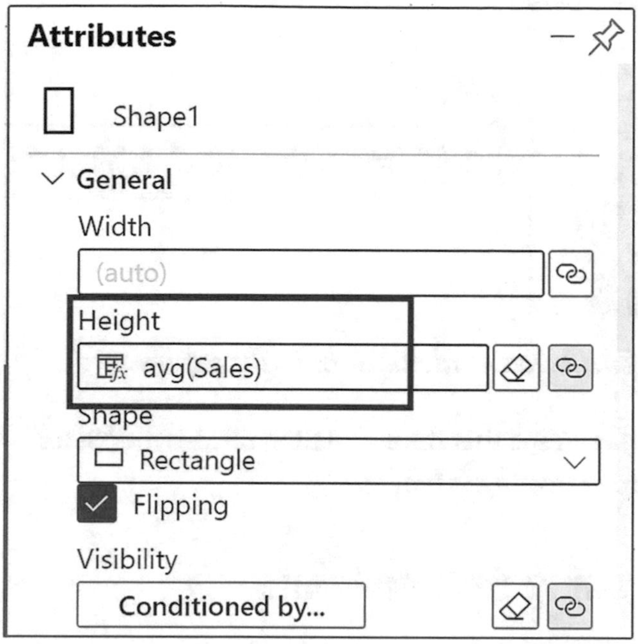

Figure 8-4. *Numerical fields use the "avg" function by default*

The reason the "avg" function is used is because, unless you use the "Group by..." attribute, each shape represents a single row from the underlying data. Therefore, expressing the average of one value is that value (as indeed would using "sum," "max," "min," "first," or "last"). In this case, there is no advantage to changing the function. The exception to this is when you group your data using "Group by...."

What you can also do in these numerical expressions is to use simple arithmetic within the braces. This can be useful to express numerical values in units such a "K" or "M" in the Text attribute of text marks. For example, in Figure 8-5, you can see two versions of a text mark showing the sales value, one showing the full value and the other expressing the same value in the "M" unit. You can see how the version expressed in "M" saves valuable space on the canvas.

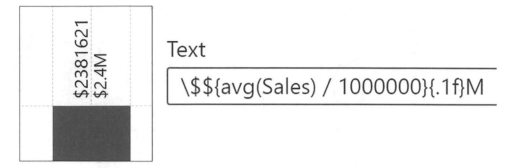

Figure 8-5. *Using arithmetic calculations in the expression*

In Figure 8-5, you can see that the calculation divides the "Sales" value by 1,000,000, and this calculation sits inside the braces.

Expressions Using Grouped Data

If you are using the "Group by…" attribute of the plot segment, then you can edit the function according to the calculation you want to plot. For instance, in Figure 8-6, we've grouped by the "Year" field and bound the "Sales" field to the Height attribute of a rectangle. We have also added a text mark to show the value of the "Sales" field. We have then changed the function used by the Height attribute from "avg" to "min." To do this, we clicked into the Height attribute and selected "Min" from the function dropdown. Notice that the text mark has also been edited to reflect the function being used by the Height attribute; see Figure 8-6.

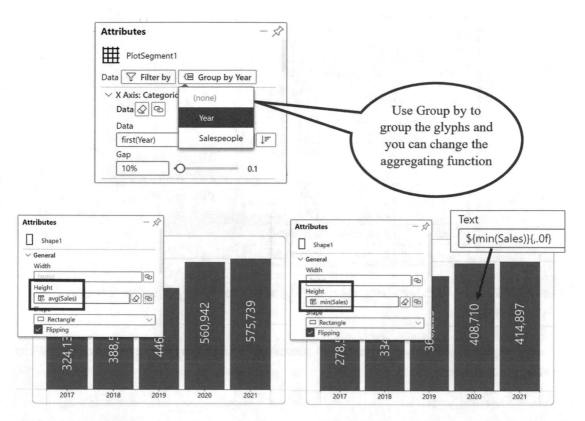

Figure 8-6. *Using Group by..., you may want to change the aggregate function*

It's important to note here that these are aggregations of the data behind the visual that you see when you view the data in the Fields pane, as shown in Figure 8-7, not aggregations of the source data. In other words, our expression is calculating the minimum of the aggregated sales for each year for each salesperson (e.g. 278,519 for "Abel" in 2017).

Main 30 rows, 3 columns		
Year	**Salespeople**	**Sales**
2017	Abel	334915
2017	Blanchet	278519
2017	Charron	368127
2017	Denis	362843
2017	Leblanc	285395
2017	Reyer	315013
2018	Abel	387531
2018	Blanchet	334486
2018	Charron	414859

The aggregate functions aggregate these values

Figure 8-7. *Charticulator aggregates the data comprising the visual (not all the rows are shown)*

In Chapter 11, I'll show you how you can use the "Group by..." attribute to great effect in your chart designs.

Formatting Numerical Expressions

When you bind numerical data to a text mark, Charticulator will apply a default numeric format using one fixed decimal place, indicated by the format string inside the curly braces; see Figure 8-8.

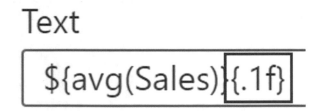

Figure 8-8. *Charticulator's formatting syntax, known as d3-format*

Charticulator uses a numeric formatting syntax based on the "d3-format" specification used by JavaScript. You may never have heard of "d3-format," but have you ever created custom Excel formats? If so, you'll be familiar with the idea of placing format specifiers in specific positions to determine the format of a number (e.g., Excel's custom format uses "positive ; negative ; zero ; text"). Well, d3-format is a bit like that, only a little more complicated. Here are the d3-format specifiers:

[[fill]align][sign][symbol][0][width][,][.precision][~][type]

You can find more information regarding this syntax here:

https://d3-wiki.readthedocs.io/zh_CN/master/Formatting/

But for the moment, we are just going to concentrate on what we need to know to format our numerical data in Charticulator. In this respect, it is just the specifiers listed in Table 8-1 that we will be using in our examples.

Table 8-1. *"d3-format" identifiers used in Charticulator expressions*

Specifier	Value	Description	Example	Result
[type]	f	Fixed decimal	${avg(Sales)}{.2f}	334915.00
[type]	%	Percent	${avg(Sales)}{.2%}	33.49%
[type]	r	Round to significant digits	${avg(Sales)}{.3r}	33500
[type]	s	For M or K units	${avg(Sales)}{.5s}	334.92
[.precision]	.n	For n decimal places	${avg(Sales)}{.2f}	334915.00
[,]	,	Comma separator	${avg(Sales)}{,.0f}	334,915

Note   You can find information on the other "type" identifiers in the documentation on GitHub.

For a currency format, just type the currency symbol at the start of the expression. If you want to use a dollar sign, precede it with a forward slash (\ ); see Figure 8-9.

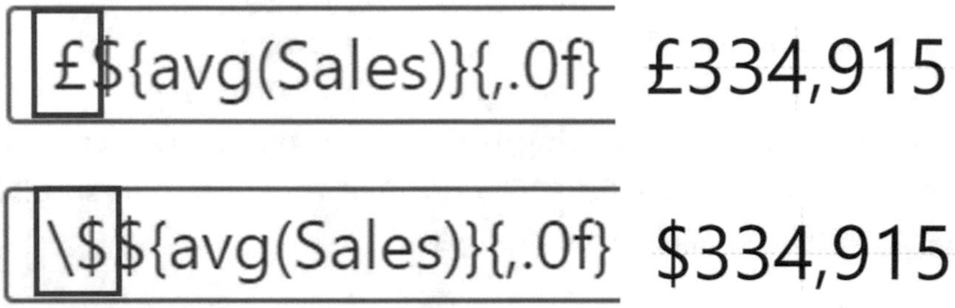

£${avg(Sales)}{,.0f}   £334,915

\$${avg(Sales)}{,.0f} $334,915

Figure 8-9.   *Formatting as currency*

There is an alternative way to generate currency formats that we explore in the last section (see the section on "Using the DAX FORMAT Function" below).

Formatting Tick Labels

You can use any of the preceding format specifiers to format a numerical axis, a legend, or a data axis (see Chapter 14 for details of the data axis). Use the "Tick Format" attribute and type the required format into the attribute, remembering to enclose the format in curly braces. An example of formatting the y-axis using the dollar currency format is shown in Figure 8-10.

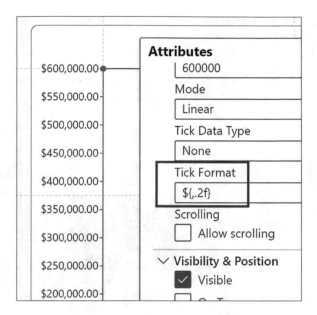

Figure 8-10. *Use the Tick Format attribute to format a numerical axis*

Note the use of the currency symbol typed outside the braces.

Using the DAX FORMAT Function

You might be relieved to know that there is an alternative to using d3-format. Using a DAX measure, you can create an alternative version of a numerical field that converts the field into a text string that includes the numerical format you require. To do this, you create a new measure and use the FORMAT function. You can see an example of creating a currency format using DAX in Figure 8-11.

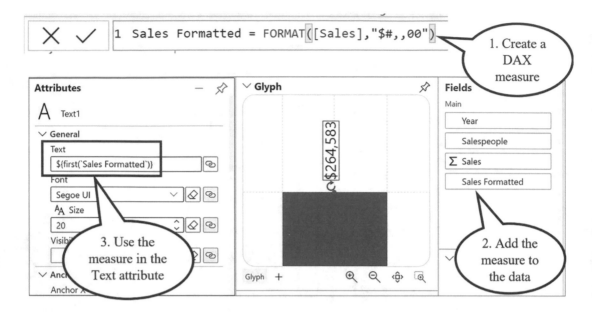

Figure 8-11. *Using the DAX FORMAT function to format a numerical value*

The measure that defines the format is added to the data that comprises the chart and so it then shows in the Fields pane. It can then be used in the Text attribute of a text mark.

For more information on the DAX FORMAT function and format strings that you can use, follow this link:

https://docs.microsoft.com/en-us/dax/format-function-dax

I appreciate that all of this has been a bit dry. Nevertheless, it's very frustrating if you don't know how to format your numerical data, and Charticulator does not make it very user-friendly! However, in this chapter, you have learned how to reference field names and how to work with expressions involving both categorical and numerical data. You also now understand a little more about d3-format and can use it to format numerical expressions for the Text and the Tick Format attributes.

I know that you're itching to get back to building visuals, but before we can do so, there's a mandatory topic that we have yet to address. In order to move forward with more challenging charts, we need to get to grips with the rather odd world of Charticulator's scales and legends, which are the subject of the next chapter. I know we've already been using legends, and we've touched on the workings of the Scales pane, but like always with Charticulator, there remains a lot more to say. I don't think you'll find that very surprising.

CHAPTER 9

Scales and Legends

In Chapter 3, you learned that whenever you bind data to an attribute, a scale will arrive in the Scales pane. You've also generated many charts that use both a numerical and a categorical legend. In the light of what you already know, you can now move forward with your knowledge of Charticulator's scales and legends because in this chapter we will take a more detailed look at what they are and how we work with them. You will learn about the different scales that Charticulator generates and how you can edit and manage these scales. More importantly, you will at last get to grips with the challenging aspects of the numerical scale. For instance, what do the Domain and Range attributes of this type of scale do and what will be the impact on the chart by editing the values in them? In this chapter, we will answer these questions. What you will also understand is that inextricably linked to the scales are Charticulator's legends, and therefore you'll want to edit and control the look and format of legends too.

However, the starting point for this chapter will be to focus on Charticulator's scales and then move forward to explore the various types of legends that can be added to a chart.

Charticulator Scales

Charticulator creates a scale for you whenever you bind data to an attribute, and then you will need to create a legend explaining the scale yourself. The scale determines how the data is mapped to the visual elements of the chart to determine the height, color, and size of marks, symbols, and lines. You can see these scales in the Scales pane that lists all the scales used by your chart along with the legends that describe each scale. It would be unusual to have a scale without an associated legend, and so you can think of a "scale" in Charticulator as any attribute of a shape or symbol where the bound field requires an explanation in a legend.

© Alison Box 2022
A. Box, *Introducing Charticulator for Power BI*, https://doi.org/10.1007/978-1-4842-8076-8_9

There are three types of scale in Charticulator – color scales, numerical scales, and scales that map images to the icon mark – but in this chapter, we'll be exploring just the first two types (we looked at binding images to icons in Chapter 3). You can see examples of these two types of scale in Figure 9-1. "Scale1" is a numerical scale associated with the Height attribute of the rectangle shape and also contains a numerical legend on the y-axis explaining the numerical values mapped to the height.

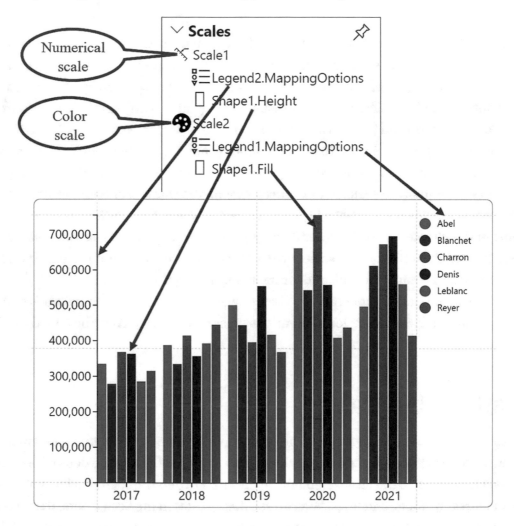

Figure 9-1. *Numerical scales and color scales in Charticulator*

"Scale2" is a color scale associated with the Fill attribute of the rectangle, and a legend has been added on the right to explain the colors used.

Properties of the Scale

Notice that in Figure 9-1 the mapping of the data by the scale is defined by a specific property listed under the scale, for example, "Shape1.Fill" or "Shape1.Height". Each scale will have listed under it similar properties that identify each attribute to which a field has been bound and whose data is mapped by that scale. In Figure 9-2, we have set out three examples of how these properties may appear in the Scales pane.

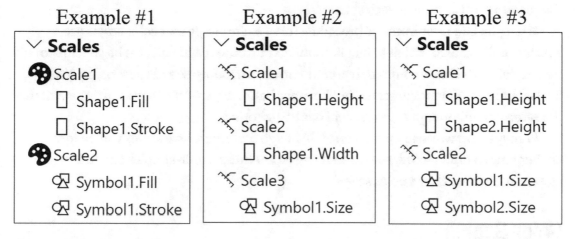

Figure 9-2. *Examples of the properties of scales that define the attributes to which data has been bound*

In Example #1, two different categorical fields have been bound to attributes generating two color scales. In "Scale1," a categorical field has been bound to both the Fill and Stroke attributes of a shape. In "Scale2," a *different* categorical field has been bound to the Fill and Stroke attributes of a symbol. Each scale maps a different collection of colors to the items in each categorical field.

In Example #2, the same numerical field or three different numerical fields have been bound to three *different* attributes. Either scenario would result in the generation of three separate numerical scales. Binding a numerical field to a different numerical attribute always generates a new scale, even if the field bound to the attribute is the same.

In Example #3, the same numerical field or different numerical fields have been bound to the *same* attribute of two different shapes and two different symbols. With respect to the rectangles, this could be because either the chart contains a glyph comprising two rectangle shapes or the chart contains two separate glyphs comprising a single rectangle shape (we will be using multiple glyphs in Chapter 11). This same arrangement could also apply to the two symbols. In both cases, each field that is bound to the same attribute will share the same scale. We take a detailed look at this scenario in the section on "Numerical Scales" below.

What you can infer from the preceding three examples is that color scales are specific to the categorical field that is bound to attributes (and can also be specific to numerical fields that are bound to nonnumerical attributes; see the section on "Color Scales" below). Numerical scales, on the other hand, are specific to the attribute whether the same or a different numerical field has been bound.

Perhaps, you will also appreciate at this stage that numerical scales will be more challenging to understand, so let's start with something a little simpler and look more closely at Charticulator's color scales.

Color Scales

A color scale is created when you bind a field to an attribute that has a color associated with it such as Fill, Stroke (for borders), or Color (for text marks). If you bind a categorical field to one of these attributes, Charticulator will map different colors to each member of the category, creating the associated color scale. If you bind a numerical field to the attribute, this will create a *gradient* color scale to define high and low values; see Figure 9-3.

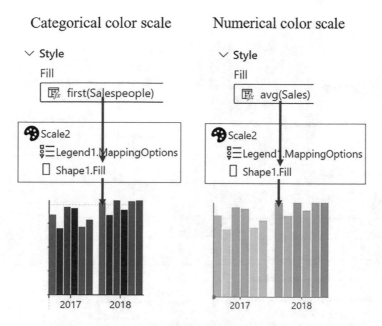

Figure 9-3. *Categorical and numerical color scales*

We looked briefly at editing color scales in Chapter 3, so now let's just recap on what we have learned regarding how color scales can be managed.

Editing Color Scales

You can edit the colors of the scale either by clicking the attribute or by clicking the property name in the Scales pane that defines the color you want to edit. For instance, if you click on the "Shape1.Fill" property in the Scales pane, a dialog will open to allow you to edit the colors used for either the fill of the rectangle shape for a categorical field such as "Salespeople" or for the gradient color used by a numerical field such as "Sales"; see Figure 9-4.

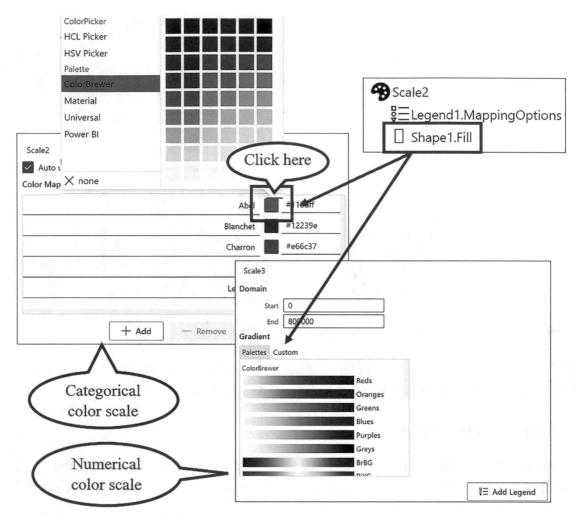

Figure 9-4. *Editing color scales in Charticulator*

To edit the categorical colors, click a color and then reselect a color from the color palette. To edit a gradient scale, select from the Palettes tab or use the Custom tab to create your own custom gradients.

It's now time to turn our attention to the more problematic numerical scale.

Numerical Scales

A numerical scale is created when you bind a numerical field to a numerical attribute such as Height, Width, Size, or X Span/Y Span. For example, in Figure 9-5, we have bound the "Sales" field to the Height attribute of a rectangle shape and to the Size attribute of a symbol.

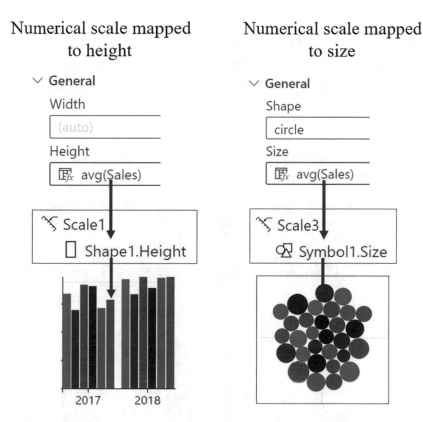

Figure 9-5. *Creating numerical scales*

One of the most important things to understand when working with Charticulator's numerical scales is that once Charticulator has generated a numerical scale to map a numerical field to a numerical attribute, *that scale will be used for all subsequent mappings to that same attribute*. Each mapping is listed as a property under the scale that has been set by the first bound field. For example, under "Scale1," there may be two properties, "Shape1.Height" and "Shape2.Height," where two different numerical fields have been bound to the Height attribute of two different rectangles that comprise the glyph (we will be doing this presently). When the second numerical field was bound to the Height attribute of the second rectangle, *the scale had already been set by the first field that was bound.* Therefore, the order that you bind the numerical fields is critical. Not understanding the impact of the order in which numerical fields are bound can result in unexpected behaviors of the glyph.

Consider the chart in Figure 9-6 where we are plotting two numerical fields, "2019 sales" and "2020 sales," that have been bound to the Height attribute of two rectangle marks.

Note   These two numerical fields are two separate measures and are being used here solely as an example of how numerical scales are generated. We will be focusing on the different ways that multiple measures are managed in more detail in Chapter 14.

You can see that the rectangle mark for "2019 sales" is plotted correctly, but the rectangle mark for "2020 sales" spills outside the plot segment.

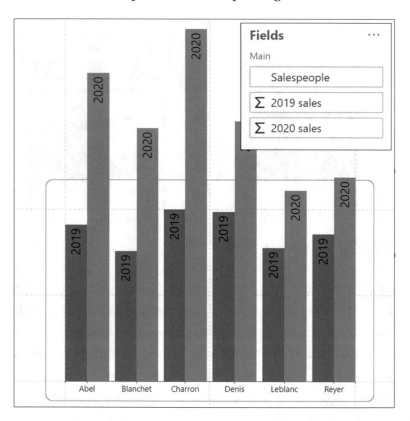

Figure 9-6. *The rectangle mark for "2020 sales" spills out of the plot segment*

Why is the rectangle mark for "2020 sales" exhibiting this bizarre behavior? Before we answer this question, let's get to grips with how the glyph comprising the two rectangles was generated.

The building of this glyph was a little more challenging than simply adding two rectangles to the Glyph pane and then dragging the numerical fields into the Height attribute, so we have set out in Figure 9-7 how the glyph was constructed.

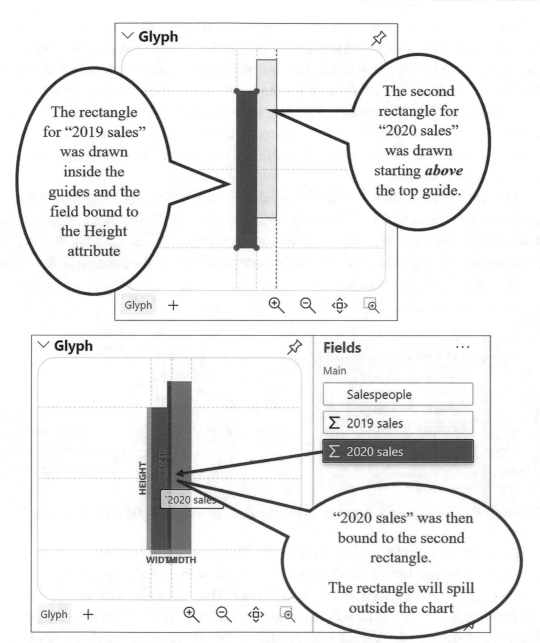

Figure 9-7. *Creating the glyph to bind two numerical fields to the Height attribute of two rectangles. The order the fields are bound is critical*

To start, the first rectangle was drawn inside the guides of the Glyph pane, ensuring that the rectangle was anchored to the top, vertical middle, side, and bottom guides of the glyph. The intuitive action to take next was to bind the first numerical field, that is, "2019 sales," to the Height attribute of this shape generating "Scale1" in the Scales pane.

The second rectangle was drawn *starting above* the top guide of the glyph and then anchored to the vertical middle, side, and bottom guides. "2020 sales" was then bound to the Height attribute of the second rectangle, but this resulted in the rectangle spilling outside the plot segment.

The reason that the rectangle for "2020 sales" is too tall for the plot segment is that we bound the "2019 sales" field *first* to the Height attribute and therefore set the Domain Start and End values for "Scale1", mapping the height of the rectangles to "2019 sales." Because the maximum value for "2019 sales" is 368127, this set the Domain End value of "Scale1" to 370000. See Figure 9-8.

Figure 9-8. *The Domain End value for "Scale1" is set by the field that is bound first*

If you were to insert a numerical legend for "2019 sales," this would also reflect this scale. When we then bound "2020 sales" to the Height attribute of the second rectangle, this rectangle was also scaled according to "Scale1". This in itself isn't necessarily the problem. It's the fact that the maximum value for the "2020 sales" is 755892 which is greater than the Domain End value of "Scale1", and what you see in Figure 9-6 is the result of this mismatch. What we should have done was to bind "2020 sales" to the Height attribute *first*, setting the correct scale for both rectangles. This would also entail drawing the rectangles in the glyph in a different order as shown in Figure 9-9.

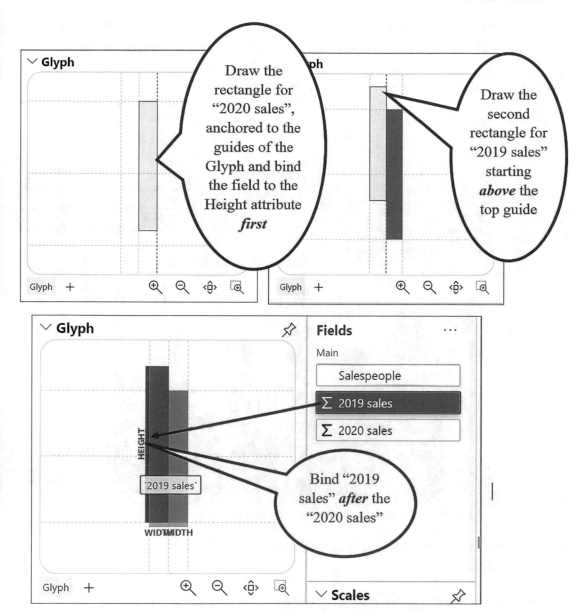

Figure 9-9. *Creating the glyph to bind two numerical fields to the Height attribute of two rectangles. The order the fields are bound is now correct*

Doing this will generate the correct Domain End value that can be used for both numerical fields (see Figure 9-10), and both rectangles will be plotted correctly.

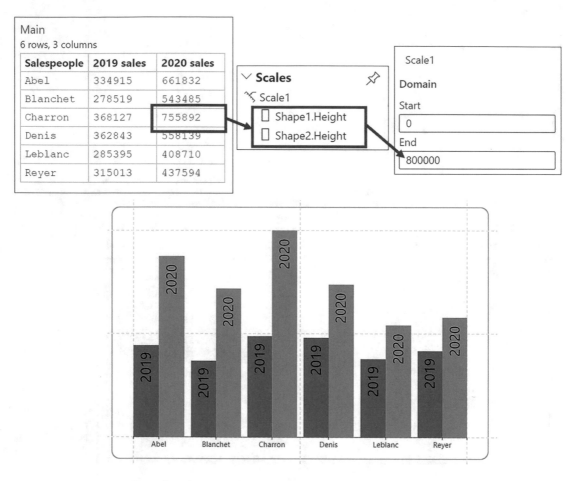

Figure 9-10. *Binding "2020 sales" first sets the correct scale for the second numerical field*

The takeaway from this section is *not* the specifics of building the clustered column chart using the two numerical fields, which you may feel at this stage is overly complicated. The takeaway is understanding how Charticulator calculates numerical scales and its implications on how the data is plotted on the chart: that binding the first numerical field always sets the numerical scale. You will have another shot at building a similar clustered column chart in Chapter 14 when we explore working with multiple measures, and we'll find easier ways to construct it correctly.

Editing Numerical Scales

Just as with color scales, you can edit a numerical scale either by clicking the attribute or by clicking the property in the Scales pane, for example, by clicking "Shape1.Height". When you edit a numerical scale, you have a choice of editing the Domain and the Range attributes; see Figure 9-11.

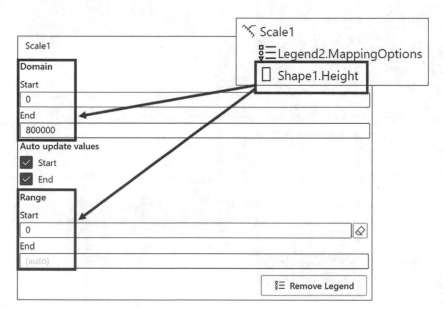

Figure 9-11. *Editing numerical scales*

We look at editing the Domain attribute in the section on legends (see the section on "Editing the Scale of a Numerical Legend" below), but for now, let's focus on what the Range attribute can do for us.

Well, in fact, if you're working with a mark or line as opposed to a symbol, changing the Range attribute won't do that much for you. The Range attribute of the scale determines the difference between the smallest glyph and the biggest. In our chart, this is the difference in height between the shortest rectangle and the tallest. If you're using a mark or a line, when you first bind numerical data, Charticulator will automatically scale the height, width, or span of the mark or line to fit the plot segment. This means that if you change the size of the plot segment, the glyph automatically rescales. Therefore, if you put measurements into the Start and End values of the Range, you will constrain the size of the glyph; see Figure 9-12.

Auto-scaling in the Range attribute allows you to resize the plot segment and the glyphs resize proportionally

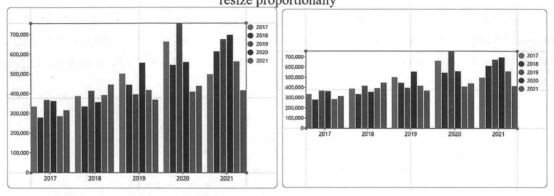

Entering values in the Range attribute constrains the size of the glyphs

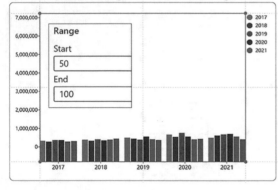
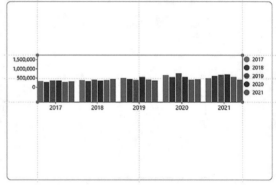

Figure 9-12. *Editing the Range attribute of the "Shape1.Height" scale*

You may find more reason to change the values in the Range attribute if you're using a symbol as your glyph and have a numerical field bound to the Size attribute. Editing the Range values allows you to resize the symbol proportionally. When you click the "Symbol1.Size" property in the Scales pane, you'll see that unlike the rectangle mark, the symbol has a specific End value in the Range attribute (628.32), constraining the size of the symbols irrespective of the size of the plot segment. If you edit the End value however, you will increase the relative sizes of the symbols; see Figure 9-13.

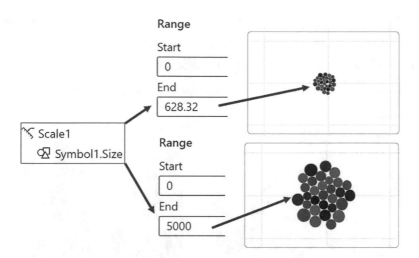

Figure 9-13. *Editing the Range attribute of "Symbol1.Size"*

Another example of using the End value of the Range attribute to control relative sizes is when you bind a numerical field to the Size attribute of a text mark. This will ensure that the text remains legible for small values but is never too big for the larger ones.

Creating Additional Scales When Mapping Data

You have already learned that when you bind the first numerical field to the Height attribute of a rectangle, this will set the height scale for all subsequent mappings to that attribute. The properties generated under the scale that map the values to the height of the rectangles are specific to the Height attribute rather than to the field, so different fields will always share the same numerical scale for heights. But what if your numerical fields hold values that require *different* scales to be used by the Height attribute? For example, you may want to compare sales and quantity in the heights of two rectangles in a clustered column chart.

With regard to categorical fields, there will only be one color scale generated for each categorical field, regardless as to which attribute it is bound. But what if you want different colors being used for each of your categorical items when bound to different attributes?

You can see in Figure 9-14 that we have resolved these problems by generating *new* scales. In the top chart, we have used a *second* scale for the Fill attribute of the symbol so that we can use a color scale to "group" the salespeople, either red or green, according to their team (the colors mapped don't have to be different for each categorical item). In the chart underneath, we have used a *second* scale for the Height attribute of the second rectangle that is plotting the "NoOfSales" numerical field.

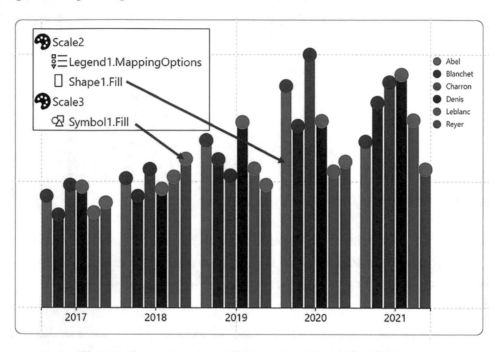

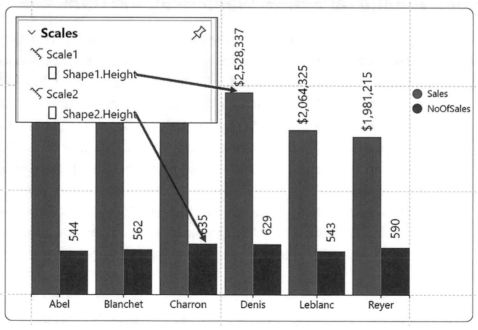

Figure 9-14. *Using different scales for the same attribute*

To generate a new scale in this way when binding a field to an attribute, you must hold down the SHIFT key as you drag the field into the attribute, as shown in Figure 9-15.

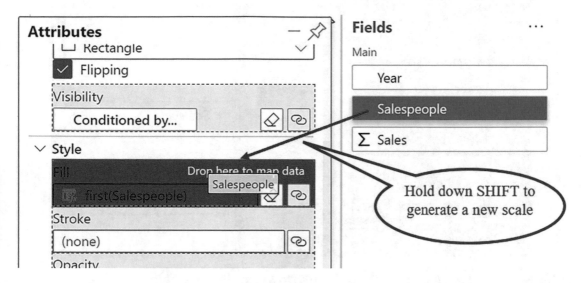

Figure 9-15. *Creating new scales when binding data*

When you do this, you will see a new scale has been created in the Scales pane. New numerical scales will be generated accordingly, but with color scales, you can now edit the colors used by the new scale and use the same color for different categorical items if required.

Reusing Scales

As well as being able to create new scales, you can reuse existing scales by dragging and dropping them into an attribute. For instance, to use the same colors for the borders of a rectangle as you have for the fill color, you can drag and drop the "Shape1.Fill" property into the Stroke attribute; see Figure 9-16.

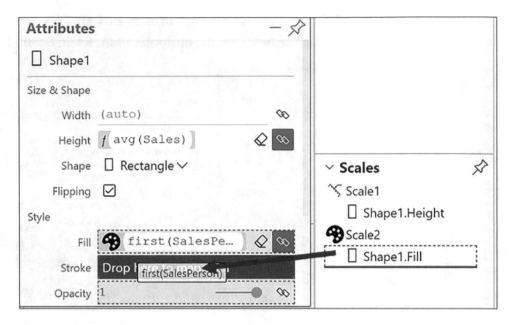

Figure 9-16. *Reusing scales in different attributes*

We've been focusing on Charticulator scales, learning how they are generated and how to manage them. However, once a scale has been created, you'll want a way to visualize the values represented by the scale. Specifically, you'll need an explanation of the height or width of a mark or the colors that represent the categories or gradients. This is where you'll need to add Charticulator's legends to your chart, so let's move forward and take a closer look at how legends are created and edited.

Charticulator Legends

In Charticulator, there are two types of legend: "column names" and "column values." You can select either type by using the Legend button on the toolbar as shown in Figure 9-17. The most commonly used legend and indeed the only type that we have added so far to our charts is the "Column values" legend.

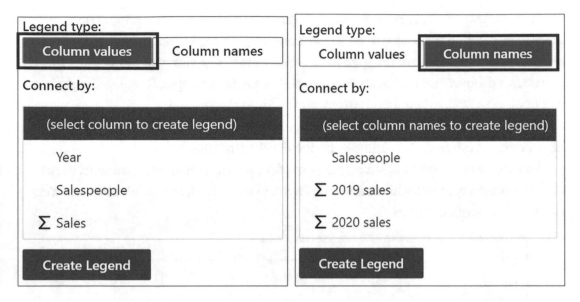

Figure 9-17. *Two different types of legend*

We will explore presently when we need to use a column names legend, but first let's work through the different ways that legends can be created.

Creating Legends

There are several ways to create legends. The most intuitive way is to use the Legend button on the toolbar, and this is the only way that you can create a column names legend. This button lists all your fields, and you can select the field for which you want a legend. You can hold down the CTRL key to select multiple column names for the column names legend.

However, there are several drawbacks to using this method to add column values legends. The list of fields on the button dropdown doesn't depend on the binding of data to an attribute, so it provides only "default" legends. Because of this, it's ambiguous as to which scale the legend will be mapped. For instance, you may need two legends for the "Sales" field, one for a gradient color scale and one for a numerical scale, but you can only insert a legend for the numerical scale from the toolbar button.

A better way to create column values legends is to use the Scales pane. The advantage of using the Scales pane, as we have seen earlier, is that it's here that you can also edit the colors that are mapped to the scale or the behavior of a numerical scale. If you click a property under a scale in the Scales pane, for example, "Shape1.Height," this will open up a Scales dialog from where you can add the Legend.

If you prefer, you can also click the attribute where the data has been bound and that has generated the scale, for example, on the Height attribute.

To place a numerical legend on the x-axis for the Width attribute, you must either click the property in the Scales pane (see Figure 9-18) or click the Width attribute. You can't use the toolbar button.

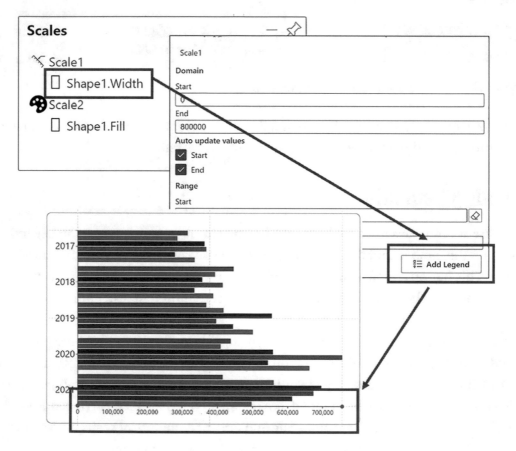

Figure 9-18. *Creating a numerical legend for the x-axis*

Using the Scales pane to generate legends in this way therefore gives you the option to both edit the scale and add the legend. Let's now explore the differences in the two legend types: column values and column names.

Column Values Legends

When you create a column values legend in Charticulator, it's listed in the Scales pane along with the scale whose data it maps.

Charticulator will create one of three different column values legends depending on the scale that it represents (see Table 9-1):

1. A category legend – The legend will map the colors to the categories.

2. A gradient legend – The legend will show the values represented by the gradient.

3. A numerical legend – A numerical legend that sits on the x- or y-axis. The numerical legend resembles a value axis, but as detailed in Chapter 4, it has no effect on how the data is plotted in the chart.

Table 9-1. *Charticulator column values legends*

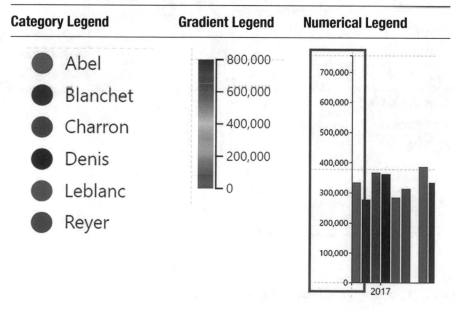

All these legends are visual representations of the data that has been mapped by the scales.

Column Names Legends

The column names legend is used when you have plotted multiple numerical values in your chart. We had an example of this in the chart in Figure 9-10 where we plotted data for "2019 sales" and "2020 sales," both of which had been bound to the Height attribute of two rectangles comprising the glyph.

To add a legend that describes the colors used by each numerical field represented by the rectangles, you need to select the **Column names** option on the Legend dropdown and select the fields to be displayed in the legend. Hold down the CTRL key to select the required fields. The legend that is placed on the chart will use the default colors from the Power BI theme, and so you will need to manually map the fill colors of the rectangles that represent each numerical field yourself. Use the Attributes pane of the legend and click the **Edit scale colors** button. See Figure 9-19.

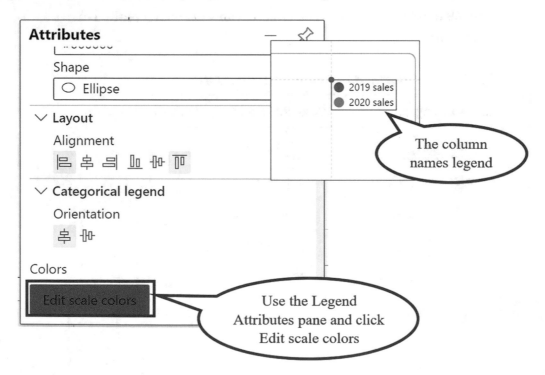

Figure 9-19. *Creating a column names legend*

Note how by creating a column names legend this will generate a new scale in the Scales pane that maps the colors to each column name.

Using the column names legend in this way will be important to you when we explore Charticulator's data axis in Chapter 14 and we understand the difference between plotting "wide" and "narrow" data.

Formatting and Moving Legends

All your legends are listed in the Layers pane under the Chart group. You can then click a legend name to open the Attributes pane. From here, you can reformat the legend, change the order of the items (for categorical legends), and change its position; see Figure 9-20.

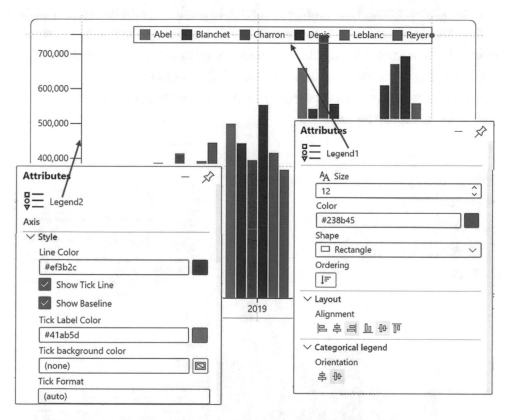

Figure 9-20. *Attributes for categorical and numerical legends*

In the examples in Figure 9-20, we have moved the categorical legend to the top of the plot segment and changed the shape to a rectangle.

Note   If you want to move a categorical legend elsewhere on the canvas, you'll need to anchor the legend to a guide or guide coordinator, the subject of the next chapter.

In the numerical legend, the tick color has been colored green and the tick line color changed to red. The font size has also been increased.

Editing the Scale of a Numerical Legend

Click on the property under the scale, e.g. "Shape1.Height" to edit the scale used by a legend. The Domain attribute of the scale shows the range of values in the numerical field to which the numerical legend is mapped. For example, our data is mapped from 0 to 800,000 which is the maximum value in the "Sales" field (rounded up). If you want to change the Start value of the legend, edit the Start attribute under the Domain attribute of the scale; see Figure 9-21.

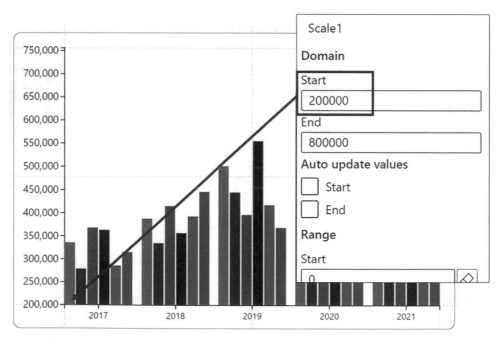

Figure 9-21. *Edit the Start attribute of "Domain" to change the Start value of the legend*

Changing the End value of the legend is a little more problematic. By default, your chart will take up the entire space of the plot segment, the largest or widest shape extending to its edge. This is controlled by the automatic scaling in the Range attribute of the scale. If you want more space between the edge of the plot segment and the tallest or widest shape, you can enter an End value in the Range attribute which indicates how tall or wide you want the tallest or widest shape. This will force the legend to increase its values accordingly; see Figure 9-22.

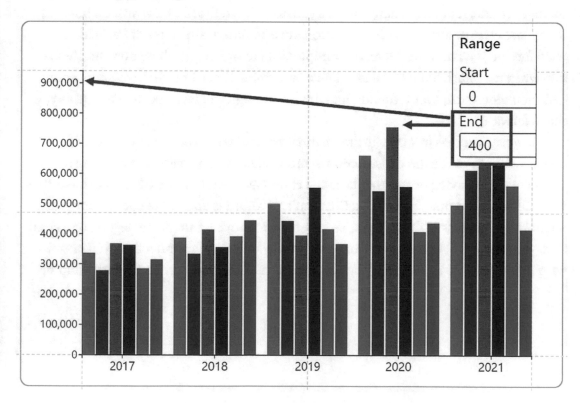

Figure 9-22. *Increasing the End value of the legend*

But as mentioned earlier when we were learning about scales, entering a value into the End option of the Range attribute will restrain the tallest shape when you resize the plot segment and generally renders the chart unpredictable.

Note   As mentioned in previous chapters, if you edit the scale, don't forget to check off the Start and End attributes under "Auto update values"; otherwise, the scale will revert when you save the chart.

If you select the Legend in the Layers pane, in the Attributes pane you can format the tick marks and change the number format as shown in Chapter 8.

Learning how to edit the scale of a numerical legend ends our journey through Charticulator's scales and legends. I hope that now you've read through this chapter, the Scales pane inside Charticulator will no longer be a mystery to you. I certainly found it one of the more unfathomable parts of the Charticulator screen when I first started out. However, you will now understand the behavior of scales, that once a scale is generated for an attribute, it doesn't change unless you hold down the SHIFT key when binding the field. You now also know what the Domain and Range attributes of the Scale are used for and how they are yet another important factor in controlling how the glyphs behave in the chart. In fact, you now know everything that's important to know about Charticulator's scales and legends, and this knowledge will be important to you as you move forward.

However, there is just one further mandatory skill you need to acquire before you can move on to tackle the construction of more challenging charts. I'm alluding to the practicalities of laying out elements on the chart canvas and in the Glyph pane. For this, you need to be competent in using Charticulator's guides and guide coordinators and anchoring elements to them. If you've ever tried to move a categorical legend or a chart title, you may have noticed that it has a habit of wandering around the chart without your permission. If you want to remedy this sad situation, read on to the next chapter.

CHAPTER 10

Guides and Anchoring

Have you been wondering why elements of your Charticulator chart won't stay where you put them when you click the Save button? Have you attempted yet to put a title on your x- or y-axis but to then find it suddenly moves elsewhere on the canvas? If the answer is yes to these questions, then read through this chapter because by doing so you will learn that to prevent elements placed on the canvas or in the Glyph pane from wandering around, they must be anchored to either one of the default guides or to a custom guide that you have placed there. In this chapter, we will be looking at how we work with the default guides, how we can create our own guides, and how to anchor elements to these guides.

Consider the chart in Figure 10-1. All the elements you see in this chart have been anchored to either default guides or user-created guides to prevent them from moving away from where they were placed. Some elements were anchored by default, including the plot segment and the rectangle mark, but other elements had to be anchored to custom guides including the chart title, the x- and y-axis titles, the legend, and the black circle symbols in the glyph.

© Alison Box 2022
A. Box, *Introducing Charticulator for Power BI*, https://doi.org/10.1007/978-1-4842-8076-8_10

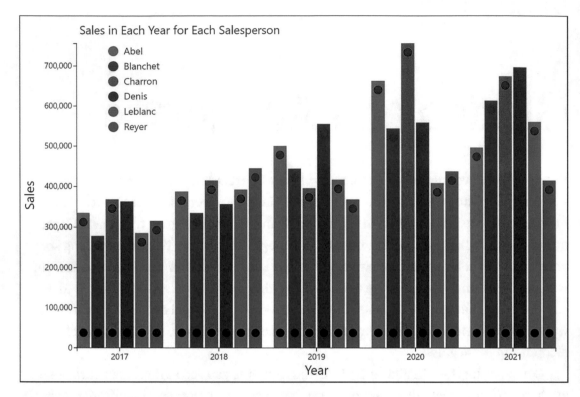

Figure 10-1.   *Chart elements are anchored to prevent wandering*

When we save this chart, all these elements will stay where you see them now and won't suddenly appear someplace else. To see how we arrived at this happy state of affairs, let's first look at the two different types of guides to which we can anchor elements, that is, the default guides and user-created guides, and then we will focus on the anchoring process itself.

Default Guides

When you first create a chart, you have a number of default guides created for you both on the canvas and in the Glyph pane. On the canvas, they appear as faint gray lines, and they mark out the margin space and the center points horizontally and vertically. The plot segment must be anchored to these guides; see Figure 10-2.

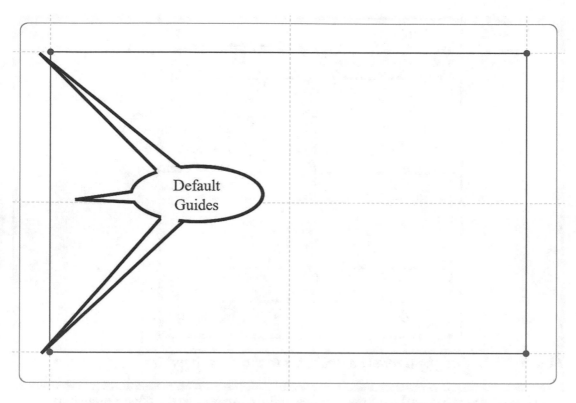

Figure 10-2. *The plot segment anchored to the default guides on the canvas*

You will also spot the green dots at the intersection of the margin guides. These are visual indicators that the plot segment (or any other chart element) has been anchored to the guides. If the dot is white, then the element has not been anchored (see the section on "Anchoring to Guides" below).

In the Glyph pane, the guides mark out the boundary of the glyph and also the center points, both horizontally and vertically. The marks and symbols comprising the glyph must be anchored to these guides; see Figure 10-3.

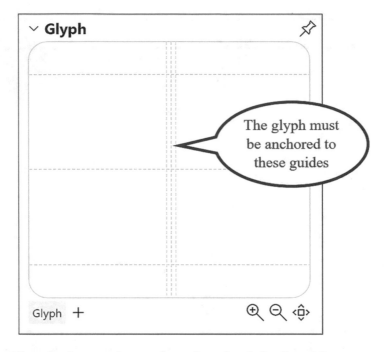

Figure 10-3. *The glyph must be anchored to the default guides*

However, you can add your own guides to the canvas or to the Glyph pane and anchor elements to them.

Creating Your Own Guides

You can create your own horizontal or vertical guides by clicking the **Guides** button on the toolbar and selecting either Guide X or Guide Y. Confusingly, there are two of each on the dropdown, but Figure 10-4 shows which are *guides* and which are *guide coordinators*. We need to select a *guide*.

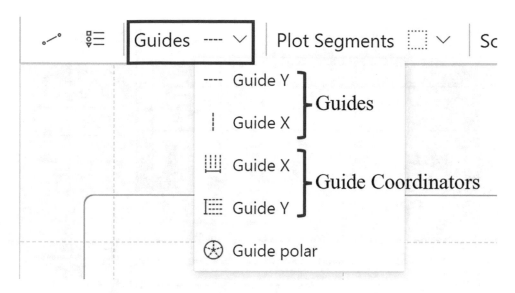

Figure 10-4. *Selecting guides or guide coordinators from the toolbar*

Now click into either the chart canvas or the Glyph pane to create the guide. The custom guide will now be listed in the Layers pane. You can change the position of your custom guide by selecting the guide in the Layers pane and open the Attributes pane for the guide. The custom guide can be offset from one of the default guides on the canvas or in the Glyph pane. For example, for horizontal guides, the guide must be offset from the Top, Middle, or Bottom guide. In Figure 10-5, for example, we have offset the custom guide from the default guide at the Top of the canvas.

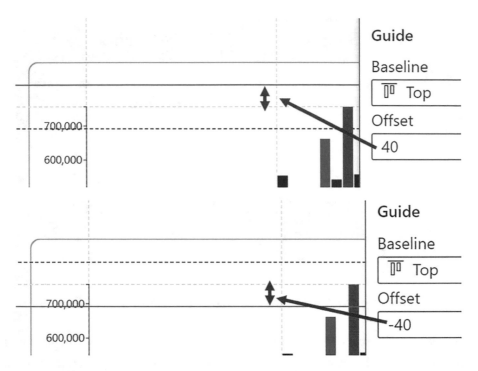

Figure 10-5. *Offsetting a custom guide from a default guide on the canvas*

Of course, you can also just drag on a guide to reposition it. Any chart element anchored to the guide will move accordingly.

Creating Guide Coordinators

Guide coordinators are a set of multiple vertical or horizontal guides that are evenly spaced. You are given two guides by default, but you can increase the number as required. You can add horizontal or vertical guide coordinators to either the canvas or the Glyph pane by clicking the **Guides** button dropdown on the toolbar and selecting, for example, Guide X or Guide Y; see Figure 10-4. To secure the guide coordinator, you must anchor it to a default guide by dragging along the guide (Figure 10-6). You can then edit the number of guides in the coordinator by using the Attributes pane of the guide coordinator.

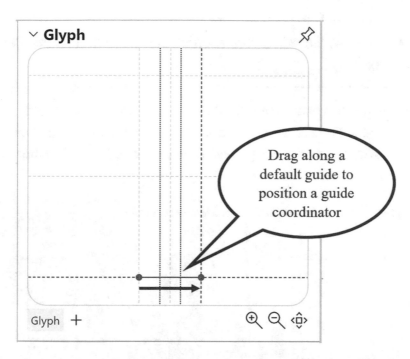

Figure 10-6. *Positioning a horizontal guide coordinator in the Glyph pane*

Once positioned on the canvas or in the Glyph pane, you are not able to drag to adjust their spacing as you can with vertical or horizontal guides.

Anchoring to Guides

Once you've added your guides or guide coordinators to the canvas or Glyph pane, you can start to anchor elements to them. Every element in your Charticulator chart *must* be anchored to either a default guide or a custom guide or guide coordinator. All chart elements have anchor handles that show as green dots. To anchor an element, either drag the anchor handle onto the intersection of a horizontal and a vertical guide or drag and draw the element inside the boundaries of a guide. For anchoring text marks, you can just click onto the intersection of a guide. You must ensure that the green anchor handles are anchored to a guide, or the element will move of its own accord when you save your chart.

Tip   If the dots are white with a green border, this indicates that the element has not been anchored.

For instance, to add a chart or an axis title to the canvas, first add guides so you can anchor the text mark. Then click the text mark button on the toolbar and click onto the canvas at the intersection of two guides when you see the green anchor point; see Figure 10-7.

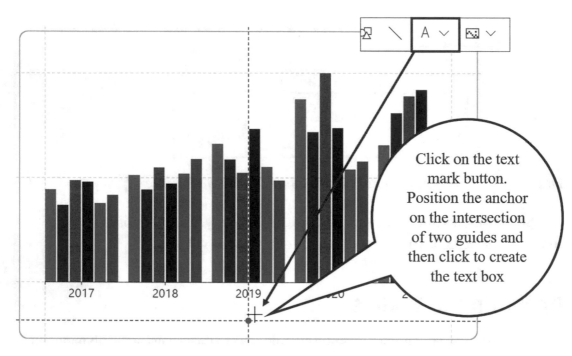

Figure 10-7.   *Adding a text mark to the canvas for a chart or axis title*

You can see some more examples of anchoring chart elements and glyph elements to guides in Figure 10-8.

Anchoring a text mark to the top and middle guides in the Glyph pane.

Anchoring two rectangle marks to the default guides in the Glyph pane.

Anchoring a legend to the default guides on the canvas

Anchoring multiple marks to guides generated by a horizontal and a vertical guide coordinator

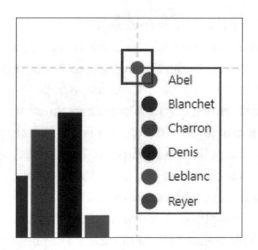

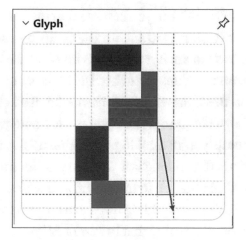

Figure 10-8. *Anchoring chart elements and glyph elements to guides and guide coordinators*

The guides that were used in the chart in Figure 10-1 to anchor the different elements are shown in Figure 10-9.

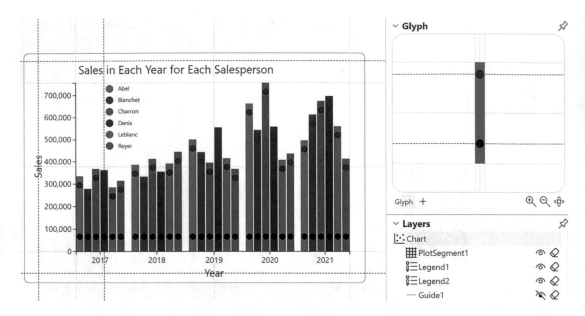

Figure 10-9. *Guides used on the canvas and in the Glyph pane*

In Figure 10-9, you can see that on the chart canvas we have added two vertical guides (Guide X) to anchor the y-axis title and the legend and two horizontal guides (Guide Y) to anchor the x-axis title and the chart title. In the Glyph pane, there are two horizontal guides to anchor the black symbol in the correct position on the glyph.

In this chapter, you've learned that all elements of a Charticulator chart must be anchored to a guide, and you must create your own guides to anchor any additional elements you're thinking of placing on the canvas or in the Glyph pane. The upshot of this is that at long last you can put titles on your chart and on your x- and y-axes, something that up to this point, you weren't able to achieve successfully. You may be thinking that adding titles to a chart is much simpler in a Power BI visual, but just consider the reality that in Power BI, you can't place chart elements at specific positions, and so you've little control over where the elements lie.

Being able to anchor elements of your chart to custom guides also now enables you to move forward with exploring another key feature of Charticulator charts, and that is using multiple plot segments, each of which must be anchored to guides, in effect creating visuals within visuals. This is definitely one of Charticulator's unique selling points, so without further ado, let's move on to the next chapter where you will discover that by using more than one plot segment, you can step up your game in designing engaging visuals that truly tell the story of your data.

CHAPTER 11

Working with Multiple 2D Region Plot Segments

In Chapter 5, you learned how to create your own 2D region plot segment by dragging and drawing it within the default guides on the canvas. However, when you first open up Charticulator, there is already a 2D region plot segment anchored on the canvas, and consequently you're not yet in the habit of adding your own, and indeed as yet you've not had any reason to do so. In this chapter, that is about to change because you will learn that one of the benefits of creating plot segments for yourself is the ability to design visuals that use multiple plot segments, in effect creating multiple complementary charts within a single visual.

You may not be surprised to hear that you can create as many plot segments as you require, but what you will also learn in this chapter is that each plot segment can contain a different glyph, and this is one of the many unique features to be discovered when you use Charticulator to generate your visuals. You can see an example of the type of visual to which I'm alluding in Figure 11-1.

© Alison Box 2022
A. Box, *Introducing Charticulator for Power BI*, https://doi.org/10.1007/978-1-4842-8076-8_11

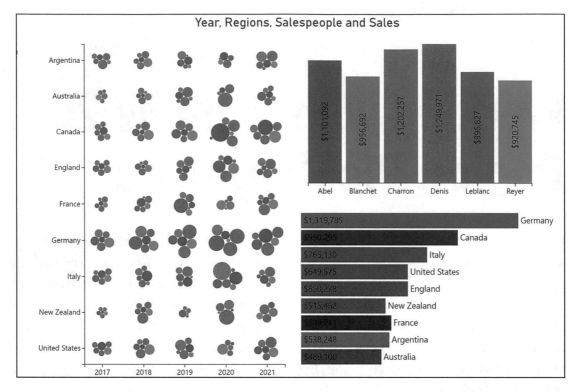

Figure 11-1. *This visual uses multiple plot segments, each with its own glyph*

However, it's not just the use of different glyphs that is a reason to use multiple plot segments. Each plot segment has its own set of attributes, and one of these attributes is designed particularly to be used with additional plot segments. This is the "Group by..." attribute. Using this feature, you can design visuals that can analyze total values (or indeed any aggregation) across your categorical data, and this is something that we are also going to explore later in this chapter along with its companion attribute, "Filter by...."

Using a Second 2D Region Plot Segment

However, let's not get too carried away to start. Why don't we generate just two 2D region plot segments on the canvas and see what we can do with them? To do this, let's start with a new chart and use our default data: "Year," "Salespeople," and "Sales." Remove "PlotSegment1" from the Layers pane, and then using the **Plot Segments** button on the toolbar, draw two new 2D region plot segments along the horizontal guides to make two "landscape" style plot segments. Remember you must anchor the plot segments to the guides; see Figure 11-2.

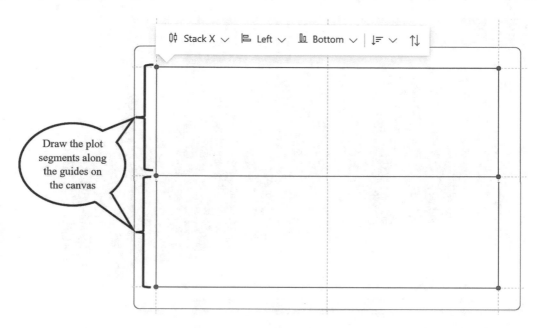

Figure 11-2. *Anchor the two 2D region plot segments to the guides on the canvas*

Now add a rectangle mark to the Glyph pane and bind your numerical field, for example, "Sales," to the Height attribute and your categorical field, for example, "Salespeople," to the Fill attribute. You will notice that the charts in both plot segments show the same data. The purpose of the two plot segments is to make two *different* charts. What we could do here is change the chart in the top plot segment by binding a categorical field, such as "Year," to the x-axis and use the Opposite attribute to place it at the top. Then, in the bottom plot segment, we could sort by our numerical field and use the Top alignment. Finally, we could add a legend for our categorical field; see Figure 11-3. Note the legend is added to the chart and not to any specific plot segment.

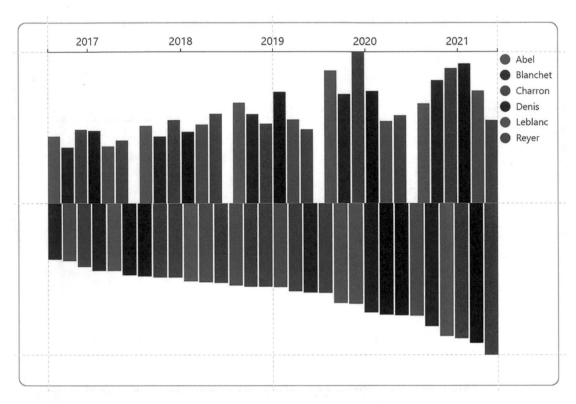

Figure 11-3. *Two different charts in the two plot segments*

I don't know how you feel about the visual in Figure 11-3, but by all accounts, it could be improved. The axis at the top doesn't work for the chart at the bottom, and there doesn't seem to be any good reason to show the data in two different plot segments within the same chart. Expressing this data in two separate charts would work better.

The problem is that at the moment we are confined to using the same glyph in both plot segments. However, we might want the glyph in the bottom plot segment to be a different shape, color, or size and have different data bound to it, but at present we don't know how to do that. If we could use *different* glyphs for different plot segments, that would give us greater scope in the design of the visual. This is the first time we've considered using more than one glyph in any of our visuals, so let's see how using a second glyph can make the visual a little less predictable.

Using Additional Glyphs

We could, for instance, redesign the bottom chart in Figure 11-3 to use a different glyph and generate the visual as shown in Figure 11-4. Here, we have a reason for the two charts presented together: to compare the salespeople's performance in each year and the yearly performance for each salesperson.

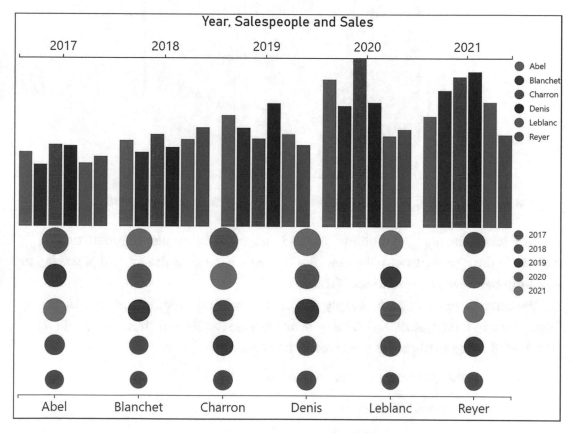

Figure 11-4. *Using separate glyphs for each plot segment gives more scope for the design*

To create the chart in Figure 11-4, delete PlotSegment2 from the Layers pane. We must now create the second glyph before we can create the second plot segment that will use it. To create the second glyph, click the plus at the bottom left of the Glyph pane. You will then see a message in the Glyph pane prompting you to create the new plot segment; see Figure 11-5.

Figure 11-5. *Creating a second glyph requires a second plot segment*

By clicking the new glyph button *first* and then creating the plot segment, this associates the new glyph with the new plot segment. Now draw the second plot segment as we did before inside the guides of the canvas.

We can now design our second glyph. For this, we used a symbol and bound the "Year" field to the Fill attribute and the "Sales" field to the Size attribute. We could then edit the following attributes of the second plot segment:

- Bind the "Salespeople" field to the x-axis.

- Use the Stack Y sub-layout.

- Sort descending by "Sales."

Adding a legend for the "Year" field completes the visual. To position the legend correctly, you will need to drag the green anchor handle of the second legend and anchor it to the middle guide on the canvas.

Using Group By...

Let's now move on to explore another reason to use a second plot segment, and that is to group the data in a categorical field to enable summarization of the data in each group. Consider the visual in Figure 11-6. You can see that in the bottom plot segment, there is a rectangle mark that represents the total year's sales, while in the top plot segment, sales are broken down into the respective salespeople's values.

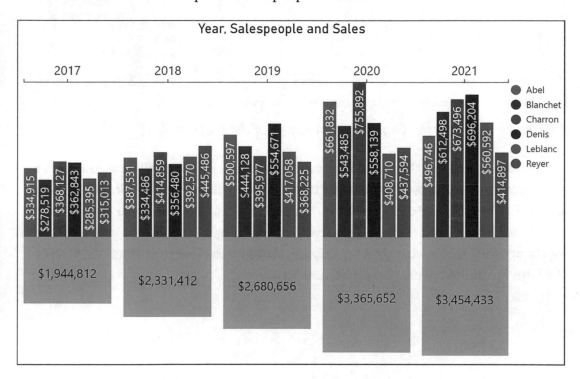

Figure 11-6. *Using the Group by... attribute allows you to summarize your data in a second plot segment*

To create the chart in Figure 11-6, we can start over with a completely new chart, and because we will need to generate a new scale for the Height attribute in the top chart, we must start with the *bottom* plot segment that groups the data by the "Year" field. In the new chart, delete PlotSegment1 from the Layers pane, then draw your new plot segment within the guides at the bottom of the canvas.

In this plot segment, we are going to use the Group by... attribute to group the data by the "Year" field as shown in Figure 11-7.

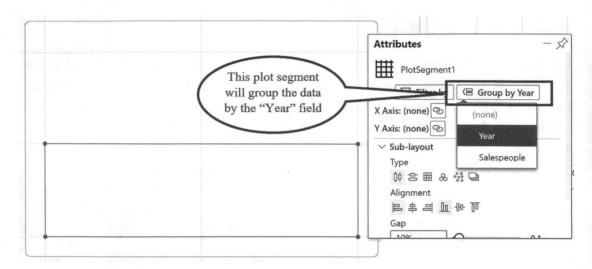

Figure 11-7. *Using the Group by… attribute of the plot segment*

We can now design the glyph that uses this plot segment and will represent sales for each year. For this, we used a simple rectangle mark, changed the fill color to gray, and bound the "Sales" field to the Height attribute. Notice that the Height attribute defaults to show the average of the sales value, but we want the height to reflect the sum of the sales. To change the function used by the attribute, click into the Height attribute and select the Sum function from the pop-up list; see Figure 11-8.

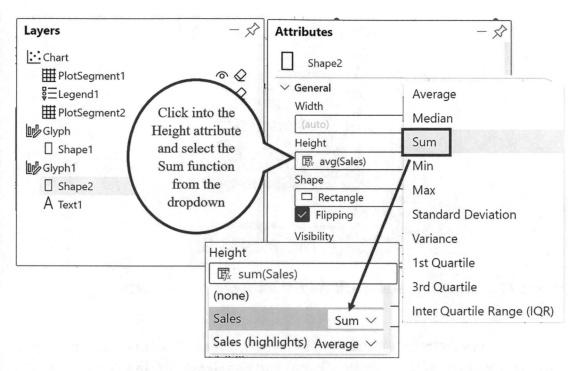

Figure 11-8. *Remember to change the aggregate function used by the Height attribute*

To label the total sales value in the rectangle glyph, we used a text mark and bound the "Sales" field to the Text attribute. Note that you must also change the aggregate function used by the text mark. If you want the text mark to show the sum of the sales, edit the Text attribute as shown in Figure 11-9. The final touch to this plot segment is to align the glyphs at the top.

Figure 11-9. *You may need to edit the Text attribute to show a different aggregation*

You can now create the second glyph followed by a second plot segment that sits at the top of the visual. This is a simple column chart that shows sales by salespeople that we've created many times in earlier chapters. There is just one caveat to the creation of the second glyph that is used in this chart. When you bind the "Sales" field to the Height attribute, hold down the SHIFT key while you drag and drop the field into the dropzone of the Height attribute. This is because you must create a *new scale* for the Height attribute that maps the average sales and not the sum. We looked at managing Charticulator's scales in Chapter 9. This will complete the creation of this chart.

Filter By…

You will find that mostly if you want to filter the data displayed in your Charticulator visual, you can use the normal Power BI filters such as slicers or the visual level filter. However, there is a reason why you may want to use Charticulator's Filter By attribute, and that is to analyze different categorical items in different plot segments. Consider the chart in Figure 11-10. It comprises two plot segments, each one showing sales for a different year.

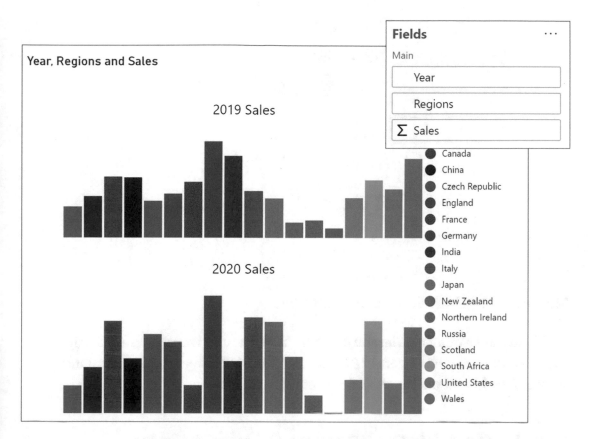

Figure 11-10. *A visual showing two plot segments, each filtered by different years*

This chart uses two 2D region plot segments and two glyphs. Each glyph is a rectangle that has the "Sales" field bound to the Height attribute and "Regions" bound to the Fill attribute. Then we used the Filter by… attribute of each plot segment, selecting the "Categories" filter type and filtering by each year, respectively; see Figure 11-11.

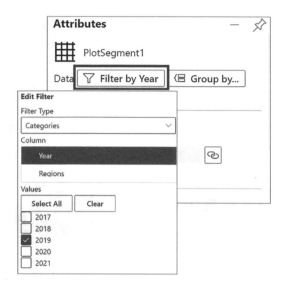

Figure 11-11. *Using the Filter by... attribute*

If you want a numerical legend for both charts, the chart must be created using a data axis which we will explore in Chapter 14. You could instead just use a text mark anchored to the rectangle to show the sales values.

Hands-On with Plot Segments and Glyphs

Using the techniques you've learned earlier to generate multiple plot segments, to add additional glyphs, and to group your data and indeed all the skills in Charticulator you've acquired along the way, why don't you see if you can re-create the chart shown in Figure 11-1? This visual uses three categorical fields, "Year," "Salespeople," and "Regions," and one numerical field, "Sales." To help you, in Figure 11-12, I've identified the three plot segments that this visual comprises by outlining them in red. Note the use of guides to position and anchor these plot segments, and seeing the Layers pane should also help you.

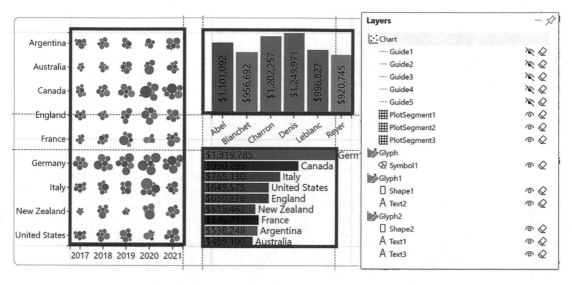

Figure 11-12. *This visual uses three plot segments, three glyphs, and custom guides*

How did you do? This was quite a challenging exercise that requires more detailed knowledge of Charticulator, so congratulations if you completed the task successfully. You're fast becoming a Charticulator expert!

What you've learned in this chapter is that by using multiple 2D region plot segments, you can design visuals that are multifaceted, and whether this is to show complementary charts inside one visual or to show ad hoc summarizations of your categorical data, I'm sure you'll find many reasons to add plot segments to your chart canvas and work with additional glyphs.

However, there is another important aspect of a Charticulator chart that impinges on plot segments and that we've yet to even mention in this book. This is the little understood world of Charticulator's X and Y scaffolds. What are they and why would you need to use them? We will find out in the next chapter.

CHAPTER 12

Horizontal and Vertical Line Scaffolds

Imagine a cartesian chart created with Charticulator where there are no fields bound to the x- or y-axis and there is an absence of any sub-layout but where the glyphs are stacked either horizontally or vertically within the plot segment. How is Charticulator able to lay out the glyphs like this when there is nothing driving the layout? What Charticulator will be using in this scenario is a *scaffold*. A scaffold determines the stacking layout of the glyphs in the absence of fields bound to the axes and replaces any sub-layout that has been applied. It's in this chapter that we are going to explore how Charticulator's horizontal line and vertical line scaffolds provide an alternative approach to laying out the glyphs in your chart.

However, before we delve into the world of horizontal and vertical line scaffolds, it's important that first we recap on what we already know about controlling the placement of glyphs in the plot segment. Reminding ourselves what we learned in Chapter 5, you will know that there are two key drivers in the layout of the chart: fields bound to the axes and sub-layouts. For instance, you will get different layouts if you bind the "Year" field to the x-axis and change the sub-layout to "Stack Y" or if you bind "Year" to the y-axis and change the sub-layout to "Stack X" (Figure 12-1).

© Alison Box 2022
A. Box, *Introducing Charticulator for Power BI*, https://doi.org/10.1007/978-1-4842-8076-8_12

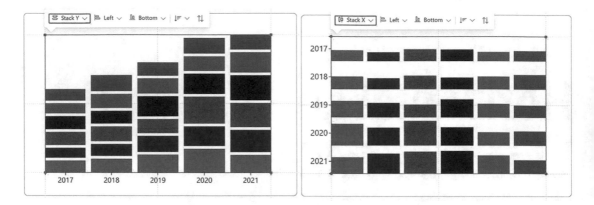

Figure 12-1. *Fields bound to axes and sub-layouts determine the layout*

However, there is a third factor that contributes to the layout of a chart, and that is the scaffold that's been applied to the plot segment. The horizontal and vertical scaffolds drive the layout where there are no fields bound to the x- or y-axis. Scaffolds always take precedence when used and will remove any sub-layouts that have been applied to the plot segment. Consider the chart in Figure 12-2. There is clearly no field bound to the x-axis, and the numerical scale on the left is a legend, not a numerical y-axis. What is determining the layout? The answer is that both a horizontal line and a vertical line scaffold have been applied to the plot segment. This seems an intriguing idea; no Power BI chart supports such a notion of building charts with a nonexistent x- or y-axis, so let's explore how this chart came into being.

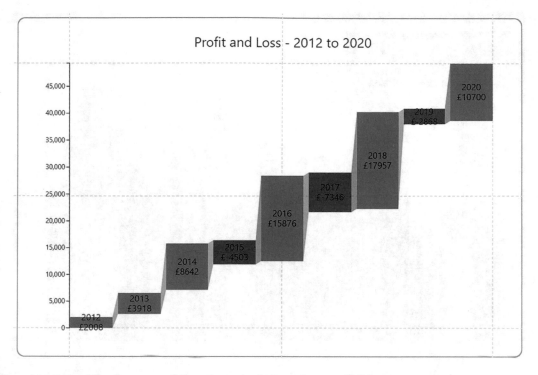

Figure 12-2. *The layout of the chart is driven by scaffolds*

We will build the chart in Figure 12-2 presently. However, our starting point will be with the chart in Figure 12-3 where the "Sales" field is bound to the Height attribute of a rectangle glyph and the "Salespeople" field is bound to the Fill attribute, but note that no fields are bound to the x- or y-axis.

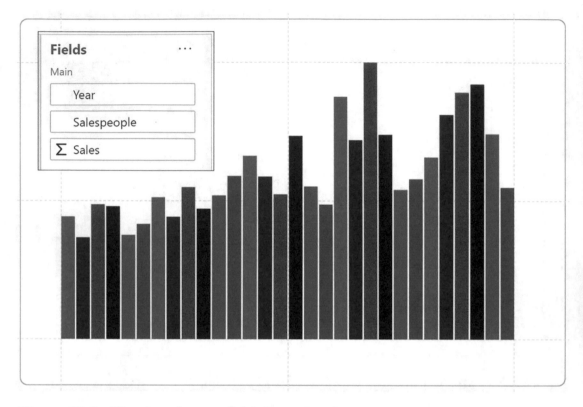

Figure 12-3. *The chart has no fields bound to the axes*

The reason we've bound no fields to the axes is because we're going to use scaffolds to determine the layout of the glyphs, not fields bound to the axes or any sub-layouts.

Applying Scaffolds

You apply a horizontal line or vertical line scaffold to a plot segment by selecting the scaffold from the **Scaffolds** button and then dragging the scaffold into the plot segment. In Figure 12-4, we've used the vertical line scaffold that has now stacked the glyphs horizontally up the y-axis.

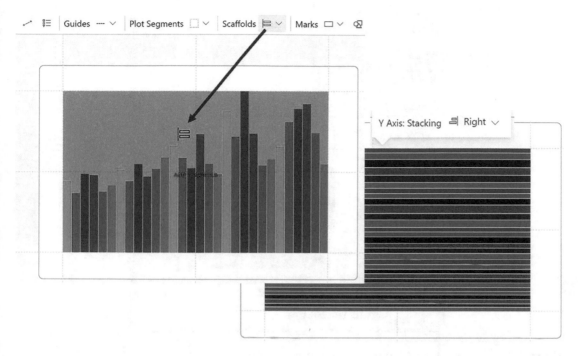

Figure 12-4. *Applying a vertical line scaffold*

If you look at the plot segment Attributes pane, you will see that the Y Axis attribute is set to "Stacking" instead of having a field bound to it (Figure 12-5).

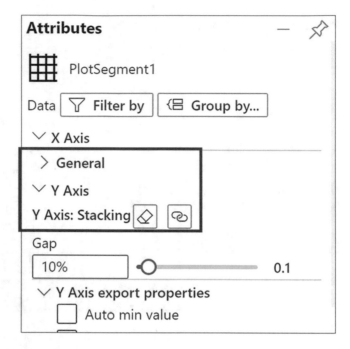

Figure 12-5. *The Y Axis attribute is set to Stacking*

Notice that it's here also that you can remove the scaffold by clicking the eraser. If you now apply a horizontal line scaffold, it will be bound to the X Axis attribute along with the Y Axis Stacking; see Figure 12-6.

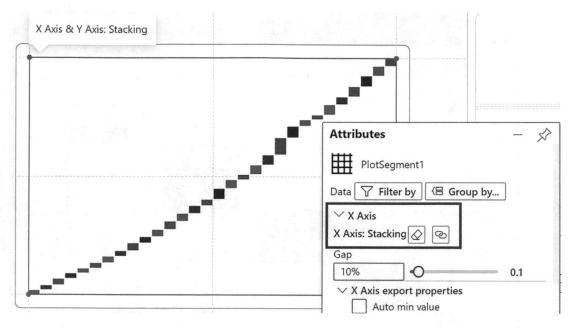

Figure 12-6. *X Axis and Y Axis stacking applied to the chart*

So now we have scaffolds controlling the layout of both the x- and y-axes, but you can "mix and match" scaffolds with fields bound to either the x- or y-axis, creating either categorical or numerical axes. Let's look at the combination of scaffolds and categorical axes first.

Combining Categorical Axes

Using the chart in Figure 12-3 where we've bound the "Sales" field to the Height attribute of the rectangle mark, we can combine a categorical x-axis using the "Year" field with a vertical line scaffold. Note how the scaffold controls the layout of the y-axis (Figure 12-7).

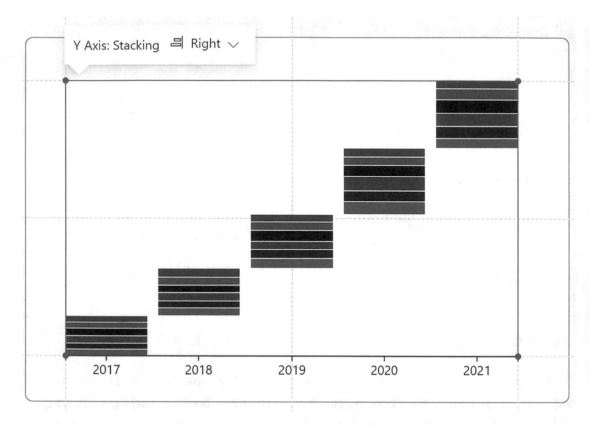

Figure 12-7. *Vertical line scaffold with a categorical x-axis*

Starting over with the chart in Figure 12-3, we can combine a categorical y-axis with a horizontal line scaffold. Again, note how the scaffold controls the layout of the x-axis (Figure 12-8).

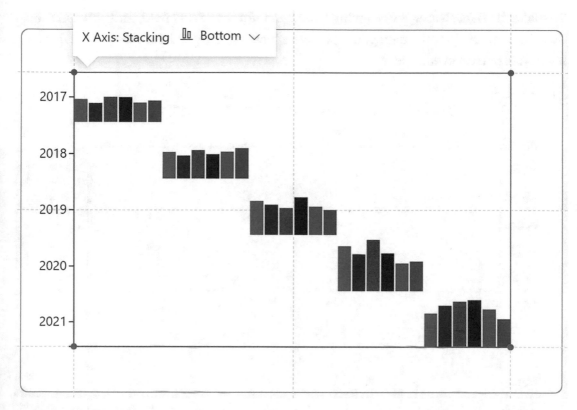

Figure 12-8. *Horizontal line scaffold with a categorical y-axis*

At this stage, you may wonder to what purpose you can put these layouts. We will find a reason to use them presently.

Combining Numerical Axes

You get more interesting (and possibly more useful) layouts if you combine a scaffold with a numerical axis. Using this method, you can create "scatter" charts without having to use both a numerical x-axis and a numerical y-axis as is the case with a Power BI scatter chart.

Consider the chart in Figure 12-9 which has been built from scratch using the "Year," "Salespeople," and "Sales" fields. This time, we're using a symbol as our glyph, and the "Sales" field has been bound to the y-axis, generating a numerical axis. The "Year" field has then been bound to the Fill attribute of the symbol. We have then applied a horizontal line scaffold, so we are now combining the scaffold with a numerical y-axis.

To make the data clearer, we've included a legend for the "Year" field, and you can see that the symbols (i.e., the data points) create a "scatter" type chart showing the sales for each salesperson in each year.

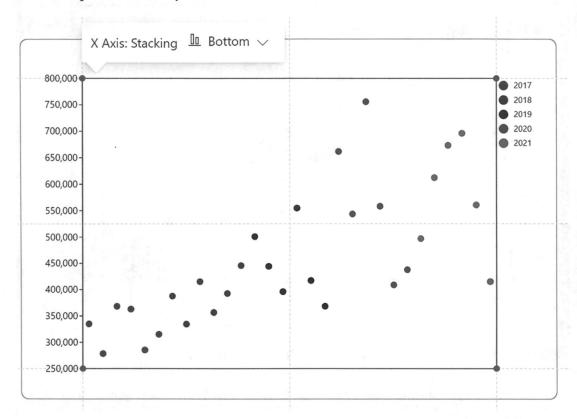

Figure 12-9. *Horizontal line stacking with a numerical y-axis using symbols*

Let's compare the chart in Figure 12-9 with what we know so far about plotting data against a numerical y-axis. If we remove the scaffold and bind the "Year" field into the x-axis instead of the scaffold, the data points would now overlap by default and line up for each year accordingly; see Figure 12-10.

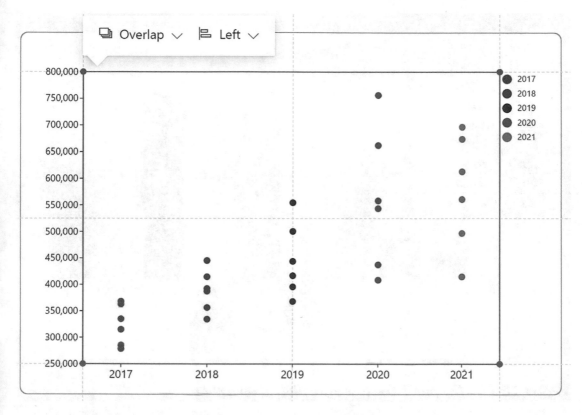

Figure 12-10. *Using "conventional" numerical and categorical axes*

You can see that using a scaffold in conjunction with a numerical axis can create interesting scatter charts without resorting to using two numerical axes. But what else can we use scaffolds for? Let's now turn our attention to the chart in Figure 12-2, plotting profit and loss data. This chart is using scaffolds to great effect because we've constructed a chart with no fields bound to x- or y-axis but just using scaffold to lay out the glyphs correctly.

In Figure 12-11, you can see how the chart started out. Using just a rectangle glyph and putting the "Profit" field into the Height attribute and the "Sign" field into the "Fill" attribute and using text marks for "Year" and "Profit," a simple column chart showing positive and negative values is generated.

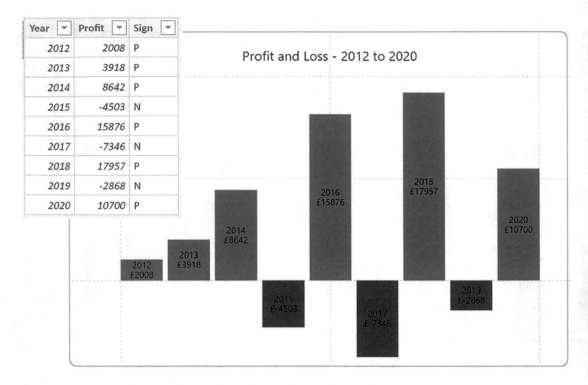

Year ▼	Profit ▼	Sign ▼
2012	2008	P
2013	3918	P
2014	8642	P
2015	-4503	N
2016	15876	P
2017	-7346	N
2018	17957	P
2019	-2868	N
2020	10700	P

Figure 12-11. *The profit and loss data plotted on a chart*

If we now apply both a vertical and a horizontal line scaffold to the chart, it will be laid out as shown in Figure 12-12.

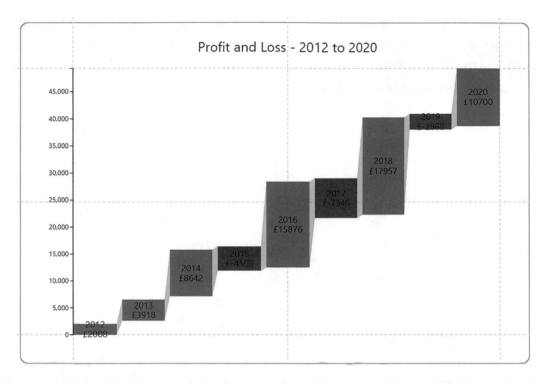

Figure 12-12. *The chart with both vertical and horizontal line scaffolds applied*

To finish this chart, I've added a legend on the left for the "Profit" field and linked the rectangles using a band (we look more closely at band links in Chapter 15). Notice that I've used no fields on either the x- or y-axis.

Therefore, to summarize what we've learned about scaffolds, you can *either* use a scaffold to lay out glyphs *or* use a sub-layout. At this point, having seen the use of these scaffolds you may be thinking that vertical and horizontal line scaffolds are a little rarefied and would only be required in a few specific instances. How often do you need to create scatter charts with no numerical axes or plot positive and negative values cascading upward? Probably not that often. I think therefore we can conclude that most likely we'd rather use sub-layouts, not scaffolds, to lay out the glyphs of our charts, primarily because sub-layouts provide us with many more design choices.

Why then don't we now move on to look at another type of scaffold whose use is more mainstream? Think on it; I haven't yet shown you how to create a simple pie or donut chart using Charticulator. This might seem a little strange considering we are now up to Chapter 12! The reason I haven't yet broached the subject of pie charts and all their variations is that to create such charts you need to use Charticulator's polar scaffold, and this will be the topic of the next chapter. It's now time to turn our attention to designing circular and radial style charts rather than square and rectangular ones.

CHAPTER 13

Polar Scaffolds

In the last chapter, you learned how to use horizontal and vertical line scaffolds to lay out the glyphs in your chart as an alternative to sub-layouts. We also concluded that their use was limited to a few specific chart designs. However, there is another type of scaffold that *does* provide us with a wealth of design options. If you want to design circular types of chart such as pies, donuts, or radar charts, you will need to apply the polar scaffold, and, unlike horizontal and vertical line scaffolds, with this scaffold you're supplied with a comprehensive choice of sub-layouts to work with. In this chapter, you will learn how to use the polar scaffold to generate not only conventional circular charts, such as the pie chart, but also more unusual and interesting ones too. We will also take a look at the custom curve scaffold which includes a tool for generating spiral and wavy style charts.

It might also be worth iterating at this point that the general consensus among data analysts is that pie charts and the like are not always the best choice of visualization. This is primarily because they can be difficult to decode when cluttered with many categorical fields. However, the purpose of this book is not to tackle the issue of which visuals are better than others but to teach you to use the tools and let you decide. We also know that by using charts generated by Charticulator, we can move away from the standard Power BI pie or donut charts with their cumbersome data labels and limited formatting options and instead design visuals that *are* able to engage with the consumers of our reports.

Just to whet your appetite with what can be achieved using the polar and custom curve scaffolds, consider the charts in Figure 13-1.

© Alison Box 2022
A. Box, *Introducing Charticulator for Power BI*, https://doi.org/10.1007/978-1-4842-8076-8_13

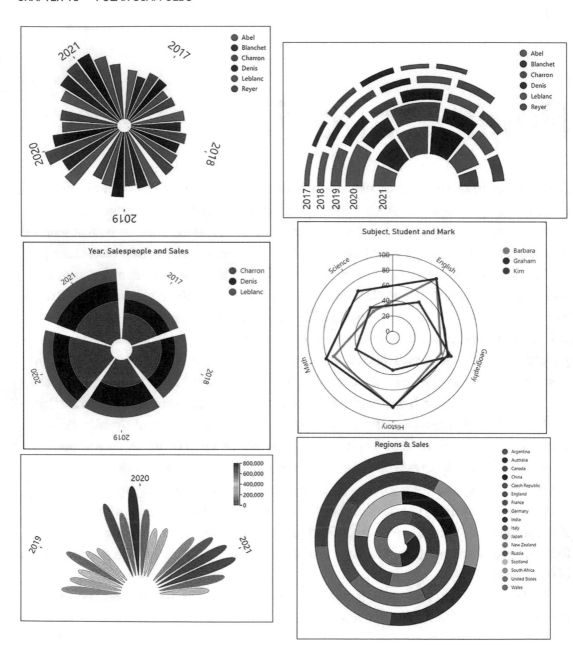

Figure 13-1. *Charts created with the polar or the custom curve scaffold*

If you think that these types of visualization have a place in the design of your reports, then read on and you'll learn how to build them.

Applying a Polar Scaffold

Before applying the polar scaffold, start afresh and create a regular column chart similar to the one in Figure 13-2.

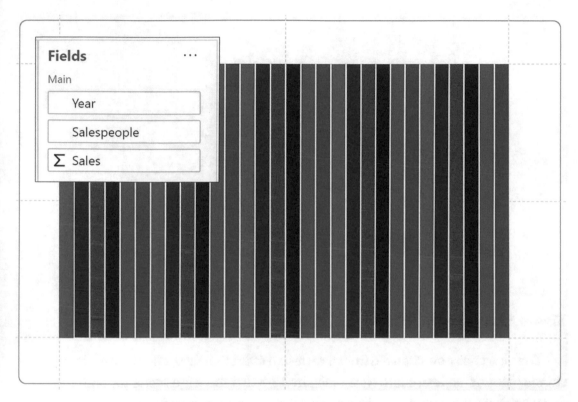

Figure 13-2. *To apply a polar scaffold, start with a chart similar to this*

This chart uses two categorical fields, one numerical field, and a rectangle mark in the Glyph pane. We've then bound the categorical "Salespeople" field to the Fill attribute.

To apply the polar scaffold, click the **Scaffolds** button on the toolbar and select **Polar** from the dropdown. Then drag the polar scaffold onto the plot segment as in Figure 13-3.

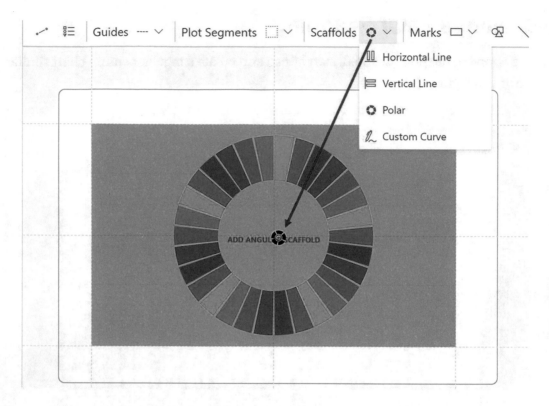

Figure 13-3. *Apply a polar scaffold to the chart*

The chart has now changed from a cartesian chart that uses x- and y-axes to a circular "donut" style of chart. Note in Figure 13-3 that there is a sector for both the category and subcategory, in other words a sector for every year for every salesperson, 30 sectors in all.

Tip   To convert the polar plot segment back to a 2D region plot segment, apply a horizontal line scaffold.

Already this donut chart is significantly different from a Power BI donut or pie chart where colored sectors can only define a single category. Also notice that applying a polar scaffold creates a polar plot segment. This can be identified in the Layers pane because of its different icon.

Reshaping the Polar Chart

Charticulator presents you with a donut-shaped chart when you first apply the polar scaffold. However, you can now easily change the donut shape into a pie shape by dragging inward on the inner radius of the chart. If you want to increase the circumference, drag outward on the circumference, and you can also drag between the glyphs to increase the spacing between them; see Figure 13-4.

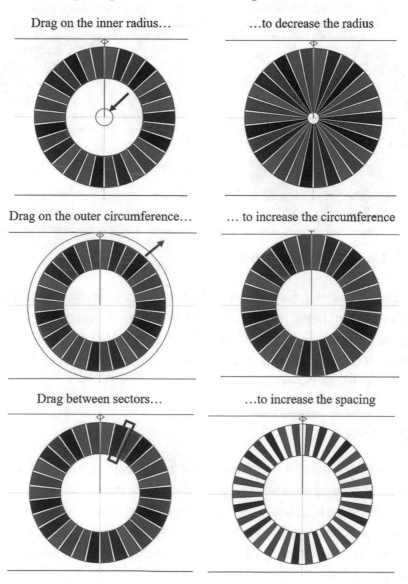

Figure 13-4. Reshaping the polar chart

If you want to fine-tune these adjustments, you can also use the attributes of the polar plot segment where you can resize the plot segment and change the gap between categories and the spacing between glyphs.

To create an arc layout, where the plot segment starts and ends at specific angles, you can drag on the handles at the top of the chart in a circular direction, for instance, creating an angle of between 270° and 450°; see Figure 13-5.

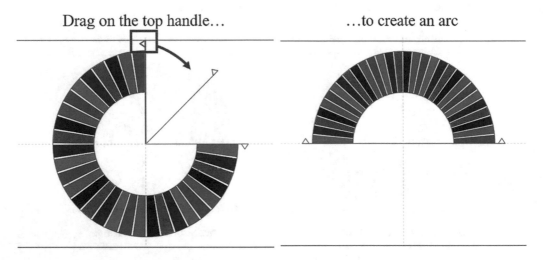

Figure 13-5. *Creating an arc layout*

To move the arc shape to the bottom of the canvas, turn on the Automatic Alignment attribute under "Origin" in the plot segment Attributes pane. You can then move the bottom guide of the canvas upward to reposition the chart in the middle of the canvas. Another approach to moving the arc into the middle of the canvas is to drag the bottom guide of the canvas below the canvas.

Creating a Pie Chart

In Figure 13-6, we have styled a very simple pie chart using Charticulator. You will notice the chart only comprises one category, the "Salespeople" field. This is because a conventional pie chart is typically used to show the percentage breakdown of a total value across a single category and works best with fewer sectors. To create this chart, all that is required is to bind a numerical field to the Width attribute of the rectangle shape and close the gap in the plot segment attributes.

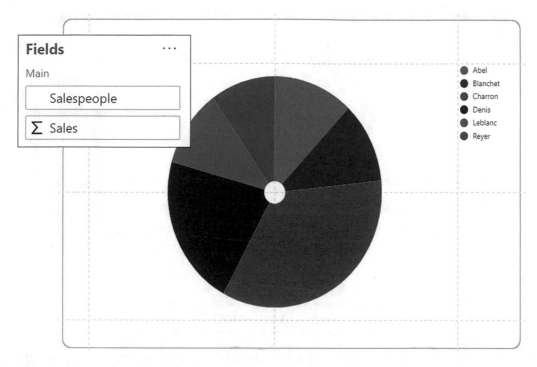

Figure 13-6. *A Charticulator pie chart*

The downside of using Charticulator to build standard pie charts is that displaying "detail labels" (e.g., the values or percentages as a callout) is problematic on two accounts.

Firstly, binding the "Salespeople" field to the angular axis (see the section on "Binding Fields to Polar Axes" below) would size the glyphs so they are equally spaced around the axis according to the value of the field bound to the Width attribute; see Figure 13-7.

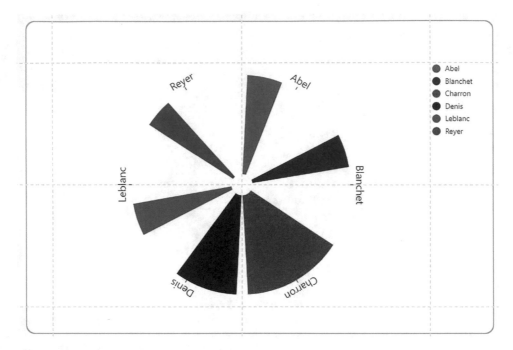

Figure 13-7. *Binding the category to the angular axis spaces the glyphs equally according to their value*

Secondly, if you were to use a text mark anchored to the rectangle glyph to show the labels, the text mark will retain its alignment irrespective of the angle at which the glyph sits within the chart. The upshot of this is that the text marks may sometimes sit upside down. This wouldn't happen to the detail labels on a Power BI pie chart. However, to remedy this problem, you could use a polar guide.

Using a Polar Guide

The polar guide allows you to anchor chart elements to positions either inside or outside the circular chart. Select the polar guide from the **Guides** dropdown on the toolbar and draw the guide onto the canvas, anchoring it to the top, bottom, and side guides of the canvas. To use the guide, anchor your text marks to the anchor points of the guide at the center of the circle. You can then drag your text marks and position them around the outside of the circle; see Figure 13-8.

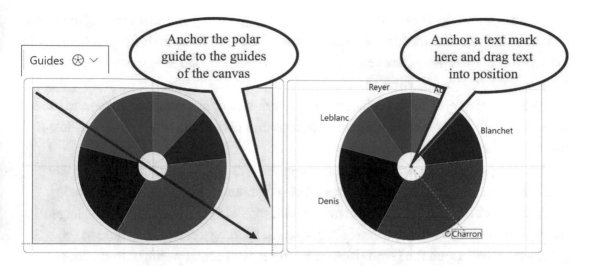

Figure 13-8. *Using the polar guide to anchor labels around the outside of the chart*

Unfortunately, these text marks won't respond to the data changing. We might conclude therefore that if we want to use a simple pie chart, we'd probably be better off building it in Power BI.

What we must do now, therefore, is to see how we can generate circular style charts that are not so easily constructed in Power BI, if at all. If we start to explore the attributes of the polar plot segment and bind fields to these attributes, we will learn how easy it is to morph the pie chart into a host of other designs. The starting point for this is to understand how the axes of the polar plot segment are used to change the design of the chart and control the layout.

Binding Fields to Polar Axes

A polar plot segment has two axes: angular and radial. You can bind categorical or numerical fields to either the angular or radial axis by dragging directly onto the plot segment or by using the Attributes pane.

Binding numerical fields to either axis doesn't typically generate meaningful charts, so in this chapter we concentrate on using just categorical data on the angular and radial axes. If you want to plot numerical data onto the axes of a polar plot segment, it's easier to use a data axis (see Chapter 14) as you have more control over how the data will be represented. However, there is an exception to this and one compelling reason to use a numerical radial axis, and that is in the construction of the radar chart, and we look at this specific example later in this chapter.

Working with the polar plot segment's angular axis will be more intuitive for you as it's the only axis that is used in Power BI pie or donut charts. The field you use for Charticulator's angular axis is synonymous with the field you would put in the Legend bucket when constructing the Power BI pie chart. Binding a categorical field to the angular axis will group the glyphs in sectors around the center point, with the labels sitting around the outside of the chart.

The radial axis may be a little more challenging to get to grips with at first as there is no equivalent in a Power BI chart. With a categorical field bound to a radial axis, each axis category now comprises a concentric circle and is labeled accordingly; see Figure 13-9.

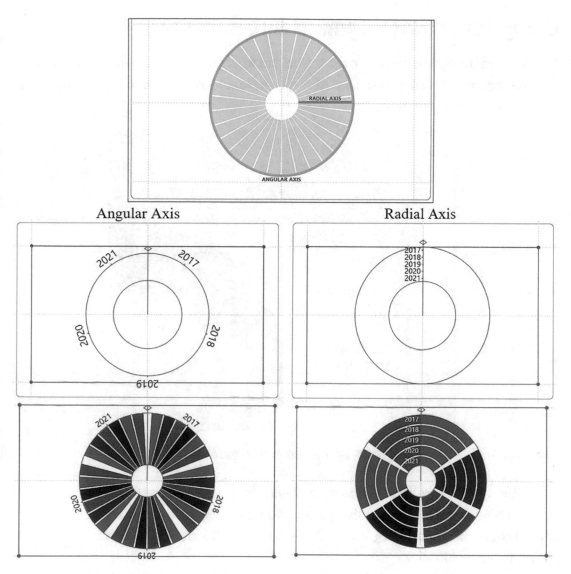

Figure 13-9. *The angular and radial axes of the polar plot segment*

Once you have plotted the axis you require, you can then further change the layout of the polar plot segment by using one of the sub-layouts. Let's see how these sub-layouts can enable you to design the charts of your choice.

Using Polar Plot Segment Sub-layouts

You will find the option to change the sub-layout at the bottom of the Attributes pane of the plot segment, but it's easier to use the options on the dropdown of the plot segment toolbar as shown in Figure 13-10.

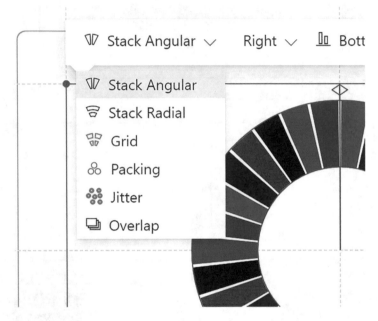

Figure 13-10. *The sub-layouts of a polar plot segment*

Although there are six sub-layouts to choose from, we're going to focus on just the stack angular and stack radial sub-layouts as these are the ones used in most circular chart designs. In all the examples of sub-layouts that follow, we will be using the fields as shown in Figure 13-11.

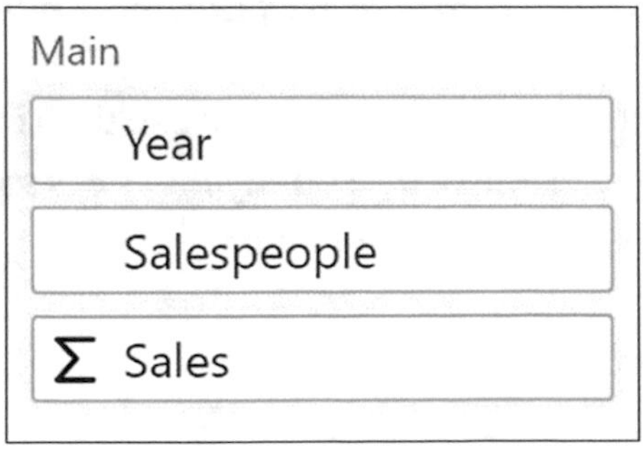

Figure 13-11. *The fields used for all the examples in the section on sub-layouts*

We now have four combinations of axis and sub-layout to work through, each one generating a different style of chart:

1. Stack angular with angular axis

2. Stack radial with angular axis

3. Stack angular with radial axis

4. Stack radial with radial axis

These four combinations are set out in Figure 13-12 where the "Year" field is plotted onto the axis and "Salespeople" field provides the subcategory.

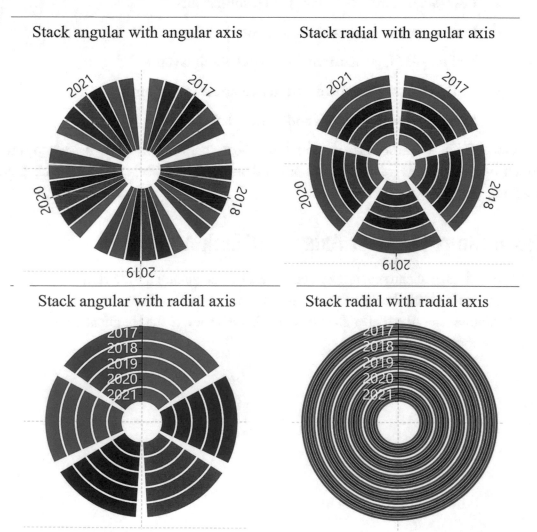

Figure 13-12. *Combinations of sub-layouts with angular and radial axes*

As with cartesian charts, the fields you bind to the axes take precedence. With an angular axis, the years are represented by sectors, but with the radial axis, the years are represented in concentric circles. The sub-layouts then stack the glyphs representing the subcategory (in our examples, the salespeople) side by side (stack angular) or one on top of the other (stack radial).

These various permutations can be a little bewildering when you first meet them, so let's now take a more detailed look at how we can fashion different chart types using each of these four combinations of axes and sub-layouts. We will look specifically at building the following chart types:

- Rose (angular axis and stack angular sub-layout)

- Peacock (angular axis and stack angular sub-layout)

- Nightingale (angular axis and stack radial sub-layout)

- Radial chart #1 (radial axis and stack angular sub-layout)

- Radial chart #2 (radial axis and stack radial sub-layout)

Once you have learned how you can build these charts, we will then leave it to you to self-explore the myriad of other options and permutations when working with a polar scaffold.

Rose Chart (Angular Axis and Stack Angular)

In Figure 13-13, you can see how we can transform the default pie chart into a rose type chart. To do this, with the default stack angular sub-layout applied and the "Year" field on the angular axis, the "Sales" field has then been bound to the Height attribute of the rectangle shape.

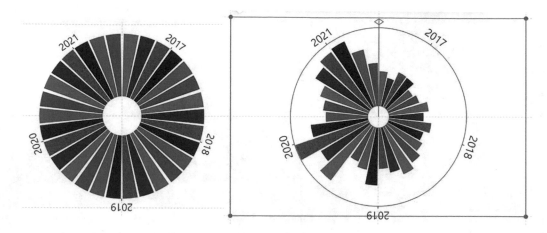

Figure 13-13. *Using an angular axis and stack angular sub-layout with a numerical field bound to the Height attribute of the rectangle*

The angular axis arranges glyphs around the axis in the same way as an x- or y-axis and that is to arrange them *equally* around the axis according to the value bound to the Width attribute. The result of this is that a gap will be produced for smaller values (see Figure 13-7).

Peacock Chart (Angular Axis and Stack Angular)

In Figure 13-14, we have set out the steps to create a peacock chart. Starting with the default chart, you will need to drag on the handles at the top of the plot segment to create an arc (i.e., an angle of 270° to 450°), and you can then bind a numerical field to the Height attribute of the rectangle. If you then change the shape of the mark to an ellipse, this will produce the peacock shape. In our example, the final step was to use the "Sales" numerical field in the Fill attribute, giving the chart a spectral gradient fill.

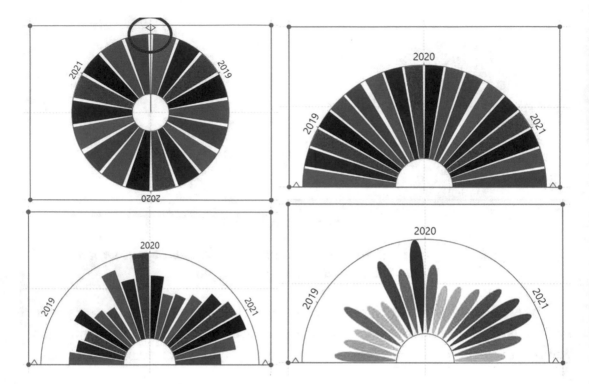

Figure 13-14. *A peacock chart uses an angular axis and a stack angular sub-layout*

You will notice that we have also filtered the "Year" field to show only three years. This type of visual, like pie charts, generally works better when you have fewer categories.

Remember to turn on the Automatic Alignment attribute to move the peacock chart to the bottom of the canvas. You can then adjust the bottom guide of the plot segment to move the chart into the middle.

Nightingale Chart (Angular Axis and Stack Radial)

To create a nightingale chart, you will need to use the default angular axis but change the sub-layout to radial. It's not until you bind a numerical field to the Height attribute of the rectangle that the chart is transformed into the nightingale chart, seen in Figure 13-15. Reducing the subcategories and closing the gap on the angular axis can result in a less cluttered chart.

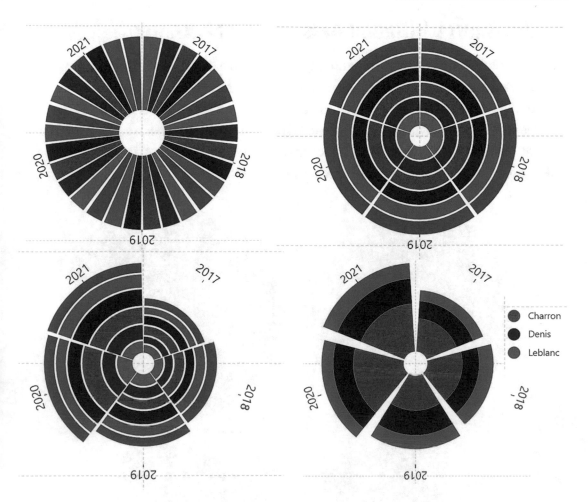

Figure 13-15. *Transforming the default chart into a nightingale chart using an angular axis with a stack radial sub-layout*

Using the stack radial sub-layout, the glyphs are grouped by year and stacked in concentric layers to show values for the salespeople. The real benefit of this chart is that not only can we analyze our salespeople's performance and see that "Charron" is doing nicely, but we can also easily see that the years 2020 and 2021 were the better years. It's the binding of a numerical value to the Height attribute of the rectangle that gives this visual its strength.

Radial Chart #1 (Radial Axis and Stack Angular)

To explore sub-layouts that are combined with a radial axis, let's start by designing a radial style chart that uses a stack angular sub-layout. As soon as we then bind the "Year" field to the radial axis, the glyphs are rearranged accordingly where each year is now represented by a concentric circle and the glyphs are grouped by each salesperson in sectors. If we now apply some techniques that we've already learned, the chart can be redesigned into an arc shape radial chart; see Figure 13-16.

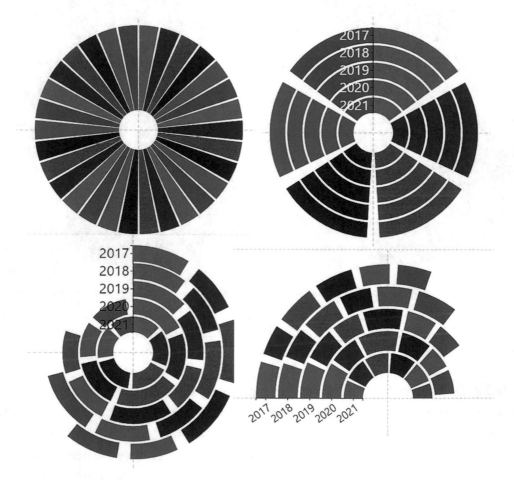

Figure 13-16. *Binding a categorical field to the radial axis and using the stack angular sub-layout*

In this chart, we bound a numerical field to the Width attribute of the rectangle to plot the data. However, the radial axis for the years by default sits vertically at the top of the chart. If you change the angle of the plot segment (i.e., an angle of 270° to 450°), this would move the axis so it sits horizontally.

You will get some more interesting layouts if you experiment with the plot segment's horizontal and vertical alignment options or the gap and sorting options.

Radial Chart #2 (Radial Axis and Stack Radial)

The last combination of axes and sub-layouts that we will explore is when a categorical field is bound to the radial axis and then a radial sub-layout is applied. This again will generate a radial style chart but with a completely different look and feel. In Figure 13-17, starting with the default chart with a stack angular sub-layout, we can apply the "Year" field to the radial axis and change the sub-layout to stack radial. The glyphs representing each salesperson now sit in concentric circles. To plot data onto the chart, we need to bind the "Sales" field to the Width attribute of the rectangle, but it's difficult to see what's what in the chart at this stage. Filtering the number of salespeople showing, increasing the gap on the radial axis, and changing the shape of the glyph to an ellipse renders the chart a little more promising.

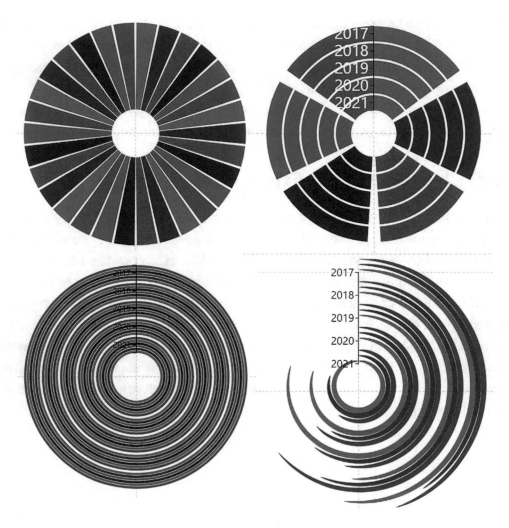

Figure 13-17. *Redesigning the default chart to use a radial axis with a stack radial sub-layout*

Having worked your way through these four permutations of axis and sub-layout, you must understand that you are still at the very tip of the iceberg with regard to the number of interesting and unusual charts that you could possibly design by applying the polar scaffold. Why don't you go on a voyage of self-discovery and see how many variations on the humble pie chart you can create by applying a polar scaffold and then changing different attributes of the plot segment and glyph? In Table 13-1, I've set out a few suggestions as to which attributes you might try modifying to see how many variations of a polar chart you can discover and invent.

Table 13-1. *Attributes you can modify to generate interesting polar charts*

Attribute to Modify	Example
• Alignment	We've only used the "Bottom" and "Left" alignments, but you could try to edit these and see what impact it has on your chart.
• Shape	Explore using triangles or ellipses. You could even experiment with symbols in the Glyph pane.
• Angle	As we have seen, creating arc-shaped charts by changing the angle can produce an interesting variation on a circular chart.
• Gridlines	You can show radial or angular gridlines using attributes of the relevant axis.
• Binding data	We've always bound numerical fields to the Height attribute for the angular axis and to the Width attribute for the radial axis, but there is no rule regarding this.

Height to Area

The Height to Area attribute is an attribute of the plot segment, and we need to take a more detailed look at it. Toggling the attribute on or off will affect the way the numerical data is plotted in the chart.

When you bind a numerical field to the Height attribute of a rectangle glyph, when plotted on a polar plot segment, the *heights* of the glyphs will be proportional, but the *areas* will be skewed for smaller values as the radius decreases. The outcome is that smaller values look disproportionally smaller relative to the area. The reason for this is that the "Height to Area" attribute of the polar plot segment is checked off by default.

If you want the area of the glyph to reflect the value bound to the Height attribute rather than its height, check on the Height to Area attribute. In Figure 13-18, we have an example of how this works. You can see that the green sector has a value of 4000 and so by default will be twice the *height* of the red sector whose value is 2000. When Height to Area is turned on however, the green sector has an *area* that is twice the area of the red sector.

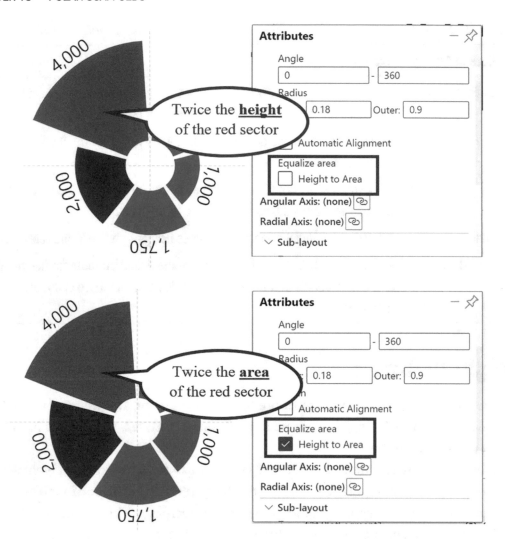

Figure 13-18. *The Height to Area attribute*

Use the Height to Area attribute by checking it on to ensure that the numerical value bound to the Height attribute drives the *area* of each sector, as opposed to the *height*.

Numerical Radial Axis – The Radar Chart

So far in this chapter, we have only used categorical fields on the angular or radial axis of the polar plot segment, and this is because most polar charts use categorical axes. However, there is a good reason to use a numerical field on the radial axis of the polar plot segment and that is to generate a radar chart, an example of which you can see in Figure 13-19.

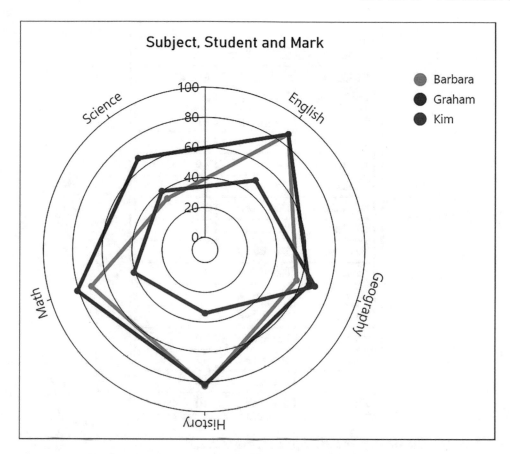

Figure 13-19. *The radar chart uses a numerical radial axis*

This radar chart analyzes three students' examination marks across five subjects, and we can easily infer from this visual that Graham is the most successful student overall, although in Geography, all three students are pretty much on a par with each other. The chart uses the data that is shown in Figure 13-20.

Main		
15 rows, 3 columns		
Student	**Subject**	**Mark**
Barbara	English	87
Barbara	Geography	47
Barbara	History	83
Barbara	Math	70
Barbara	Science	35
Graham	English	87
Graham	Geography	66
Graham	History	82
Graham	Math	80
Graham	Science	65
Kim	English	49
Kim	Geography	70
Kim	History	34
Kim	Math	42
Kim	Science	40

Figure 13-20. *The data plotted onto the radar chart*

Let's now explore how this chart was built. We started with a new chart and then applied the polar scaffold to the plot segment. We know that when we use a numerical axis on a cartesian chart, the default sub-layout is Overlap, and the norm is to use a symbol in the Glyph pane. This is no less true for numerical axes in polar charts. With a symbol in the Glyph pane, the "Student" field was then bound to the Fill attribute of the symbol and the "Subject" field was bound to the angular axis. The "Mark" numerical field was bound to the radial axis, generating a numerical radial axis that has all the same attributes as a numerical x- or y-axis. The Range attribute of the plot segment was set from 0 to 100.

To create the "radar" aspect of the chart, we used the Gridline attribute of the radial axis to apply the radial gridlines, and then using the **Link** button on the toolbar, inserted a Line link, linking the "Student" field. The last action was to ensure that the Close Link attribute was checked on; see Figure 13-21.

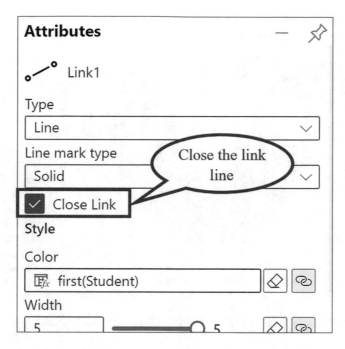

Figure 13-21. *Close the link line to create the radar chart*

You may also find that you need to change the link line type to "line" rather than "Bezier."

The Custom Curve Scaffold

It's now time to look at the last of Charticulator's scaffold types and that's the custom curve scaffold. Charticulator allows you to generate charts where you can *draw* the shape you require on the canvas such as curvy, wavy, circular, or square. In Figure 13-22, you can see we have drawn a curvy chart. However, just as with the use of the pie chart, we need to think carefully whether such charts can provide any valuable information. It might be a case of just because you can doesn't mean you should! But I don't want to be a spoilsport, and if Charticulator provides us with the tools to design such charts, we will include them in this chapter.

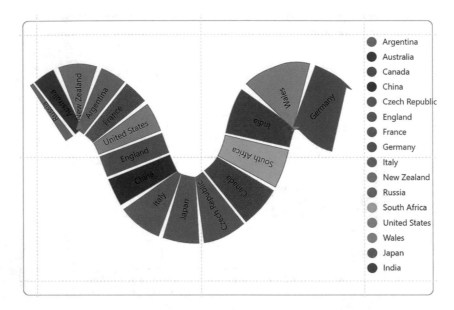

Figure 13-22. *A visual created with the custom curve scaffold*

To use the custom curve scaffold, begin afresh with a new chart that uses two fields, one categorical and one numerical, and then put a rectangle mark into the Glyph pane. You can then bind your numerical field to the "Width" attribute of the rectangle and categorical field to the "Fill" attribute. In the visual shown in Figure 13-22, we used the "Regions" categorical field and the "Sales" numerical field and also sorted the glyphs ascending by numerical value, but the sorting isn't essential.

Applying the Custom Curve

You are now ready to apply the custom curve scaffold. To do this, from the **Scaffolds** button on the toolbar, drag the custom curve scaffold into the plot segment; see Figure 13-23.

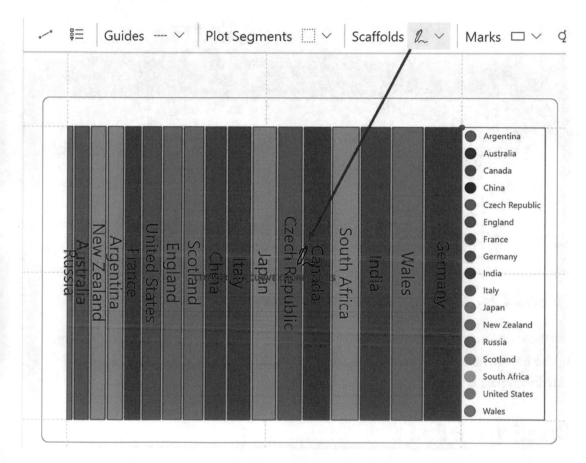

Figure 13-23. *Applying a custom curve scaffold*

A default curve is created for you, but you can then use the pencil button top right of the plot segment to draw any shape you want; see Figure 13-24.

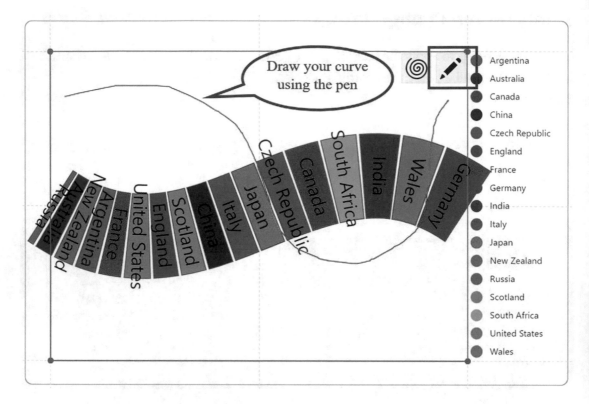

Figure 13-24. *Drawing your own custom curve*

The custom curve scaffold creates a custom curve plot segment that you will see in the Layers pane. You can bind data to the tangent and normal axis by using the Attributes pane.

Creating a Spiral

As part of the custom curve scaffold, you can also produce spiral type charts. To do this, start with a very simple chart that comprises a rectangle mark that has a numerical field such as "Sales" bound to the Width attribute and a categorical field such as "Regions" bound to the Fill. Then close the gap to zero in the plot segment attributes to pull the shapes together. It works best if you restrain the Height of the rectangle to a measurement, such as 30, but experiment here to see what works for you.

Now apply a custom curve scaffold, and a wavy chart is generated by default. Click the spiral button top right of the chart, and a spiral is now made; see Figure 13-25.

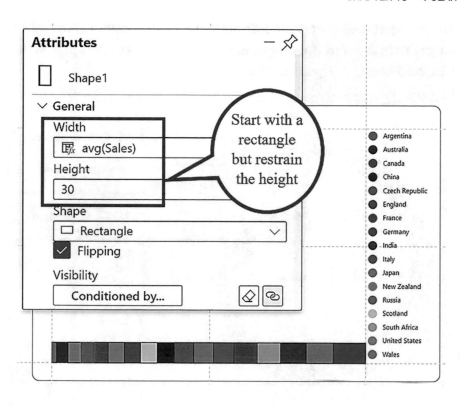

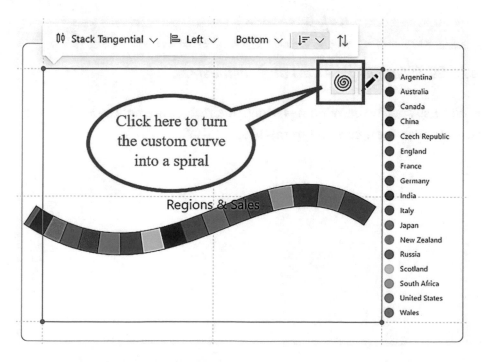

Figure 13-25.   *Creating a spiral chart*

By default, the spiral will start at the 180° point (i.e., at the bottom of the spiral), but you can change this in the Start Angle attribute. For instance, start the spiral at the top of the chart with the 360° angle (Figure 13-26).

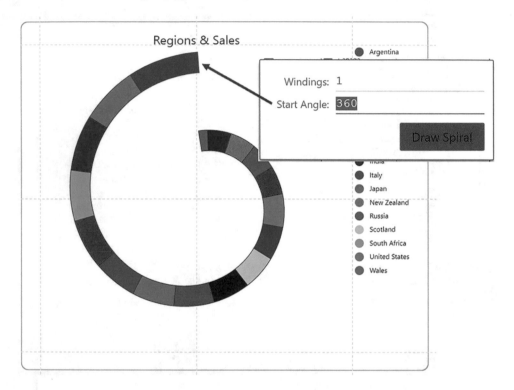

Figure 13-26. *Specifying the start angle of the spiral*

You can also specify the Windings which determines the tightness of the spiral. The bigger the number, the tighter the spiral (Figure 13-27).

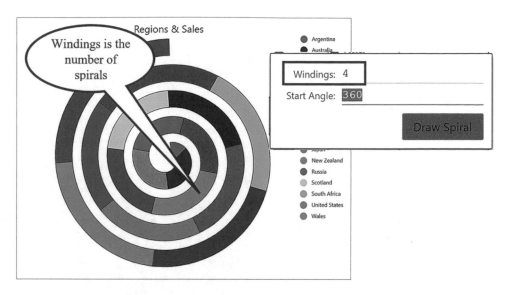

Figure 13-27. *Specifying the Windings of the spiral*

I think you'll agree that by using Charticulator's polar and custom curve scaffolds and by combining angular and radial axes with the sub-layout options, you've been able to design some engaging, interesting, and unusual visuals. You now also know how to design a radar chart. It's true that we need to be cautious in our choice of visual, and you may feel that some polar and custom curve charts are not always the best choice to do the job of reporting on your data. However, now that you know how to create pie, nightingale, and radial charts using Charticulator, at least you can make that choice for yourself.

In the next chapter, we turn our attention away from scaffolds and instead focus on the numerical data that we want to analyze in our visuals. It may not have escaped your notice that up to now, our data has mostly comprised a single numerical value, that is, the "Sales" value. This has been because designing charts that use multiple metrics often requires a completely different approach from plotting just a single numerical value against multiple categories. So let's move forward and learn how to design visuals that can compare and contrast the metrics that matter to us.

CHAPTER 14

Plotting Multiple Measures

So far in this book, you've yet to learn how to tackle the scenario of plotting more than one numerical value in a visualization so that you can compare and contrast their values, for example, compare sales in the current year to sales in the previous year or compare a target value against an actual. In this chapter, we will now fill this gap in your knowledge.

Using Charticulator, there are three alternative approaches you can take if you want to represent multiple measures in your visuals:

1. Create *separate* scales for each measure by binding data to *different* attributes of the same or different marks.

2. Create *one* scale by binding each measure to the *same* attribute of multiple marks. This requires managing Charticulator's automatic scaling of the glyph.

3. Use Charticulator's data axis.

In this chapter, we will explore all three of these approaches.

Typically, such data would be represented in Power BI in a stacked or a clustered bar chart or variations on such charts. In a Power BI visual, plotting a number of metrics is straightforward; you just ply the "Values" bucket with all your measures and leave the visual to do the rest. It will even create the corresponding legend for you. You may not be surprised to learn that in Charticulator things are not quite so easy, and this is for two reasons.

Firstly, the method that Charticulator uses to scale the glyph to fit the 2D region plot segment is particularly problematic if the glyph comprises multiple rectangles. We explored this aspect of Charticulator in Chapter 9.

A. Box, *Introducing Charticulator for Power BI*, https://doi.org/10.1007/978-1-4842-8076-8_14

Secondly, and interlinked with the first reason, you can't plot marks against a numerical axis (well, you can but they will be plotted according to the center point of the mark). We have to use attributes such as Height and Width to drive the plotting of the rectangles.

However, even before we consider how to overcome these problems, we need to step back and think about the conceptual difference between designing visuals where we need to plot just one numerical value and visuals where we need TO plot many, in other words the difference between the two types of data schemas, so let this be our starting point.

Data Schemas

When considering the shape of the data that requires plotting on a chart, we can divide the data schemas into two types: "narrow" data and "wide" data. One of the biggest differences between these types of schema is how Charticulator generates legends, so let's now consider these two schemas and how they will influence the design of our visual.

Narrow Data

Throughout this book up until now, we've always built visuals that comprise *narrow* data; this is where the data contains a *single* numerical field and one or multiple categories. With narrow data, the glyphs represent categories, not measures. An example of narrow data is shown in Figure 14-1.

Year	Salespeople	Sales
2017	Denis	362843
2017	Leblanc	285395
2017	Reyer	315013
2018	Denis	356480
2018	Leblanc	392570
2018	Reyer	445486
2019	Denis	554671

Main
15 rows, 3 columns

Figure 14-1. *Narrow data*

As we already know, to represent narrow data in a clustered column chart in Charticulator, the numerical field is bound to the Height attribute of the rectangle mark, creating a scale that drives the plotting of the data; see Figure 14-2.

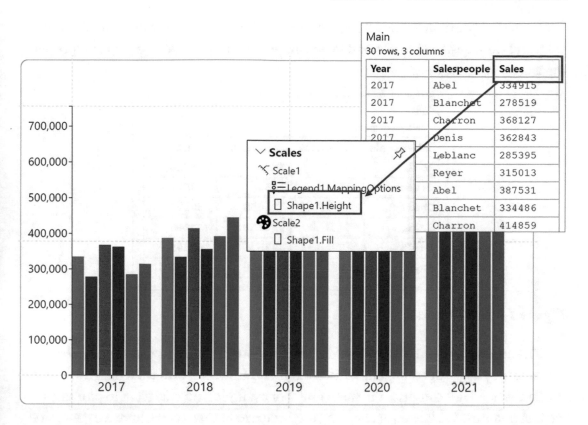

Figure 14-2. *Narrow data is plotted by using the Height attribute that generates a single scale*

This single numerical value can be represented by binding it to a number of other attributes of a shape or a symbol such as Fill, Width, or Size, and this will determine how the data is visualized. Each time you bind the value to a different attribute of the same shape, a *separate* scale will be generated. We've generated many such charts using multiple scales in earlier chapters.

When building visuals on top of narrow data, we add a categorical legend (known as a column values legend) that maps colors to categories accordingly.

Wide Data

In this chapter, we turn our attention to *wide* data, that is, data that comprises multiple measures and one or more categories. You can see an example of wide data in Figure 14-3, and this is the data for which we'll be designing visuals in the examples that follow. You can see that we have one categorical field, "Salespeople," and three measures,

"Previous Yr," "Current Yr," and "Current Target." These measures were created using DAX and were designed to respond to date filters. With wide data, the glyphs represent measures, not categories.

Salespeople	Previous Yr	Current Yr	Target
Abel	500597	387531	334915
Blanchet	444128	334486	278519
Charron	395977	414859	368127
Denis	554671	356480	362843
Leblanc	417058	392570	285395
Reyer	368225	445486	315013

Main
6 rows, 4 columns

Figure 14-3. *Wide data*

The assumption is that these metrics can be plotted against the same value axis because they share the same unit of measurement. However, with wide data the measures need not comprise the same unit. For example, you may want to plot sales against quantity. We looked at resolving this scenario in Chapter 9 where we generated new scales using the SHIFT key, or we could use a secondary line plot segment as we will do in Chapter 16. However, in this chapter, we will be considering only data that includes metrics that share the same measurement.

When building visuals that contain wide data, the legend will map a color to the rectangle or symbol representing each measure, known as a column names legend.

Now that we understand the conceptual difference between plotting narrow and wide data, we can move forward and explore the three different ways, as outlined earlier, in which we can represent wide data.

Using Separate Scales

To plot wide data, we could, for instance, bind each measure to different attributes of a mark or symbol generating separate scales. For example, in Figure 14-4 we have bound the following data:

- "Current Yr" to the Height attribute

- "Previous Yr" to the Fill attribute

- "Current Target" bound to the size of a symbol

Notice that this would create three different scales.

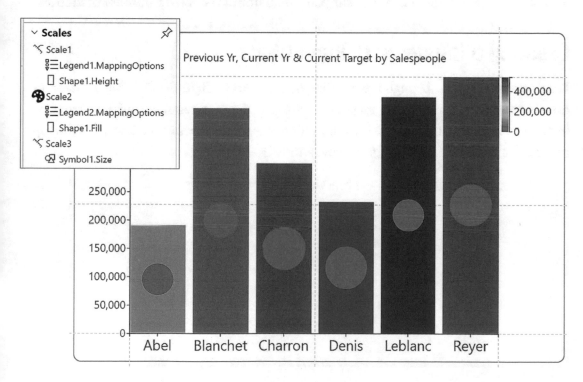

Figure 14-4. *Binding measures to different attributes of a mark and symbol creates separate scales*

However, there are two problems with this approach. Firstly, we're restricted to binding each measure to different attributes, and we quickly run out of attributes. Secondly, it's not a good representation of the data because it's not easy to understand the values being plotted.

So let's look at an alternative way to represent these metrics.

269

Using the Same Scale

A more conventional approach would be to use a clustered or stacked column or bar chart or any variation on the same idea. Such a chart requires a glyph comprising a different rectangle to represent each measure. Each measure can then be bound to the Height or Width attribute of each mark, creating just a *single* scale.

In Chapter 9, we learned that if we bind different measures to the same attribute of different rectangles, Charticulator uses the values in the *first* measure that you bind to generate the scale that is then applied to the other rectangles. All the rectangles will therefore share the same scale. Armed with this knowledge, we can now tackle rendering a clustered column and bar chart using Charticulator to visualize a number of metrics.

Creating a Clustered Column Chart

For this, we will work through the building of the chart in Figure 14-5. What we need to note in this visual is that each measure maps to a different rectangle, and we have two legends: a numerical legend on the left to show the sales values and a legend at the top to map the colors to the rectangles representing the measures.

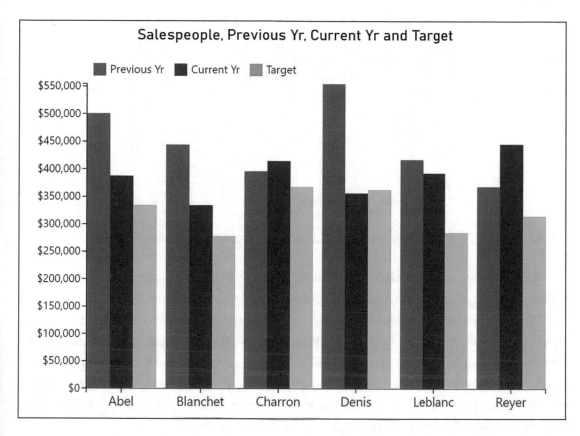

Figure 14-5. *Creating a clustered column chart plotting three measures*

As we have learned when exploring scales in Chapter 9, the first step in building this chart is to identify the measure that will determine the scale to be used by all the rectangles. This must be the measure that holds the maximum value, and we will bind this first to the Height attribute of a rectangle. We can see in Figure 14-6 that the "Previous Yr" value for salesperson "Abel" is the largest, so we need to bind "Previous Yr" to the Height attribute before we bind the others.

Main
6 rows, 4 columns

Salespeople	Previous Yr	Current Yr	Target
Abel	500597	387531	334915
Blanchet	444128	334486	278519
Charron	395977	414859	368127
Denis	554671	356480	362843
Leblanc	417058	392570	285395
Reyer	368225	445486	315013

Figure 14-6. *Finding the measure to bind first to the Height attribute*

We can now start to construct the chart. Starting with a new chart and the data in Figure 14-6, the first step is to bind the "Salespeople" field to the x-axis.

We now need to assemble the glyph that will comprise three rectangles, one for each measure. These rectangles must be anchored to guides in the Glyph pane. To do this, it's best to use a Guide X coordinator that will render three vertical guides. Now draw the rectangle that will represent the measure with the maximum value; in our data, that is the "Previous Yr" measure. Draw this inside the vertical guide, changing the Fill attribute as required, and then bind the measure to the Height attribute.

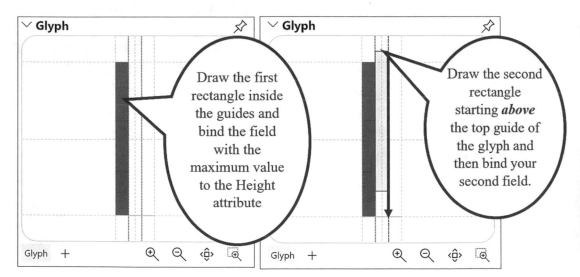

Figure 14-7. *Draw the rectangles that comprise the glyph and bind the data*

Now draw the second rectangle inside the guides of the guide coordinator. The most important point here is to ensure that the rectangle starts *above* the top guide of the glyph. The rule is that the rectangle must not be anchored to the top guide. You can then bind your second measure to the Height attribute of this rectangle and change the fill color. You can then repeat for the third rectangle; see Figure 14-7.

What's lacking now is of course the numerical legend on the left of the chart that will imitate a value axis. You can use the Legend button on the toolbar and select the measure that determines the scale. In our example, we inserted a legend for "Previous Yr." The legend is limited by being an adjunct of the scale, and as a consequence, although you can change the starting value of the legend using the Domain attribute of the scale, you can't control at what value the legend ends. You can format the legend by editing the Tick Format attribute using a format expression as described in Chapter 8.

To add the legend that maps the fill colors to the measures, see the section on "Creating a Legend for Multiple Measures" below.

Creating the Stacked Column Chart

Working with the same fields we used in the preceding clustered column chart, we will now look at how we could use a stacked column chart to visualize this data instead; see Figure 14-8.

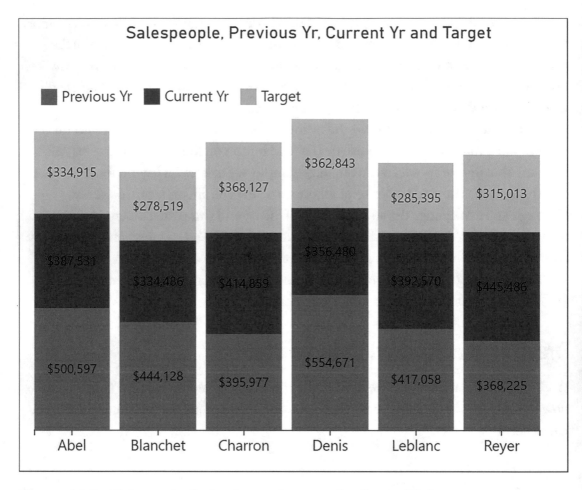

Figure 14-8. *Using a stacked column chart to plot the multiple measures*

To generate the stacked column chart, first bind the "Salespeople" field to the x-axis. To compose the glyph, draw three rectangle shapes in the Glyph pane, one on top of the other. The size of the rectangles doesn't matter, but keep them inside the guides of the Glyph pane. Ensure that the first and third rectangles are anchored to the bottom horizontal and top horizontal guides in the Glyph pane, respectively, but *don't* anchor the middle rectangle to the middle horizontal guide; see Figure 14-9.

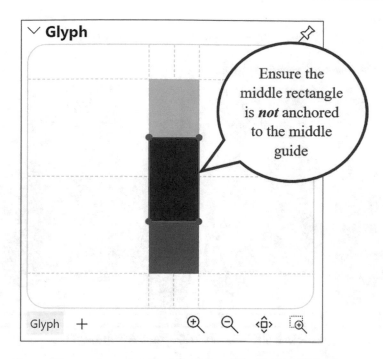

Figure 14-9. *Draw the rectangles inside the guides of the Glyph pane, but their height doesn't matter*

Change the fill colors so you can distinguish the marks. Now bind the measure that represents the maximum value (in our data, that's the "Previous Yr" measure) to the Height attribute of the rectangle that you want to represent it. Remember that this will determine the scale that will be used by the other two rectangles. Now bind the other measures to the Height attribute of their respective rectangles.

To finish the chart, you could add text marks to show the values being plotted. To add the legend at the top that maps the color to the measures, see the section on "Creating a Legend for Multiple Measures" below.

With both the clustered column chart and stacked column chart, the question has to be asked, why don't you just use Power BI to create these visuals? You've got no issue there with the scaling of the glyphs or the generation of a value axis, so wouldn't this be an easier option? One reason to use Charticulator might be to use the skills you have learned so far to give these charts a "makeover" (see Figure 14-10), but they are still, at the end of the day, just column and bar charts.

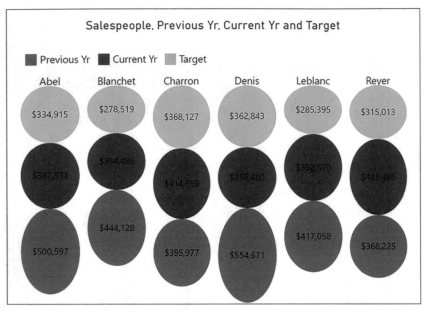

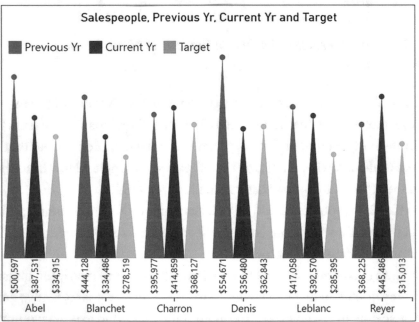

Figure 14-10. *A clustered chart and stacked chart given a Charticulator "makeover"*

Despite the makeover, the problem still persists that we must work within the confines of Charticulator's scales. Must we always have to search our data to find the maximum value so we can set Charticulator's scales? This seems, if nothing else, just awkward. You'll be glad to know that help is at hand. There is another approach to visualizing and comparing measures that doesn't involve any scale. This approach means it's not only much simpler to achieve the visual you require but provides you with greater flexibility in the design of the visual too. I'm referring to the use of Charticulator's data axis.

Using a Data Axis

Consider the chart in Figure 14-11. Can you spot the difference between this chart and the one in Figure 14-5? No? You're quite right; there is no difference in the design. However, there was a considerable difference in the way they were generated.

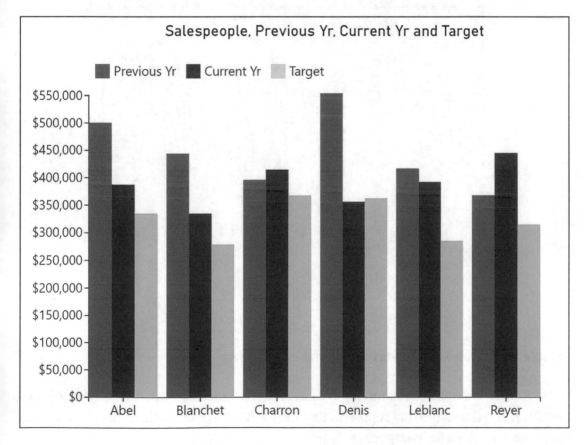

Figure 14-11. *A clustered column chart generated with a data axis*

The chart in Figure 14-11 was created using a *data axis*. A data axis is a numerical scale that is put into the Glyph pane and on which you can generate data points by plotting an example of each measure onto the axis. You can then align the marks that comprise the glyph to these data points. This is quite a verbose description of something that is relatively simple to work with.

What you will also discover is that if you use a data axis, you can go far beyond simple clustered column charts and design truly engaging and insightful visuals that are very easy to piece together. However, for the moment, let's concentrate on the job in hand and see how we used a data axis to build the chart in Figure 14-11.

Starting with a new chart, first we will add a data axis to the Glyph pane. Drag and drop the **Data Axis** button from the toolbar into the Glyph pane (Figure 14-12).

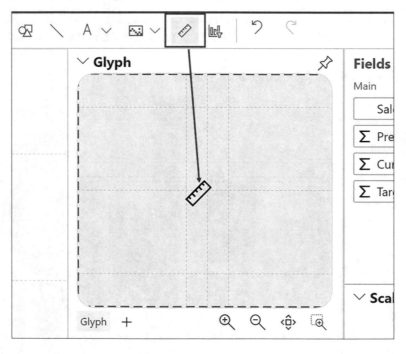

Figure 14-12. *Adding a data axis to the Glyph pane*

Now drag each measure onto the data axis, and the measure will then be plotted on the axis using the values that represent the first row in the data. For instance, in our data these are the values for salesperson "Abel."

Tip   Use the zoom button on the bottom right of the Glyph pane if the first row of the data contains very small values in relation to other values; otherwise, it'll be very difficult to see where the small value has been plotted on the data axis.

Next, add a Guide X coordinator, anchoring it to the bottom guide in the Glyph pane. You can now draw the three rectangles that will represent each value, anchoring them to the data points on the data axis and the guides; see Figure 14-13.

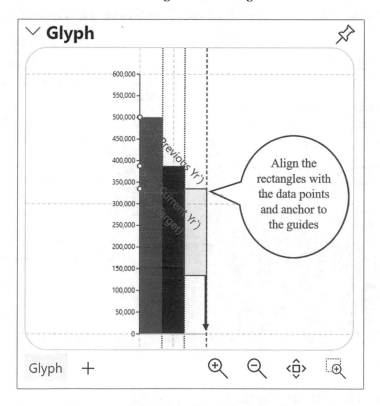

Figure 14-13.   *Ensure the rectangles are aligned to the data points on the data axis*

You'll find that as you plot the rectangles on the data axis, the rectangles are scaled accordingly, and a chart is generated automatically along with an instance of the data axis on the left, providing a numerical y-axis on the chart itself.

The data axis shares many of the same attributes as a numerical x- or y-axis with regard to editing the start and end values and formatting the tick labels (see Chapter 7). If you need to edit or remove the measures used by the data axis, use the Data Expressions attribute at the bottom of the data axis Attributes pane.

Note If you edit the Range "from" and "to" attributes of the data axis, remember to turn off the tick boxes for the Data Axis export properties in the Attributes pane of the data axis to ensure the range doesn't change on save.

However, there is a difference between a numerical axis and a data axis. The data axis is associated with the *glyph*, whereas a numerical axis is associated with the *plot segment*. We can see this more clearly if we change the Visible On attribute of the data axis to "All." The data axis is now visible in the chart for every instance of the glyph; see Figure 14-14.

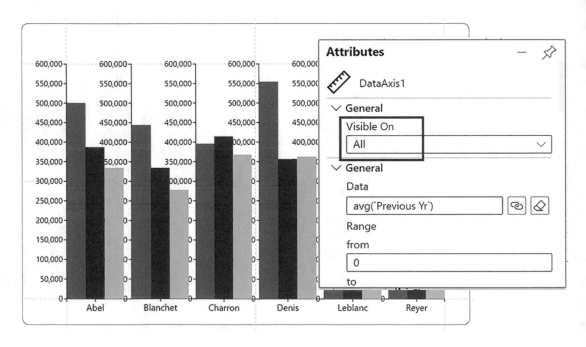

Figure 14-14. *The data axis is associated with the glyph*

Because you usually set the Visible On attribute to either first or last, you only ever see an instance of the glyph that represents the first or last row of the data, and this is how it can be used as a value axis.

Note that the Scales pane does not show a scale for the height of the rectangle because the height is driven by the data axis, not by binding the measures to the Height attribute of the rectangles.

It would seem that we are yet again using Charticulator to create charts that don't require the trouble of using Charticulator! But if I told you that now you know that the data axis exists in Charticulator, you can design a variety of bullet charts, dumbbell charts, tornado charts, box and whisker charts, and many more, would that get you more interested? Well, these are the types of visualizations that you can use Charticulator's data axis to render, and so let's now have a go at doing so. These are the charts we will be generating:

- Cartesian bullet chart

- Polar bullet chart

- Dumbbell

- Box and whisker

- Tornado

Cartesian Bullet Chart

The bullet chart (Figure 14-15) uses a categorical y-axis with the "Salespeople" bound to it and a horizontal data axis.

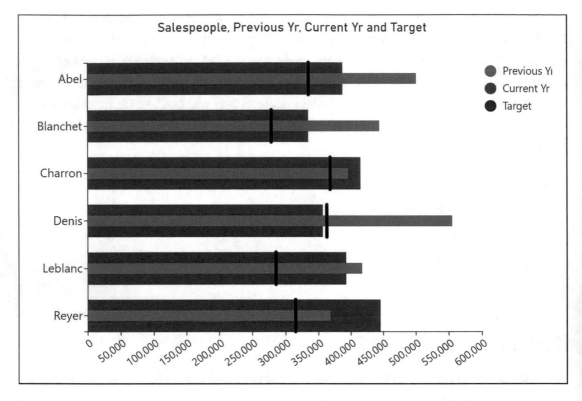

Figure 14-15. *A cartesian bullet chart*

In the Glyph pane, to create a horizontal data axis, you must draw the data axis along the bottom guide of the glyph. In the Attributes pane of the data axis, change the Visible On attribute to "last" and move the axis to Opposite using the Position attribute.

This chart uses a Guide Y coordinator drawn down the left guide of the glyph. The rectangles for the "Previous Yr" and "Current Yr" measures were then drawn inside the guides accordingly; see Figure 14-16.

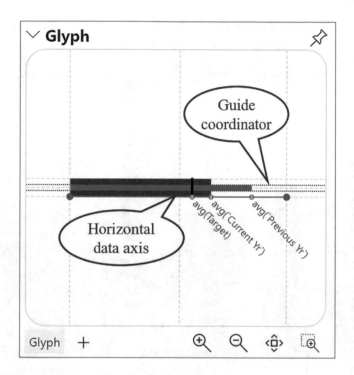

Figure 14-16. *The glyph used in the bullet chart*

The "Target" measure is represented by a line mark, with the Stroke attribute set to black and the Line width set to 5.

Polar Bullet Chart

You can use a data axis with a polar scaffold, and this is how you can generate numerical axes for polar plot segments. Remember, you can't use a numerical radial axis because we are using rectangle marks. Using the polar scaffold allows you to design an alternative bullet chart; see Figure 14-17.

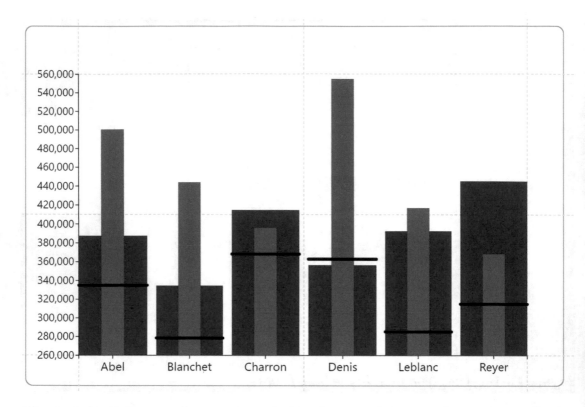

Figure 14-17. *Start with a cartesian bullet chart and then apply a polar scaffold*

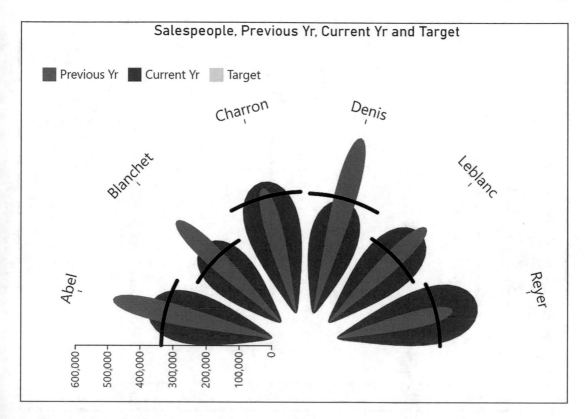

Figure 14-17. *(continued)*

Figure 14-17 shows you how you can start with a cartesian vertical style bullet chart and then simply apply a polar scaffold to the plot segment. Then change the angle of the plot segment so it lies from 270° to 450°. If you think the ellipse shape works better to represent "Previous Yr" and "Current Yr," you can change that too.

Dumbbell Chart

The dumbbell chart is a great visual to compare just two metrics, in our case "Previous Yr" and "Current Yr"; see Figure 14-18. Here, we can quickly spot the reverse dumbbells to see when sales were worse for our salespeople in the current year. In fact, only "Charron" and "Reyer" are improving their performance!

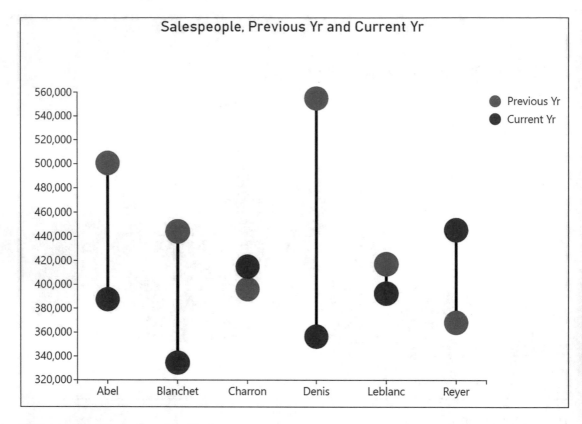

Figure 14-18. *A dumbbell chart*

This chart is particularly easy to produce using Charticulator. You can see the design of the glyph in Figure 14-19. It comprises two symbols aligned to the two measures on the data axis. A line mark then joins the two symbols, anchoring the line to the center of the symbols.

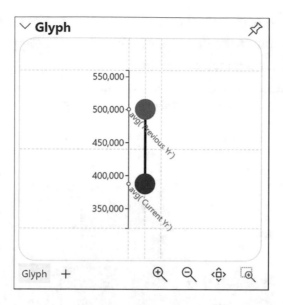

Figure 14-19. *The glyph used to create the dumbbell chart using a data axis*

You can use the Layers pane to ensure that the line sits behind the symbols by changing the order the elements are listed.

Box and Whisker

The data axis makes the generation of a box and whisker chart very straightforward as long as the data presents itself as wide data; see Figure 14-20.

Main
6 rows, 7 columns

Salespeople	Max	Quartile3	Median	Average	Quartile1	Min
Abel	661832	500597	496764	476834	387351	334915
Blanchet	612498	543485	444128	442623	334486	278519
Charrron	755892	673496	414859	521670	395977	368127
Denis	696204	558139	554671	505667	362843	356481
Leblanc	560592	417058	408710	412865	392570	285395
Reyer	445486	437594	414896	396243	368225	315013

Figure 14-20. *Wide data used in the box and whisker chart*

In other words, each of the calculations involved in the box and whisker chart should present itself as a measure in the Fields pane. You can see in Figure 14-21 the box and whisker chart we have built on top of this data.

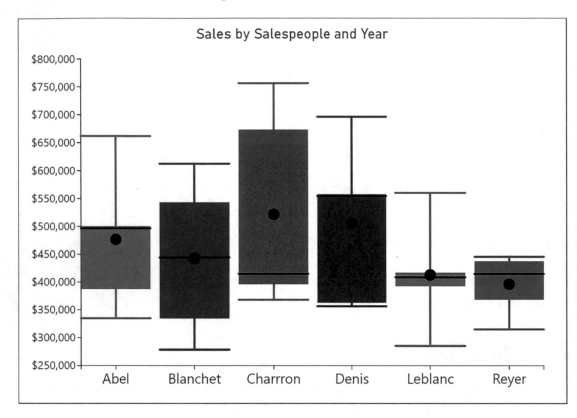

Figure 14-21. *Box and whisker chart*

Here, we are displaying our salespeople's performance across all five years by showing the distribution of their sales, salesperson "Blanchet" having the most evenly distributed sales values.

Using a data axis, in Figure 14-22 you can see the glyph that was constructed to render the box and whisker chart.

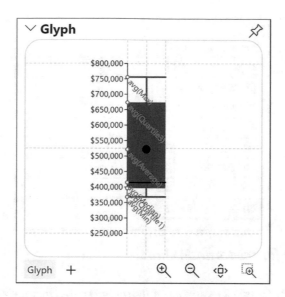

Figure 14-22. *Glyph used in the box and whisker chart*

Once the measures were plotted onto the data axis, it was then only a matter of adding the appropriate marks to build the glyph: a horizontal line for "max," "min," and "median" and a vertical line drawn between the "max" and "min." A symbol was used for the "average" and a rectangle drawn for the box.

Tornado Chart

The last example of using a data axis will be to generate a tornado chart. Because the sales data we've been using in our examples doesn't lend itself to being plotted on a tornado chart, we will use instead data comprising a set of competition scores to compare male and female contestants in different age groups; see Figure 14-23.

Main
7 rows, 3 columns

Age	F	M
20 and Less	31	29
20 to 30	33	32
30 to 40	31	29
40 to 50	28	26
50 to 60	24	24
60 to 70	23	20
70 and over	22	18

Figure 14-23. *Data for the tornado chart*

The tornado chart is a great example of using two horizontal data axes that diverge from the center of the glyph where the zero point for both axes starts; see Figure 14-24. This will allow us to plot and compare the male and female scores in each age group.

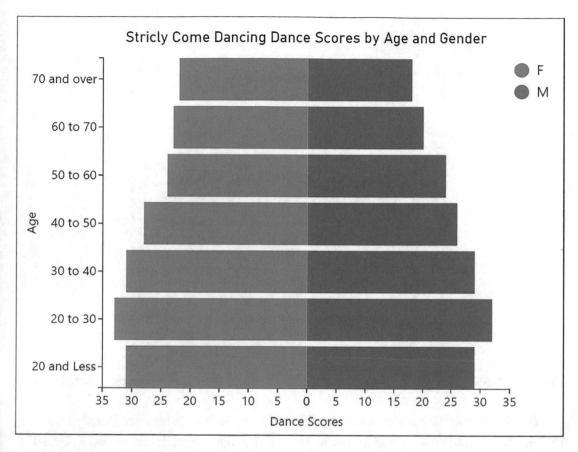

Figure 14-24. *A tornado chart*

Using a data axis, this chart was straightforward to build, despite its looks. The "Age" field was bound to the y-axis. In the Glyph pane, the two data axes were drawn by anchoring each data axis to the center guide of the glyph, dragging outward to anchor one to the left guide and the other to the right guide; see Figure 14-25.

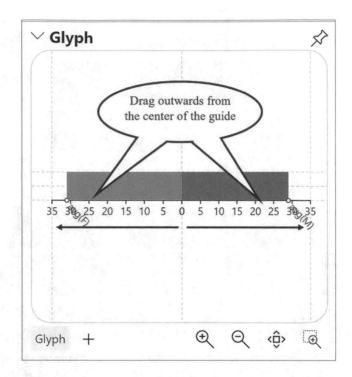

Figure 14-25. *The glyph used in the tornado chart uses two diverging data axes*

To ensure that the data axes were visible only on the first instance of the glyph, the Visible On attribute was edited accordingly, and the right-hand data axes were moved to the opposite side. All that remained was to plot the two measures "F" and "M" on the axes and draw the rectangle marks accordingly.

Creating a Legend for Multiple Measures

You will have noticed that a number of our charts have included a legend that maps the color that is used to represent each measure. Charticulator generates legends for wide data differently from narrow data and uses two separate legend types accordingly. The column values legend is used for narrow data and the column names legend used for wide data. We learned how to create a column names legend in Chapter 9. However, to recap on how this is done, use the Legend button on the toolbar as normal, but this time select column names as the Legend type and select your columns using the CTRL key. Notice that there is now a scale in the Scales pane that maps the colors to the measures. However, unlike the other scales in the Scales pane, you can't click the scale to edit the colors. You must select the Legend in the Layers pane and then use the Attributes pane, clicking on **Edit scale colors**; see Figure 14-26.

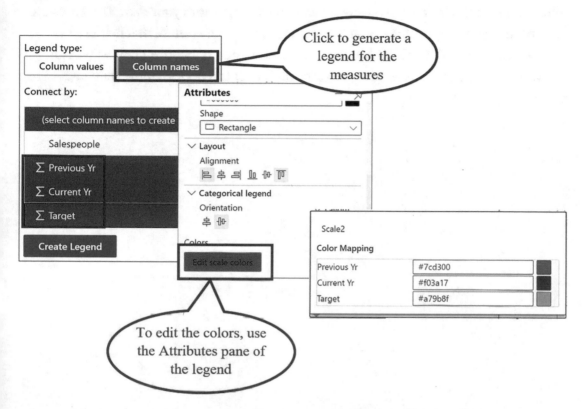

Figure 14-26. *Generating and editing a legend for wide data*

Reminding ourselves how to insert a legend to describe wide data ends this chapter that explored the different methods to visualize data comprising multiple numerical values.

You have learned that you are limited in the number of different numerical attributes to which you can bind such data and that if you then decide to bind numerical data to the same attribute of multiple instances of a mark, the scaling of the glyph will need to be controlled. The best and easiest solution is of course to use Charticulator's data axis. This is not only a very simple and easy method of accurately plotting measures, but it provides a workable numerical axis despite the choice of a rectangle mark or a line within the Glyph pane. More than this, it allows you to design visualizations that you may have thought would be more complex to build, such as bullet, tornado, or box and whisker charts. This has been another milestone along the way of understanding how Charticulator works.

Perhaps, you are also learning that Charticulator never fails to surprise us in the richness of its tools that are fit for purpose, and this allows you to design visuals that inform and inspire by unequivocally showing the insights into your data. This leads me to introduce you to yet another one of these tools, and that is a tool that has a rather unassuming name: the link. We've used links before, but in the next chapter, we will throw the spotlight on this feature and discover how it can do a lot more than just produce line charts.

CHAPTER 15

Links and Data Linking

In this chapter, we're putting the spotlight on Charticulator's *links,* where you connect glyphs within a chart to show an association between them. We're already familiar with the idea of the line chart where data points are joined to enable decoding of the data. Indeed, in Chapter 4, we successfully built line charts using the line link. However, Charticulator's links encompass a number of more complex concepts, and Charticulator provides us with not just one way but three ways to connect glyphs within the visual, as follows:

1. Link the *same* items in a particular field by using a line or band. The purpose of doing so is normally to show trends across time such as a line chart, but variations on the line chart might be the ribbon chart or a slope chart.

2. Link *different* items within the same field to show some relationship between them, the co-occurrence and chord chart being the most obvious examples.

3. The third way is to also link *different* items within the same field, but this time there is an implied categorization of the items. Often, these charts show a direction of flow, for example, in a Sankey chart, and organization charts might also fall into this method of linking.

In Figure 15-1, you can see visual representations of these three types of link.

© Alison Box 2022
A. Box, *Introducing Charticulator for Power BI,* https://doi.org/10.1007/978-1-4842-8076-8_15

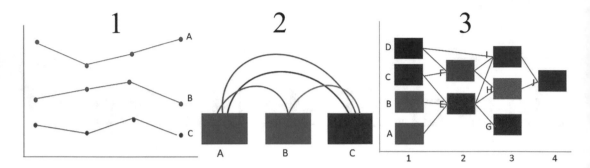

Figure 15-1. *Three ways to link glyphs*

In this chapter, we are going to delve into all three of these link types. However, Charticulator does not present the links to us in the context of these different types. Instead, it presents us with four different choices of linking glyphs depending on the composition of your chart. These are:

- Linking categories

- Linking plot segments

- Linking categories within plot segments

- Linking data

All Charticulator's links are accessed from the **Link** button on the toolbar, and you can see the four different options in Figure 15-2. Notice that each choice also allows the selection of either a band link or a line link.

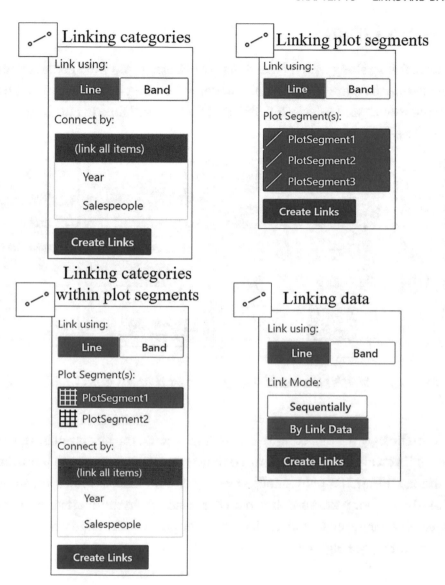

Figure 15-2. *The four linking options on the Link button*

It would seem sensible then for us to explore the links feature in the context of these four options. However, before we can do so, there is a precursor skill we need to acquire, and that is to understand how the links anchor themselves to the glyph and how to change the anchor points.

Anchoring Links

If you want to follow along with this section on anchoring, you will need to create a chart similar to the one in Figure 15-3 that has categorical x- and y-axes. Then use the **Link** button on the toolbar and select a line link and then a band link, in our examples linking by the "Year" field.

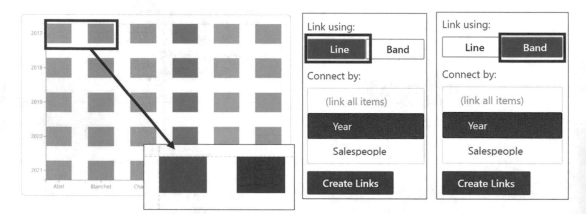

Figure 15-3. *Create this chart and use the line and band links to follow along with this section*

When you link glyphs that comprise a rectangle mark, the link is anchored either to a default point if you are using a line or to a default edge if you are using a band. However, you can change the anchor point or edge by selecting the Link in the Layers pane. When you do this, the anchor points are shown on the rectangle in the chart as green points or green edges. To change an anchor, click the anchor point or the edge where you want to move the anchor to; see Figure 15-4.

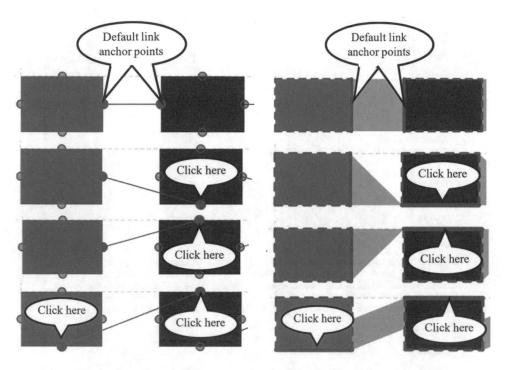

Figure 15-4. *Changing the anchor points of a line link and a band link*

Now that you know how to change the anchor points of the band or line, we are ready to move forward and look at the different ways we can connect up shapes and symbols comprising our chart. Let's start with the first of these in Figure 15-2, and that is the simple linking of glyphs that represent items in each category.

Linking Categories

Here, we can remind ourselves what we learned in Chapter 4, where we plotted symbols against a numerical y-axis and then used the links feature to select a line link for the subcategory so that we could generate a line chart. We could have then hidden the symbols so only the linking lines show (Figure 15-5).

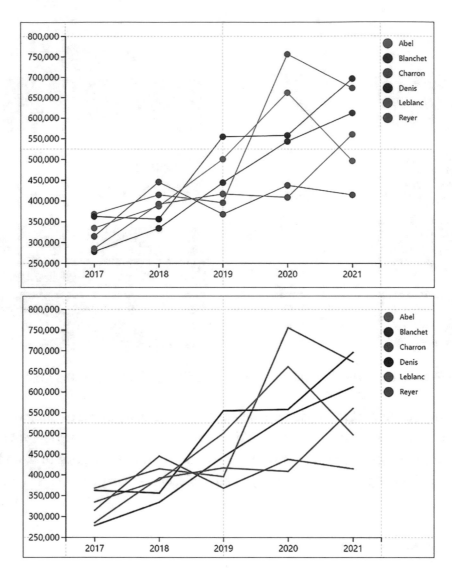

Figure 15-5. *Creating line charts using the links feature*

To give the line chart a Charticulator "makeover," you could try changing the line type to Bezier. It might be worth noting here that in Chapter 19, we will find out how to add dynamic data labels to the line chart and highlight specific categories.

Ribbon Chart

What we didn't explore in Chapter 4 was using a band to connect categories. In order to connect the glyphs, the band link needs a straight edge and so is not applicable to symbols. The band link is best used for connecting glyphs comprising a rectangle mark. In Figure 15-6, you can see that using this link and changing the Type attribute of the link to Bezier, you can produce a ribbon chart.

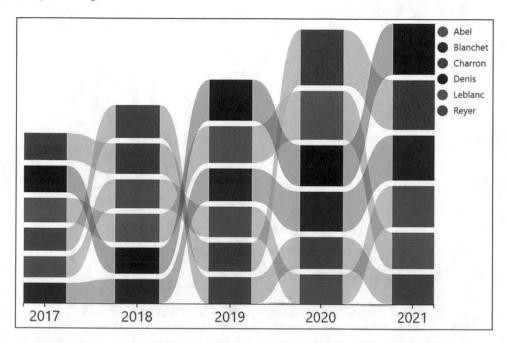

Figure 15-6. *Using the band link on a rectangle mark produces a ribbon chart*

The ribbon chart uses a Stack Y sub-layout, and changing the opacity of the band can give the ribbon a more fluid appearance.

Area Chart

If you want to create an area chart, the area or "fill" is produced by using a band link. Consider the chart in Figure 15-7 that you'll be learning to build in this section and that also shows the fields that we will be using. For this, you will need to start over with a new chart.

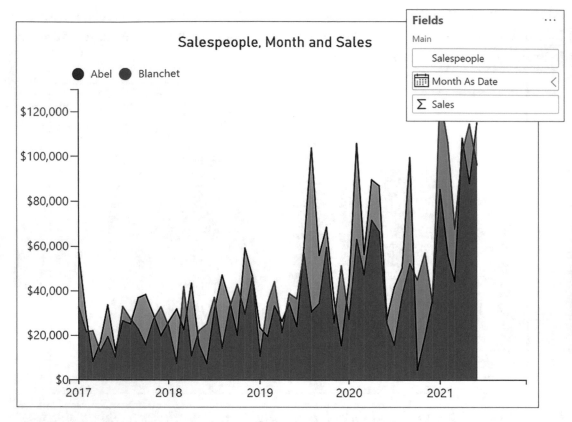

Figure 15-7. *To create an area chart, you need to use a band link*

Although we have used the "Salespeople" and "Sales" fields extensively throughout this book, we have never used the "Month As Date" field. This is because this chart also highlights another aspect of plotting data in Charticulator that you've not yet met: plotting temporal or date type data such as monthly sales across years. The "Month As Date" column is a calculated column in a date dimension that associates each month with its start date; see Figure 15-8. The purpose of doing this is to generate a temporal field type that will be plotted correctly on the x-axis, creating a date x-axis that behaves just like a numerical axis. Using a month name field here wouldn't work because that would produce a categorical field type.

X ✓   `1  Month As Date = STARTOFMONTH(DateTable[DateKey])`

DateKey	Year	Qtr	MonthNo	Month	Month As Date
01 January 2017	2017	Qtr 1	1	Jan	01/01/2017
02 January 2017	2017	Qtr 1	1	Jan	01/01/2017
03 January 2017	2017	Qtr 1	1	Jan	01/01/2017
04 January 2017	2017	Qtr 1	1	Jan	01/01/2017
05 January 2017	2017	Qtr 1	1	Jan	01/01/2017
06 January 2017	2017	Qtr 1	1	Jan	01/01/2017
07 January 2017	2017	Qtr 1	1	Jan	01/01/2017
08 January 2017	2017	Qtr 1	1	Jan	01/01/2017
09 January 2017	2017	Qtr 1	1	Jan	01/01/2017

Figure 15-8. *The "Month As Date" field is a calculated column*

Notice on the x-axis of the chart in Figure 15-7 that there are only labels for years, not months. In a similar way to Power BI, to avoid cluttering the x-axis, Charticulator will generate a "continuous" axis for temporal fields that displays just the years (or years and months if there is room on the axis).

As well as being able to plot the monthly data correctly on the x-axis, the other benefit of using a temporal field is that once bound to an x-axis, you can filter the date range you want to plot by using the attributes of the plot segment; see Figure 15-9.

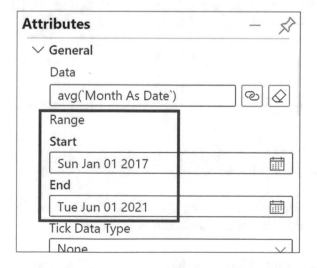

Figure 15-9. *You can edit the start and end dates of temporal data plotted on the axis*

Let's now focus back on using Charticulator's links and build the chart that uses a band link to supply the "fill" of the area chart. In a new chart, first bind "Month As Date" to the x-axis.

Now we can build the glyph. We can't use a symbol as our glyph and create a conventional line chart because you've learned that band links can only be used with rectangle marks, so we must use a rectangle mark in the area chart. However, we need a numerical y-axis to plot the "Sales" value, but you also know that rectangles can't be plotted against a numerical axis. As a consequence, our only option is to use a data axis in the Glyph pane which will allow us to plot the rectangle mark representing the "Sales" against a numerical data axis.

You can see in Figure 15-10 how to complete the chart. Using a data axis, plot your numerical field such as "Sales" onto it and align a rectangle to the data point on the axis. The rectangle can now be given a width of 2 so that it hardly shows in the Glyph pane or in the chart. Now link the rectangles by the categorical field, for example, "Salespeople," using a band, which will mimic the fill of an area chart. Once the band is in place, you can "remove" the rectangle completely by putting zero in the Width attribute.

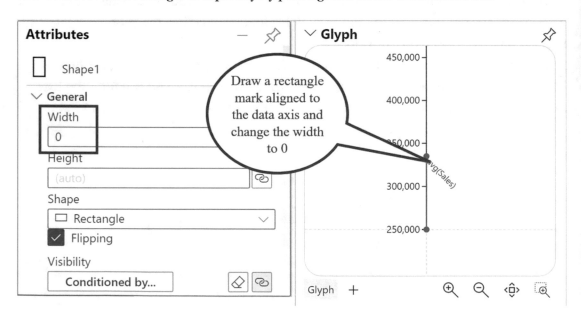

Figure 15-10. *The area chart uses a data axis with a rectangle mark aligned to the data point on the axis. The rectangle has a width of 0*

You can then bind your categorical field such as the "Salespeople" field to the fill color of the band.

Linking Plot Segments

In Chapter 11, we built a visual comprising a number of plot segments. What we can do now is link glyphs between these plot segments.

Vertical Ribbon Chart

Consider the chart in Figure 15-11, a variation on the ribbon chart where we've used a band to link glyphs in two 2D region plot segments to compare the sales and quantity in each region. Note in this chart how the regions have been sorted ascending by their sales and quantity values to show this analysis more clearly.

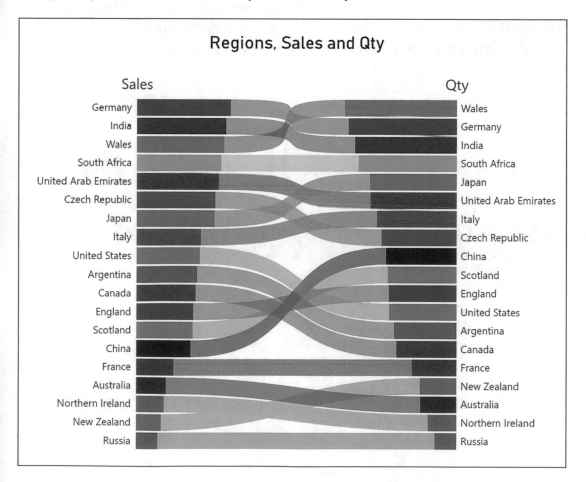

Figure 15-11. *Linking glyphs between two 2D region plot segments*

Again, it's best to start with a new chart if you want to build this visual yourself. This chart was produced by using two plot segments, each plot segment having its own glyph comprising a rectangle mark. Both plot segments use the Stack Y sub-layout, and the second plot segment is aligned on the right.

Tip   Remember you will need to create additional guides on the chart canvas on to which to anchor the plot segments.

One of the glyphs had the "Sales" field bound to the Width attribute, and the other had the "Quantity" field bound to the Width attribute. You will need to hold down the SHIFT key to generate a new scale when you bind the second numerical field to the Width attribute of the second rectangle. We then linked PlotSegments1 and 2 using a band link. The details of how the chart in Figure 15-11 was generated are shown in Figure 15-12.

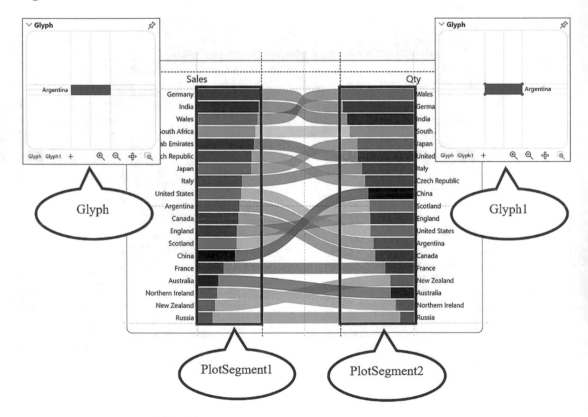

Figure 15-12. *Linking glyphs between two 2D region plot segments using a band link*

Note the use of the text mark to label the y-axes with the region names. If we had used the "Regions" field on the y-axis, it would have prevented the sorting of the rectangles ascending by their numerical value (see Chapter 5 for details on sorting axis labels).

Proportion Plot

Building the proportion plot in Figure 15-13 uses much the same techniques as the previous chart, but this time we're comparing sales in the current year to sales in the previous year. Again, start over with a new chart.

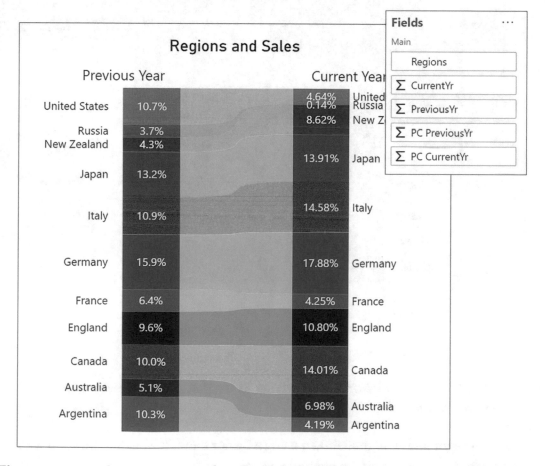

Figure 15-13. *The proportion plot also links plot segments using a band*

Figure 15-14 sets out how this visual was built. This was again created using two 2D region plot segments with Stack Y sub-layouts. The two separate rectangle glyphs were resized in the Glyph pane so they were half the width to allow room for the band link. The "Previous Yr" field was then bound to the Height attribute of the first rectangle, and just as before, use the SHIFT key when binding the "Current Yr" field to the second rectangle to generate two separate scales.

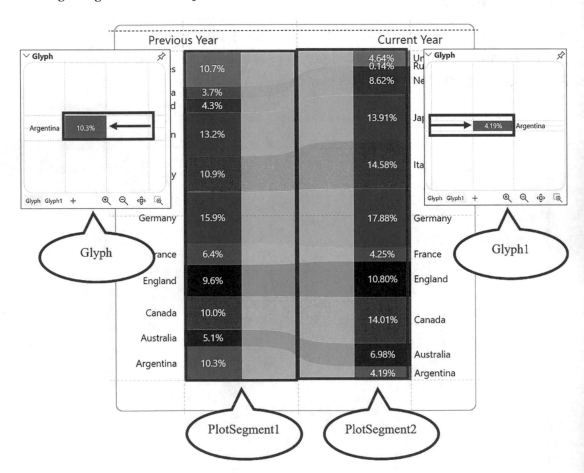

Figure 15-14. *The proportion plot uses two 2D region plot segments and two glyphs linked by a band*

The plot segments were then linked using a Bezier band. It was then finished with text marks for the regions and the percentages.

Linking Categories Within Plot Segments

One of the great advantages of using multiple plot segments is that you can design a visual that comprises multiple charts. The visual in Figure 15-15, for instance, contains a stacked column chart and line chart. The line chart at the bottom requires the glyphs to be connected by category, for instance, the "Salespeople" field. When you first click the Link button on the toolbar, it seems that you can only link the plot segments. To link categories within a plot segment, click the plot segment name in the Link dropdown, and it will expand to show the categories in that plot segment; see "Linking categories within plot segments" in Figure 15-2.

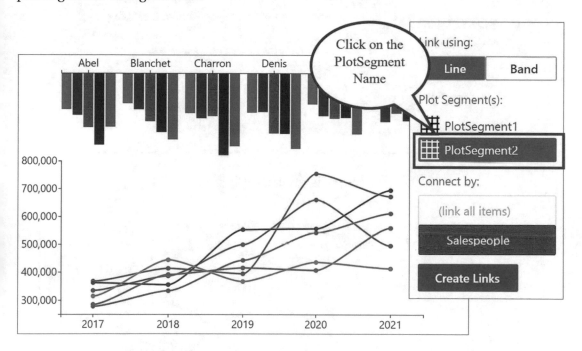

Figure 15-15. *Click the plot segment name to link categories in one of the plot segments but not the other*

Being able to build charts that comprise both linked and nonlinked glyphs in this manner allows you to mix and match charts within charts.

Linking Data

Up to now, all the links we have worked with have been linking the *same* values in a particular category, for example, linking the symbols that represent each salesperson in the line chart or linking the rectangles that represent each region when linking across plot segments. There is however another way to link glyphs, and that is by associating *different* values within the same category to find associations between them. Consider the data in Figure 15-16 which comprises a table that lists countries that export and import goods and services between each other, and below this table is a co-occurrence chart that represents this traffic.

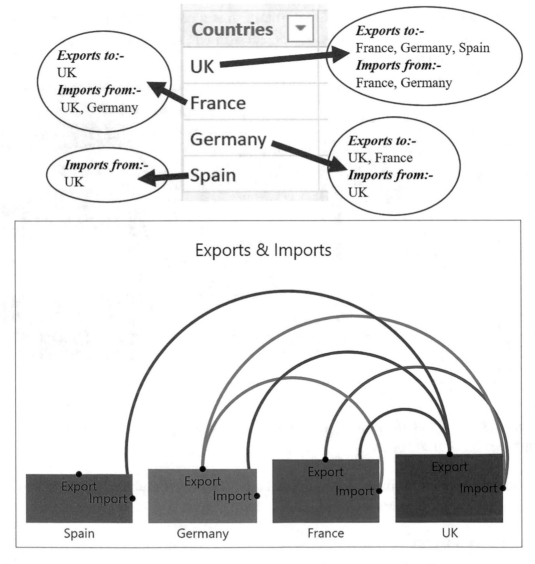

Figure 15-16. *Countries that export and import between each other*

Here, the values in the columns, that is, the country names, are interconnected between each other. In Charticulator, we can use the concept of *linking data* to link different items within the same field that share an association with each other.

Co-occurrence Chart

Let's use the chart shown in Figure 15-16 as our example and examine the source data used to generate this visual shown in Figure 15-17. The table that contains the country names is called the "Nodes" table, and it also contains a field called "Value," but this column is arbitrary. The only requirement is that the column that holds the entities in the Nodes table (the county names in our case) *must* be named "id," and the name of the column must be in lowercase.

You must then create a table that links the nodes (i.e., the countries) to their respective counterparts. This is called the "Links" table, and it must contain a column called "source_id" (that lists the nodes) and a column called "target_id" that will link the nodes. These column names must be in lowercase. Note the two-way aspect of the data in this table.

	Nodes table		Links table	
			Import From	Export To
id	Value		source_id	target_id
UK	956346		UK	Germany
France	887652		UK	France
Germany	756346		Germany	UK
Spain	683924		Germany	France
			France	UK
			UK	Spain
			Spain	

Figure 15-17. *The two tables required to generate the visual in Figure 15-16*

Also note that "Spain" must be listed in the "source_id" column (despite the fact that it doesn't export to any country) because there must be a match for every value in the "id" column with the values in the "source_id" column.

Note   Although you must name the columns "id," "source_id," and "target_id," you can rename these columns when you put the fields in to the "Data" bucket. They can have different names in your data model. You can name the tables anything you like. They don't have to be named "Nodes" and "Links."

Once these two tables have been generated, you will need to create a one-to-many relationship between them in the model view of Power BI Desktop, linking the "id" column with the "source_id" column; see Figure 15-18. This creates the links between the nodes and therefore links the data.

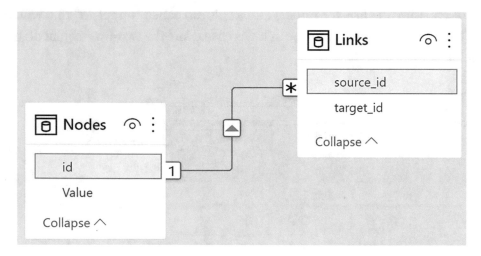

Figure 15-18. *Create a relationship between the Nodes table and the Links table*

Now all that's left is for us to create the chart and generate the links. In Power BI, when you first create the chart, put all the fields from the "Nodes" table into the Data bucket and all the fields from the "Links" table into the Links bucket; see Figure 15-19.

Figure 15-19. *Place the fields in the correct buckets*

Now in Charticulator, add a rectangle mark to the Glyph pane. If you have a numerical value, you can bind this to the Height attribute. You may also need to edit the End Range value of the Height scale to ensure the rectangles are not too high. You are now ready to link the data using the Link button on the toolbar which will invite you to use the link mode, "By Link Data"; see "Linking data" in Figure 15-2. The default is to link with a line, so all you need to do is click Create Links.

However, we're still not quite there. Unfortunately, the linking lines are linked to the wrong anchor points on the rectangle glyph. Not only this but the export and import lines have not been identified individually; we only see that there is a link between the countries. This is because the link lines are anchored to the *same* anchor points on the two rectangles, that is, the bottom center anchor, and so they don't distinguish between the "from" and "to" directions of the data.

Warning   This is an aspect of linking data that isn't always apparent, so always check out the anchor points of the linking lines.

Therefore, not only do we need to change the position of the anchor so the lines emanate from the top of the rectangles, but also we need to select two *different* anchor points, one for exports and one for imports. You learned earlier in this chapter how to change the anchor points. Select the link in the Layers pane and click onto the correct anchor points in the chart; see Figure 15-20. You might note that in correcting the anchor points of the linking lines, the visual now identifies both the exports and imports.

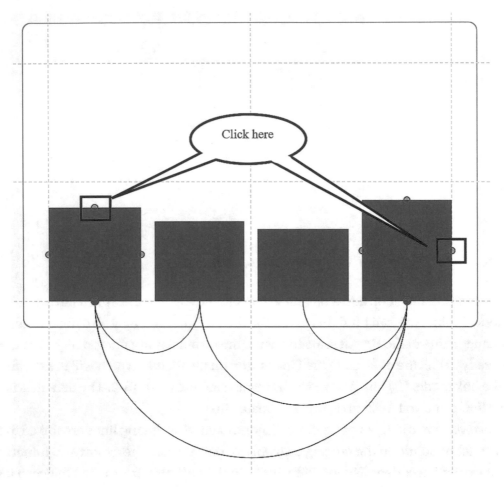

Figure 15-20. *Correcting the anchor points of the linking line separates the lines into "from" and "to"*

To change the color of the linking lines, you must bind the "source_id" field to the Color attribute of the Link. Don't use the "id" field as this won't work. You can now change the color of the rectangles by binding the "id" field to the Fill attribute and add any text marks or symbols you require. For instance, in Figure 15-16, we used a symbol with a black fill to mark the anchor points of the rectangles to identify imports and exports.

Chord Chart

If you apply a polar scaffold to the visual in Figure 15-16, you will transform it into a chord chart (Figure 15-21), but note again that you can't distinguish between imports and exports because of the anchor points that are used.

Figure 15-21. *A chord chart generated from the chart in Figure 15-16 using the polar plot segment doesn't identify "from" and "to" links*

Before we leave the co-occurrence charts, if you want to browse through more examples of using data links to generate this type of chart, visit Charticulator's video gallery:

https://charticulator.com/docs/video-tutorials.html

There, you will find the spectacular Les Miserable co-occurrence chart that uses all the techniques that you have learned in this chapter.

Sankey Chart

There is another use of data linking in Charticulator, and that is to link *different* items within the same field where there is an implied grouping of the items creating charts that plot the flow of data from one group to another.

Consider the data in Figure 15-22 where a "Nodes" table comprises a list of staff members that have been grouped by the "position" field, implying a sorting or ranking order from Team Member through to Director. In the "Links" table, we have identified which staff member reports to whom. Notice again the naming of these fields; in the "Nodes" table, the "id" field lists the staff members. In the "Links" table, each staff member is listed in the "source_id" field and to whom they report in the "target_id" field; each member of staff reports to another member of staff, and they in turn report to someone else.

Links Table

Nodes Table			This person…	…reports to this person
id	position	amount	source_id	target_id
Josie	Director	43453	Jason	Jerome
June	Director	35334	Jacob	Julian
Jules	Manager	64305	Julia	Jerome
Jenny	Manager	43201	Janet	Julian
Jolian	Manager	54770	Joseph	Jerome
JuJu	Manager	23543	Jade	Jerome
Jock	Manager	57577	Jacky	Jerome
Jill	Manager	57557	Jack	Julian
Jane	Supervisor	23109	Jim	Jerome
Jemima	Supervisor	50275	Jerome	Jane
Jeremy	Supervisor	65060	Julian	Jemima
John	Supervisor	34813	Jilly	Jules
Jerome	Team Leader	39347	Jackie	Jemima
Julian	Team Leader	23675	Jane	Jules
Jason	Team Member	16501	Jemima	Jenny
Jacob	Team Member	37539	Jeremy	Jolian
Julia	Team Member	31691	John	JuJu
Janet	Team Member	26086	Jilly	Jeremy
Joseph	Team Member	48826	Jackie	Jill
Jade	Team Member	32098	Jules	Josie
Jacky	Team Member	25597	Jenny	June
Jack	Team Member	44898	Jolian	Josie
Jim	Team Member	23463	JuJu	June
Jilly	Team Member	45724	Jock	Josie
Jackie	Team Member	32346	Jill	June
			Josie	
			June	

Figure 15-22. *Shaping data to define who reports to whom*

We want to create a visual that shows who reports to whom but with the added factor that the staff members will be grouped from the lowest ranking position to the highest. This visual is shown in Figure 15-23, which is a take on the idea of a Sankey chart.

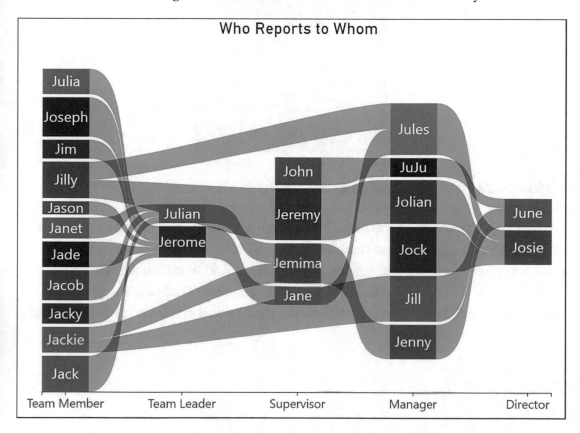

Figure 15-23. *The Sankey chart generated from the data in Figure 15-22*

Notice that it's the "position" field bound to the x-axis that is key to how the data is plotted in the chart. The "position" field identifies the groups, and this in turn drives the flow of data from left to right defining the ranking.

Let's take a step-by-step look at how the Sankey chart in Figure 15-23 was built. After shaping the data correctly into Nodes and Links tables, the next step was to relate the "id" field with the "source_id" field using the model view in Power BI Desktop. The fields were then populated into the correct buckets in the Power BI Visualizations pane (Figure 15-24).

Figure 15-24. *The Data and Links used in the Sankey chart*

Inside Charticulator, the "position" field was bound to the x-axis, and the sub-layout of the plot segment changed to Stack Y and the alignment to middle. Next, a rectangle mark was placed in the Glyph pane and the "amount" field bound to the "Height" attribute and the "id" field to the Fill attribute. You may also need to increase the gap between the x-axis labels. You can see how the chart looked at this stage in Figure 15-25.

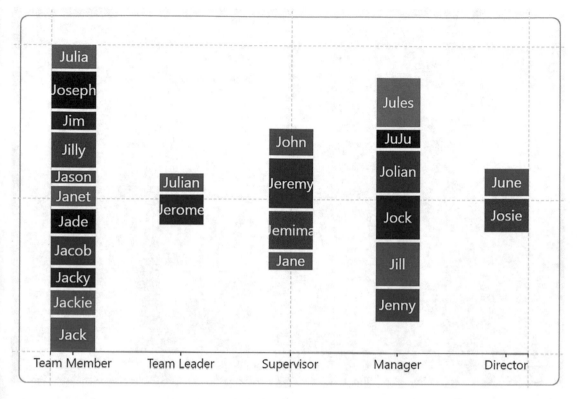

Figure 15-25. *The Sankey chart before the links are added*

We were then ready to insert the links from the Link button, ensuring to choose the band link and using the "By Link Data" link mode. At this point, the chart looked a bit chaotic; see Figure 15-26.

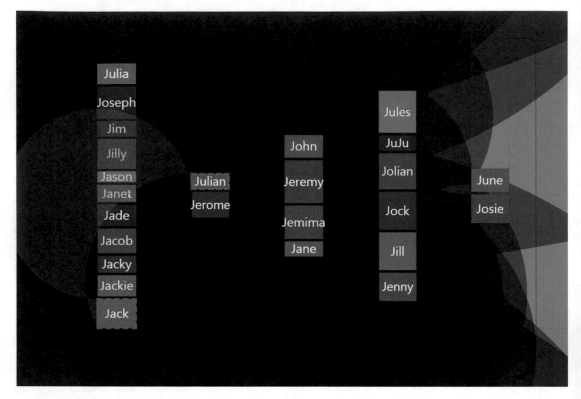

Figure 15-26. *The Sankey type chart looks chaotic at first*

However, all that was required was to change the link type from arc to Bezier and edit the anchor point of the first glyph to move it to the right side of the rectangle; see Figure 15-27.

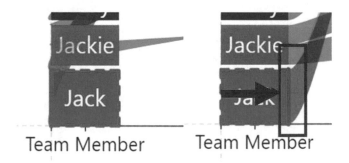

Figure 15-27. *You will need to move the anchor point of the band link in the Sankey chart*

The creation of the Sankey chart concludes our exploration of Charticulator's links. You have learned in this chapter that linking glyphs is not confined to line charts, but links can be used in a myriad of chart designs that, on first meeting, seem very different types of visual. Who would have thought that an area chart had anything in common with a chord chart? In Charticulator, we've learned to expect the unexpected, which leads us on to the next chapter where we will meet a concept that in charting terms is not to be expected either, and that is the idea of plotting data onto a single axis.

CHAPTER 16

The Line Plot Segment

When most of us think of a chart or graph, we normally think in terms of a "cartesian" chart where data is plotted on both the x- and y-axes. We've created many such charts in the course of this book. However, when working in Charticulator, there is another approach to plotting data, and that is to use just a *single* axis.

Let me introduce you to Charticulator's line plot segment, the topic of this chapter, which allows you to build charts that use a single line as their axis. What you will discover though is that using just *one* line plot segment will give you very little to work with; a chart comprising a single line axis doesn't provide much scope for analysis. However, you've already learned that you can link glyphs between multiple 2D region plot segments, and this is no less true of multiple line plot segments. When you join up glyphs plotted on multiple line plot segments, this is when this type of plot segment comes into its own, and it's this aspect that we will be focusing on in this chapter.

Consider the two charts in Figure 16-1. Both have been built using multiple line plot segments where the glyphs have been linked.

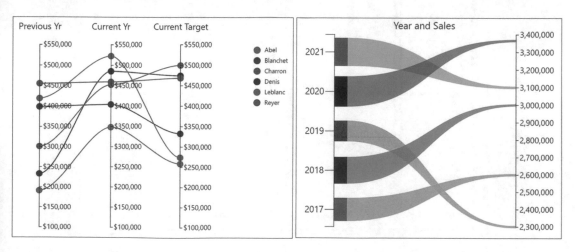

Figure 16-1. *Charts using multiple line plot segments and linking the glyphs*

© Alison Box 2022
A. Box, *Introducing Charticulator for Power BI*, https://doi.org/10.1007/978-1-4842-8076-8_16

These visuals are just variations on the slope chart but I think you'll agree are more interesting and eye-catching. In this chapter, I will take you through the process of generating these charts, and using many skills you've learned so far, you will be able to take these ideas and move forward with them.

Creating a Line Plot Segment

We will start by creating a vertical line plot segment. First, remove "PlotSegment1" from the Layers pane using the eraser button. Next, add a vertical Guide X to the canvas on which to anchor the plot segment. This is so you can reposition the plot segment once it's on the canvas.

Now click on the **Plot Segments** button on the toolbar and select "Line" and drag and draw the line along the vertical guide. This will create a vertical line plot segment that will act as a single line axis onto which you can plot data; see Figure 16-2.

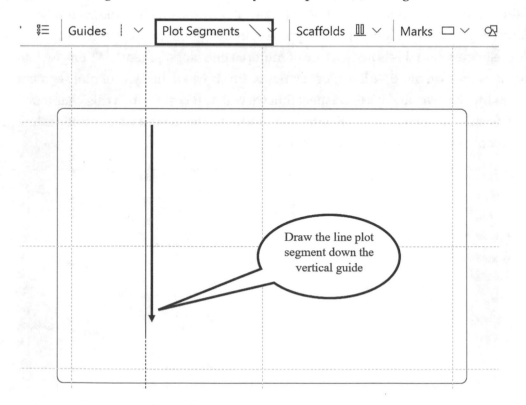

Figure 16-2. Creating a line plot segment

In a similar way to working with x- and y-axes, the line axis will be either categorical or numerical depending on the data plotted onto it and will behave differently accordingly. Let's first consider a categorical line axis.

Using a Categorical Line Axis

In this example, we will use just two fields, the categorical field "Salespeople" and the numerical field "Sales." Having drawn a vertical line plot segment, if you now create a rectangle shape as your glyph, binding the "Salespeople" field to the Fill attribute, it will be plotted onto this line. At this stage, depending on your data, the rectangles may overlap each other on the plot segment. To remedy this, bind the "Sales" field to the Height attribute and then edit the Range attribute of the Height scale to reduce the End value. Lastly, bind the "Salespeople" field to the line plot segment creating a categorical axis and if required increase the tick size; see Figure 16-3.

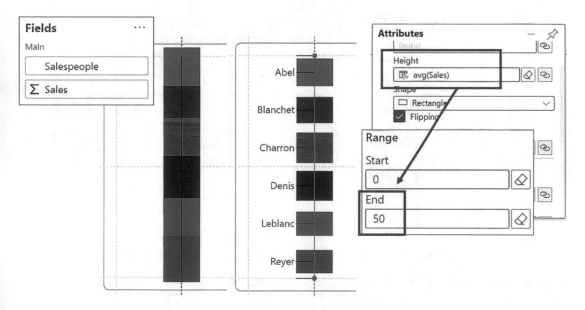

Figure 16-3. *Plotting data onto a categorical line plot segment, at first the rectangles overlap, but you can bind data and edit the scale*

You may be wondering why you would want to use a single categorical line axis. On its own, it's not going to provide particularly meaningful insights into your data. Certainly none that we couldn't glean from using a traditional cartesian chart. Where you will find a use for the categorical line axis, however, is when you combine it with numerical line axes, but before we can do this, we need to look at plotting numerical data onto the line axis.

Using a Numerical Line Axis

Starting afresh, with a new chart but with the same data as before, again remove "PlotSegment1" and add a vertical guide to the canvas. Then draw a line plot segment up the guide. The direction you drag and draw the line plot segment is important; you must drag upward to generate an ascending scale. Now you can bind the "Sales" field to the axis; see Figure 16-4.

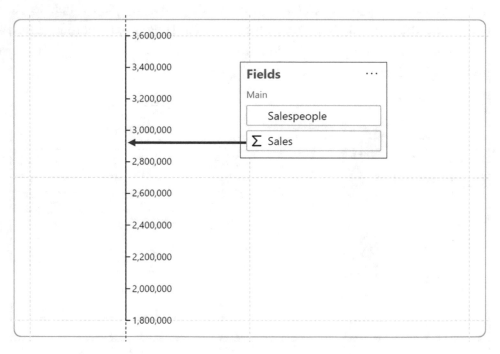

Figure 16-4. *Binding a numerical field to a line plot segment*

This will generate a numerical line plot segment that has the same attributes as the numerical axis, and therefore you can format the tick data as currency, increase the tick size, and make a number of other formatting choices (see Chapter 7).

Plotting Glyphs on a Numerical Line Axis

If you now create a rectangle glyph, you will observe the same behavior on the line plot segment as in a 2D region plot segment. The rectangles are overlapped and plotted on the line with their center point on the value being plotted. Therefore, just as on a cartesian chart, using a symbol will normally work better when binding numerical fields to the line axis. Alternatively, you could reduce the size of the rectangle mark so it resembles a symbol, and this is a strategy we will be using later.

In our example in Figure 16-5, you can see that using a symbol in the Glyph pane and binding the "Salespeople" field generates a numerical line axis.

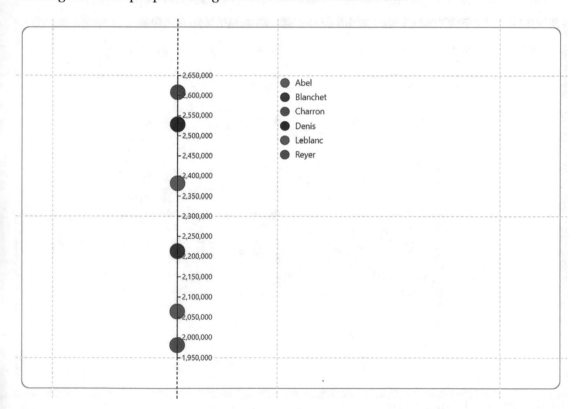

Figure 16-5. *A numerical field bound to the line plot segment and using a symbol to plot the data*

I think you'll agree though that this chart is a little underwhelming. Although we've correctly plotted the sales for each salesperson, we would probably want to compare the sales with other years or perhaps a target. Using just one numerical line axis is not going to take you very far. The real benefit of using numerical line axes is when you use a number of them in the chart and use Charticulator's links feature, so let's see if doing so can improve our unimpressive visual.

Multiple Numerical Line Axes

Using multiple line plot segments is a straightforward way to visualize multiple numeric measures and is an alternative approach to using the data axis that we explored in Chapter 14. As you also learned in Chapter 15, as soon as you have multiple plot segments in your chart, you can then link the glyphs between them. This straightforward approach can result in simple but insightful visuals. Consider the slope chart in Figure 16-6 that compares salespeople's performance over two years.

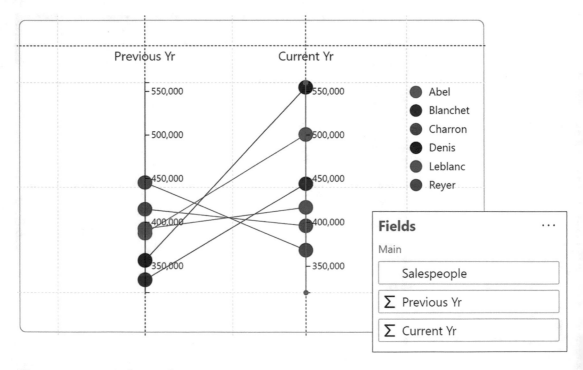

Figure 16-6. *A slope chart*

This chart uses two line plot segments and a symbol in the Glyph pane. A measure was then bound to each line plot segment generating two numerical axes. Using the Link button, we can then link the plot segments using a line. Also note that when using different metrics, it's often necessary to edit the Range attributes of the plot segments so the numerical scales are consistent, starting and ending at the same values.

Note   If you edit the scale, don't forget to turn off both the auto min and auto max "Axis Export Properties" in the Attributes pane of the line plot segments so that when you return to Power BI the scale will be saved.

Consider the chart in Figure 16-7 that uses the same techniques we've learned so far and extends the scope of the data we can analyze. Here, we've created three line plot segments and anchored them each to a vertical guide but this time used three measures in the line plot segments. By linking the line plot segments and formatting the linking line as a Bezier curve, this adds that extra visual appeal.

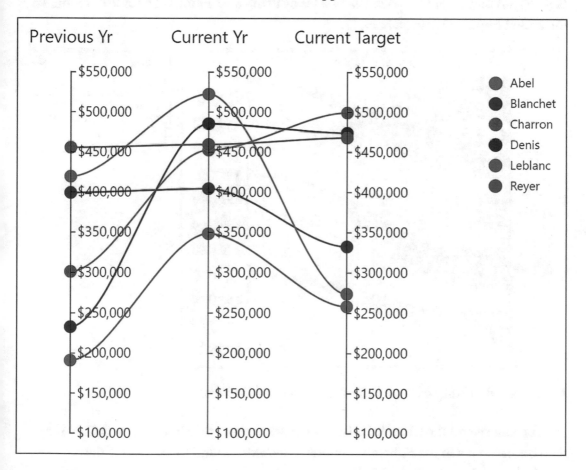

Figure 16-7. *A visual using multiple line plot segments to plot multiple measures*

We've been able to use multiple numerical line plot segments and link the glyphs between them to build variations on the slope chart. What you need to appreciate, however, is that so far we've always used the *same* symbol glyph. If you want to combine a categorical line axis with a numerical line axis, the requirement will be to use *different* glyphs associated with the different line plot segments. The next step therefore is to learn how, by linking glyphs across categorical *and* numerical line axes, we can step up our game in designing visuals using the line plot segment.

Combining Categorical and Numerical Line Axes

By combining two different axis types, we can build the type of visual shown in Figure 16-8 that compares each year's sales by using a variation on a slope chart but with the added impact of using a band link.

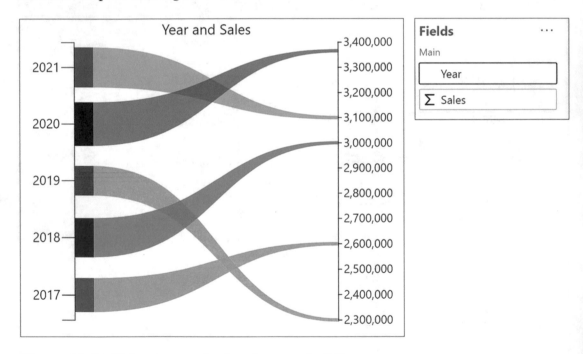

Figure 16-8. *Using categorical and numerical line axes*

You can see on the left of this visual we have a categorical line axis, with the "Year" field bound to it. On the right is a numerical line axis, bound to the "Sales" field.

We learned earlier in this chapter how to plot a category onto a line plot segment using a rectangle as the glyph. We also know that if we are using a numerical line plot segment, a symbol glyph works best. However, we are now presented with a problem. If we want to link data using a band across a categorical and a numerical line plot segment, we can't link a rectangle to a symbol. We can only link a rectangle shape to another rectangle shape.

What we can do here is to use a second glyph for the numerical line plot segment that is a rectangle shape but has been sized so small it behaves like a symbol. This is what you are looking at in Figure 16-8, where the linking band joins the glyphs in the categorical and numerical line axes.

Now that you know the secret to this chart, let's see how we can build it. Start by using a vertical line plot segment anchored to a vertical guide and a rectangle in the Glyph pane. Bind your numerical field, such as "Sales," to the Height attribute of the shape and bind the categorical field, "Salespeople," to the Fill attribute. Depending on your data, you may need to edit the scale for the Height attribute of the shape and restrain the End range; see Figure 16-9.

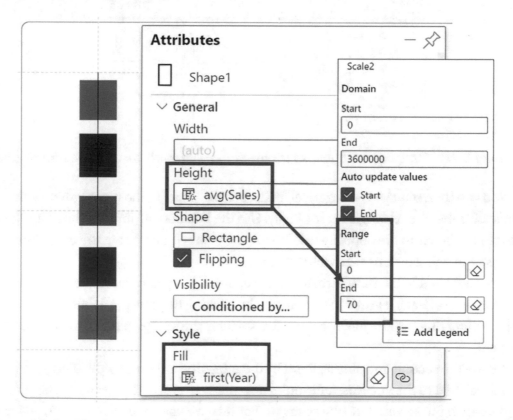

Figure 16-9. *The first steps in building the chart that uses two plot segments and two glyphs*

The rectangles look odd straddling the line axis and need to be moved so their left edge starts on the axis. To do this, in the Glyph pane drag the left edge of the rectangle so it's anchored to the center vertical guide of the glyph; see Figure 16-10.

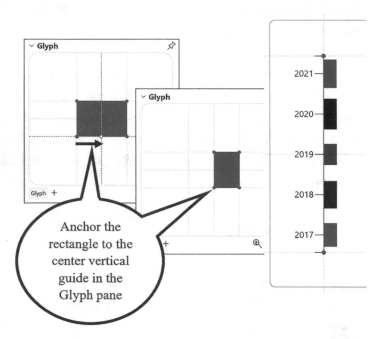

Figure 16-10. *Resizing the glyph so it's anchored correctly on the line plot segment*

You can then bind your categorical field, such as "Year," to the plot segment axis which will label the rectangles accordingly. Use the Position attribute of the plot segment to move the labels to the opposite side. To move the labels away from the axis, either increase the tick size or use the Offset attribute.

Now we can add the numerical line plot segment, but you must create a new glyph first. As we've already learned in Chapter 11, by clicking the new glyph button *first* and then creating the line plot segment, it associates the new glyph with the new plot segment.

Create the second line plot segment by dragging upward on a guide. Bind your numerical field to the line axis, and you're now ready to create the second glyph that will be plotted on the second line plot segment. For this, we used a rectangle mark, giving it a width of 1 and a height of 5; see Figure 16-11. Because the glyph is now very small, you can use the zoom button bottom right of the Glyph pane to zoom in if required.

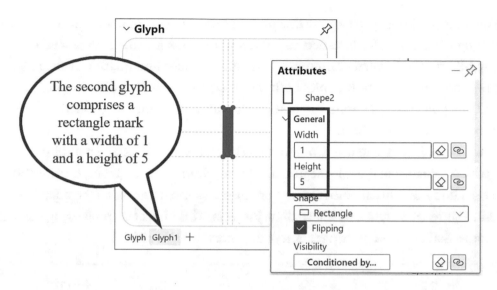

Figure 16-11. *Creating the glyph for the second line plot segment*

The rectangle is so small that you can't see it plotted on the second line plot segment. But look what happens when you add a band linking the plot segments. The glyphs are now linked accordingly, and all you need to do is edit the band to a Bezier type using the attributes of the link; see Figure 16-12.

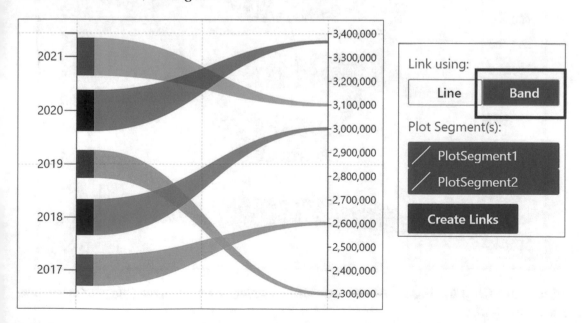

Figure 16-12. *Linking the plot segments with a band links the glyphs accordingly*

333

Now that you know you can use line plot segments to compare measures, let's think this through. We could, for instance, use different line plot segments to plot values that use different units of measurement, for instance, sales and quantity. Normally, this presents a problem; how to plot both values on the same chart. In Chapter 9, you learned that you could generate two numerical scales using the Height attribute to plot a clustered column or bar chart.

A simpler solution is to use two numerical line plot segments and combine them with a categorical line plot segment. You can then use two glyphs, one for the numerical line axes and the other to plot on the categorical line axis. Consider the visual in Figure 16-13 where we have done just this. This chart was built using the same techniques that we used in the creation of the chart in Figure 16-12.

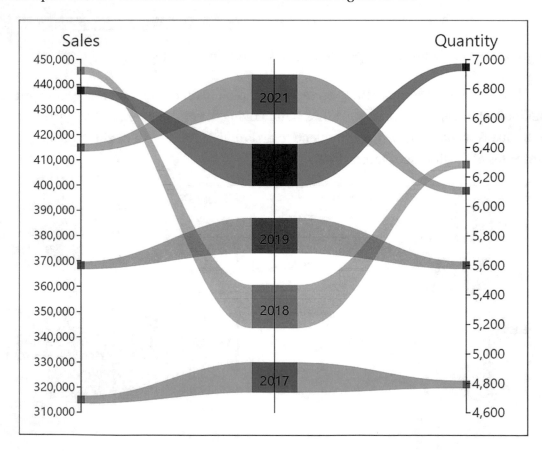

Figure 16-13. *Plotting two measures and a category using three line plot segments and two glyphs*

Having explored just a few applications of the line plot segment, I'm sure you'll find reasons to benefit from its use. However, I think you will agree that its most valuable contribution can be for comparing multiple measures by linking glyphs accordingly. Using the band link certainly makes for impressive visuals.

We are nearing the end of our journey through Charticulator, learning how to design and build customized visuals to be used in your Power BI reports. We have a few more topics in store, but in the next couple of chapters we move away from generating visuals and consider other aspects of using this software. You may think it rather strange that we are about to complete this journey by having explored such an unassuming feature as the line plot segment. If you think this, just think again. To be able to work through all the examples outlined above, you had to use skills learned in almost every single chapter of this book, so I think you'll agree that you've come a long way since those early chapters.

CHAPTER 17

Templates and Nested Charts

In this chapter, we move away from designing charts and visuals and instead look at two aspects of managing the visualizations you've learned to build inside Charticulator. The features we will be learning to use are:

1. Repurposing a chart with a different data set using a template

2. Generating small multiples of a chart to compare data across specific categories using nested charts

Saving the Chart As a Template

One of the great advantages of generating charts with Charticulator is that you can use a template to repurpose a chart and so use the same visual to analyze alternative data. Let's take the nightingale chart that we designed in Chapter 13 as our example; see Figure 17-1.

© Alison Box 2022
A. Box, *Introducing Charticulator for Power BI*, https://doi.org/10.1007/978-1-4842-8076-8_17

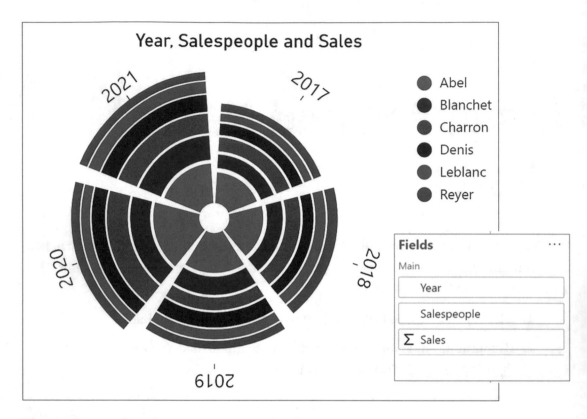

Figure 17-1. *This chart can be reused with a different data set*

It's an appealing chart that currently shows sales for each salesperson in each year, but wouldn't it be useful if we could reuse it to show instead the quantity of products sold in each region?

In Charticulator, once you've generated a chart where you've bound fields to various attributes, you can think of these attributes as containers whose contents can be variable while the chart itself remains constant. This is where the concept of mapping the original fields that comprise the chart to different categorical and numerical fields becomes important because this is what we do when we create a template.

However, before you can save a chart as a template, you must have the necessary security permission to do so. Your Power BI administrator will need to ensure that under the Tenet settings of the Admin Portal, the setting "**Allow downloads from custom visuals**" is enabled; see Figure 17-2.

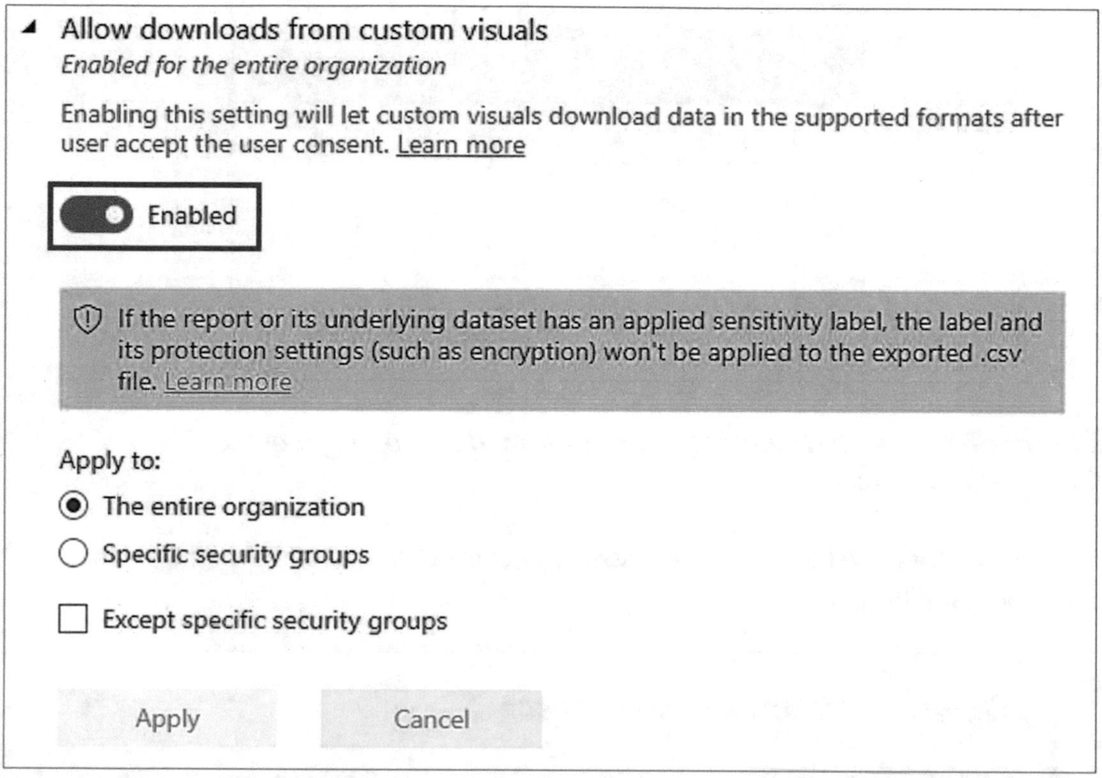

◢ **Allow downloads from custom visuals**
Enabled for the entire organization

Enabling this setting will let custom visuals download data in the supported formats after user accept the user consent. Learn more

⬤ Enabled

🛡 If the report or its underlying dataset has an applied sensitivity label, the label and its protection settings (such as encryption) won't be applied to the exported .csv file. Learn more

Apply to:

🔘 The entire organization

⚪ Specific security groups

☐ Except specific security groups

Apply   Cancel

Figure 17-2. *To save a chart as a template, you must have this setting enabled*

To create a template, open the chart you want to save as a template in Charticulator and then click the **Export template** button at the top right of the Charticulator screen (Figure 17-3).

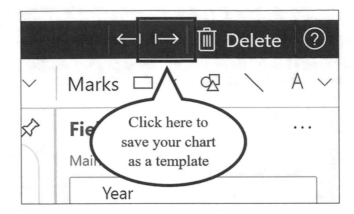

Figure 17-3. *Use the Export template button at the top right of the Charticulator screen*

You will then see the warning as shown in Figure 17-4, and at this point, you can click the **Download** button.

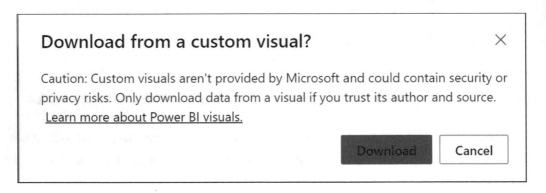

Figure 17-4. *This warning message shows prior to downloading*

You can now save the JSON file that is generated so that it can be used as a template.

To use your template, populate the Data bucket in Power BI with the new fields you want to use in the chart. In our example, these would be the "Year," "Regions," and "Qty" fields. After clicking the Edit option from the Options button in Power BI, click **Import template** (Figure 17-5) and open your template file.

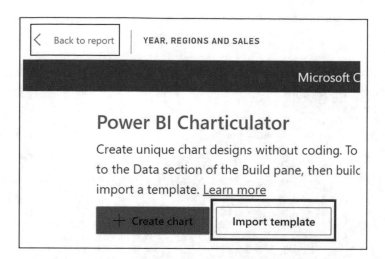

Figure 17-5. *Use the Import template option*

You will then be prompted to map your data. In our example, we must map the "Regions" field to the Salespeople entity and the "Qty" field to the Sales entity; see Figure 17-6.

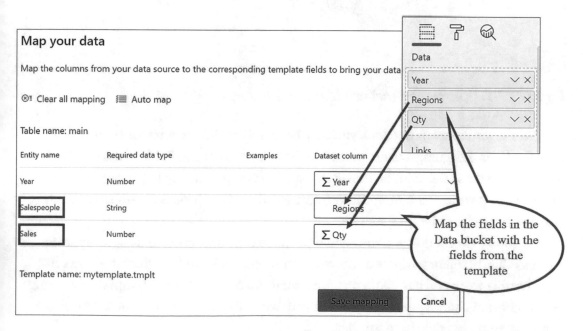

Figure 17-6. *Map your new fields to the original fields saved with the template*

You can see in Figure 17-7 that we have exactly the same nightingale chart but now visualizing the "Regions" data.

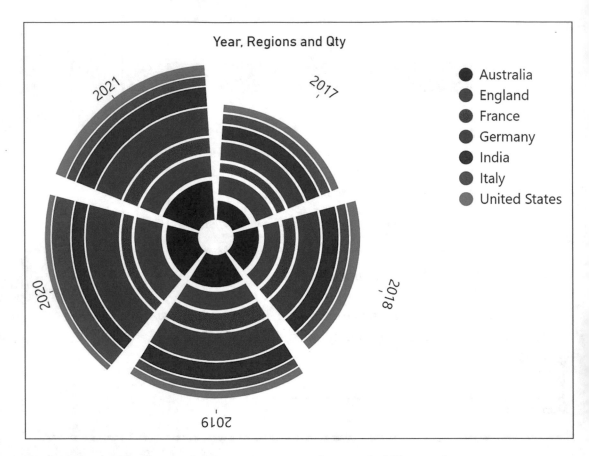

Figure 17-7. *The same chart as Figure 17-1 but with different data*

With regard to mapping data, you may have noticed that when you are inside Charticulator, designing a chart where you have bound certain fields to attributes, if you then change those fields in the Power BI Data bucket, you are again prompted to map the new fields with their counterparts in the existing chart. This is an alternative way to reuse a chart with different data sets.

It's good to know that you now can repurpose your own custom designs by saving them as Charticulator templates. However, the community of Charticulator users has been hard at work and has come up with a plethora of predesigned templates covering many different chart types and visuals. If you would like to use one of these templates, mapping your own data to them, visit

https://github.com/PowerBI-tips/Charticulator-Templates/tree/main/ templates

When you visit this page on GitHub, it's not obvious how you then download the template files. In Figure 17-8, I have shown you the process you need to follow to do this.

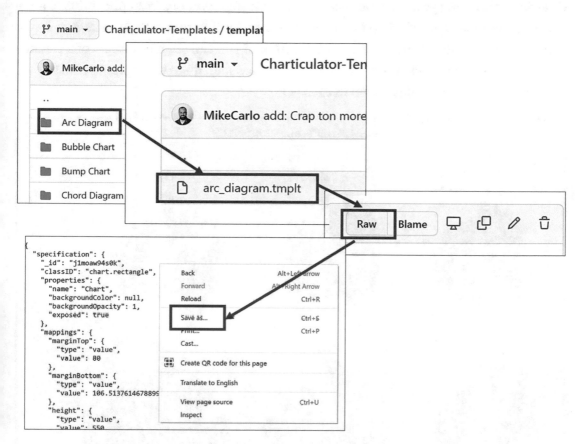

Figure 17-8. *Downloading a Charticulator template from GitHub*

After browsing for the chart you are interested in, for example, an "Arc Diagram," click the blue folder, then click the "*.tmplt" file name. This will take you to the source code for the template. At the top right of this window, click the **Raw** button. When the raw code opens, right-click the code and select **Save as...**. Now save this code with a "*.tmplt" file extension.

Using these templates is a great way to extend your knowledge of Charticulator, and I would highly recommend you take time out to explore them. After all, you don't want to reinvent the wheel!

Nested Charts

Charticulator allows you to create visuals containing *small multiples*, replications of a chart that use the same scale and axis but show data for different categorical items. In Charticulator, these are known as nested charts, and you can see an example of a visual containing nested rose charts in Figure 17-9. In this visual, there is a separate chart showing sales for each salesperson in each year.

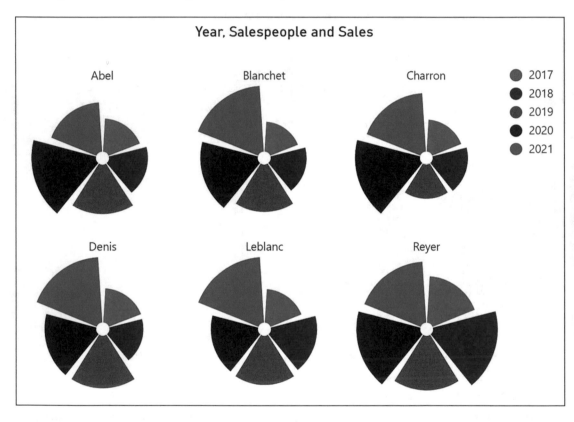

Figure 17-9. *A Charticulator visual comprising nested charts*

To use the nested charts feature, create a new Charticulator chart, including the fields used by each individual chart, but also include the field by which you want to group the data. This will be the categorical field for which there will be an instance of each chart. In our example, this is the "Salespeople" field. In the new chart, using the Group by… attribute of the plot segment, group your data by this field; see Figure 17-10.

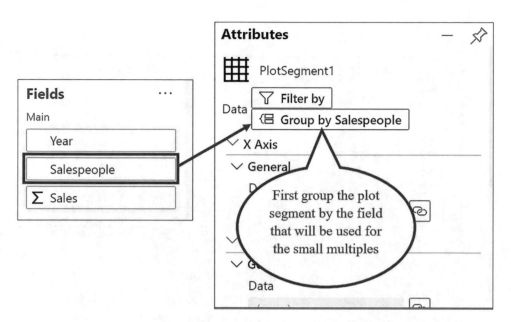

Figure 17-10. *Nested charts require a field to be used to group the data*

The first step is to generate plot segments on the chart canvas for each nested chart. To do this, drag the **Nested Chart** button from the toolbar onto the Glyph pane; see Figure 17-11.

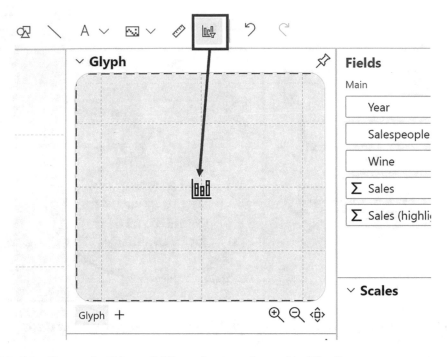

Figure 17-11. *Drag the Nested Chart button into the Glyph pane*

Because the default sub-layout of a chart is always Stack X, the canvas may look rather strange, particularly if there are many values in the grouping category. If you change the sub-layout to Grid, the canvas will look tidier. You will notice you now have a nested plot segment for every instance of the chart; see Figure 17-12.

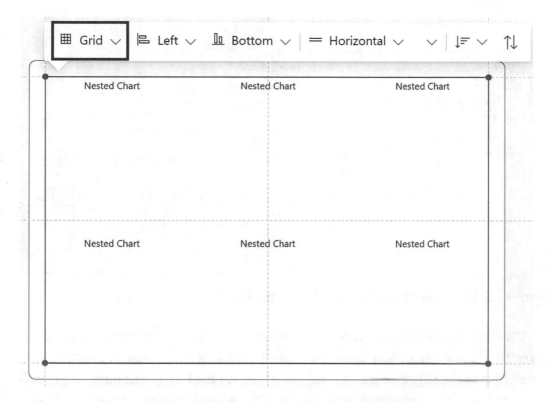

Figure 17-12. *You will probably need to change the sub-layout to Grid*

Now we are ready to design the nested chart. In the Layers pane, click on "NestedChart1", and in the Attributes pane, click **Edit Nested Chart**; see Figure 17-13.

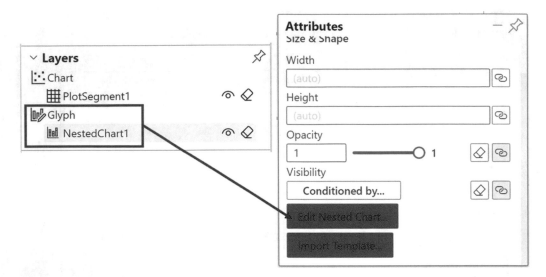

Figure 17-13. *Select Edit Nested Chart from the Attributes pane of the nested chart*

The chart canvas will now reflect the nested chart, and you can create your chart just as you would any other chart. In our example, I used a rectangle mark and bound the "Year" field to the Fill attribute and the "Sales" field to the Height attribute. To produce the rose chart, I applied a polar scaffold. You will also probably want to edit the Title mark by binding the grouping field to the Text attribute to ensure that each instance of the chart is labeled.

Click **Save Nested Chart** at the top left of the screen and then click **Close** to return to the main chart; see Figure 17-14.

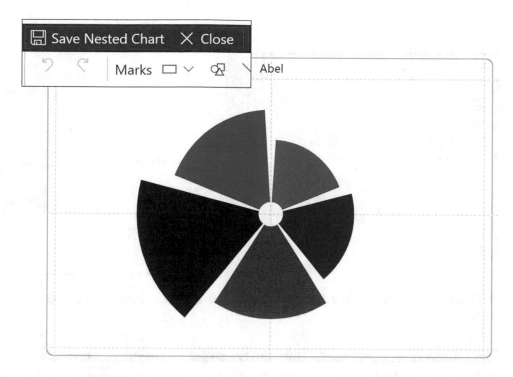

Figure 17-14. *Create the nested chart in the normal way and then save and close*

Back in the main chart, you can edit as required, for instance, you could add a legend to the canvas. Each nested chart now constitutes a glyph, and you may want to use the plot segment attributes to reduce the spacing between the glyphs.

If you don't want to generate the nested chart from scratch, you can use a chart that's been saved as a template chart. For instance, we can use the chart in Figure 17-1 that we saved as a template. To do this, after grouping the data and dragging the Nested Chart button into the Glyph pane, select the nested chart in the Layers pane, and in the Attributes pane, click **Import Template...** and open your template file; see Figure 17-15.

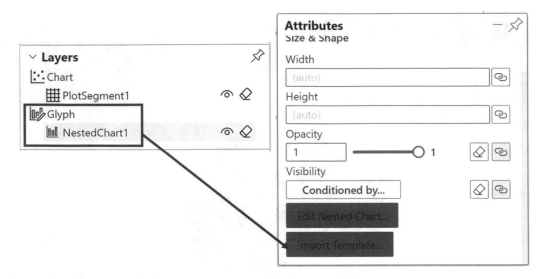

Figure 17-15. *You use the Import Template... button to use a template as a nested chart*

The template chart is now copied into the Glyph pane, and you can then click **Edit Nested Chart...** to make further edits to it. For example, you can remove the legend that displays in each nested chart and replace it in the main chart.

In this chapter, we've been focusing on how you can manage and reuse the charts and visuals that you've learned to design using Charticulator. However, there is another facet to using these visuals that we now must consider. How well will they integrate into our Power BI report and how will the users of our report interact with them? In the next chapter, we will return to the Power BI canvas and consider our consumer's experience of using Charticulator's custom visuals.

CHAPTER 18

Integrating with Power BI

It's now time for us to consider what will happen to our Charticulator charts when we close and save and return to Power BI. The charts we have built inside Charticulator should integrate seamlessly into our Power BI report, and much of this depends on how the Power BI visuals and the Charticulator charts will interact with one another on the report canvas. In this chapter, we will be looking at how we can generate appropriate interactions between Power BI and Charticulator visuals and how these interactions can be modified and controlled.

Charticulator's Interactivity Options

In Charticulator, each mark and symbol has its own set of attributes that allow you to control the interactions to other Power BI visuals on the Power BI canvas. These attributes are under the "Interactivity" heading and are shown in Figure 18-1.

A. Box, *Introducing Charticulator for Power BI*, https://doi.org/10.1007/978-1-4842-8076-8_18

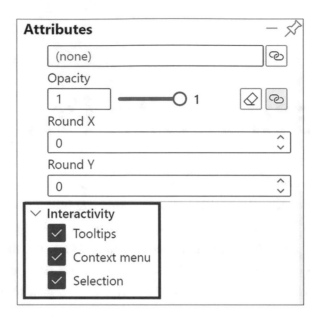

Figure 18-1. *The attributes of the mark or symbol that control the interactivity with Power BI visuals*

Let's take each of these attributes in turn and discover how they control various aspects of browsing the Charticulator visual in the Power BI report.

Tooltips

Enabling the Tooltips interactivity requires you to place a field into the Tooltips bucket in Power BI. This data will then show in the Power BI tooltip when users hover on a glyph; see Figure 18-2.

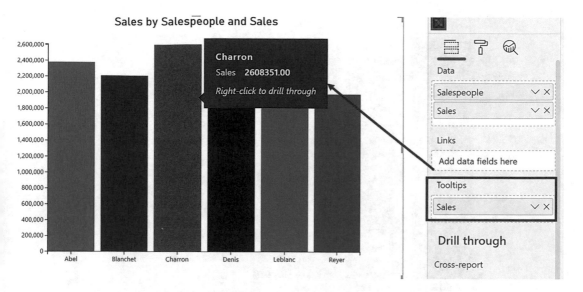

Figure 18-2. *The Tooltips interactivity allows the display of the Power BI tooltip*

You can put multiple fields into the Tooltips bucket, but all the fields must also be in the Data bucket. Dynamic tooltips using a tooltips page are not supported by Charticulator.

Context Menu

This attribute enables the display of the context menu when consumers of the report right-click on one of the glyphs in the chart; see Figure 18-3.

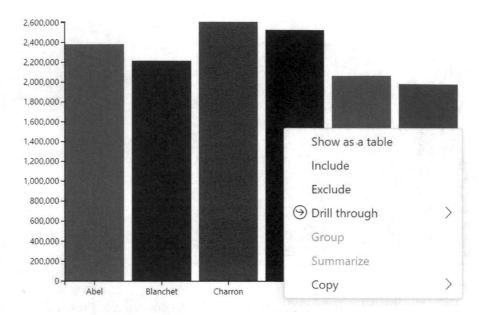

Figure 18-3. *The context menu displayed on a Charticulator chart*

The options on this context menu are consistent with all Power BI visuals.

Selection Interactivity

The Selection attribute when checked on enables the clicking or tapping on a glyph in a Charticulator chart on the Power BI canvas and invoking the Power BI interactions with other visuals on the canvas; see Figure 18-4. With Power BI bar and column charts, the default is the highlight interaction, and with line charts it's a filter, but you can use the Edit Interactions feature on the Format contextual tab of Power BI to change the interactions if required.

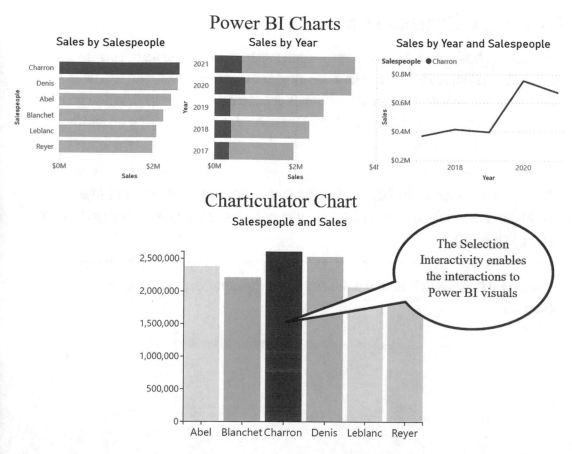

Figure 18-4. *Using the Selection interactivity to enable Power BI interactions*

Because the Selection interactivity is associated with each mark or symbol, if you have a glyph comprising many marks, ensure the interactivity is checked on for all the marks so the glyph is "clickable," if you want to enable the interactivity.

Interactions onto Charticulator Charts

We have seen that when Charticulator charts are clicked or tapped, they invoke the correct interaction on other Power BI visuals. But how will Charticulator charts respond when Power BI visuals are tapped or clicked? With Charticulator visuals, the way they respond when other visuals on the canvas are browsed is not so clear-cut. We would expect the highlight interaction to be the default and then use Edit Interactions to change the interaction to a filter. However, this is not the case as we will now explain.

Filtering a Charticulator Visual

The filtering interaction does work as normal for Charticulator visuals. However, because the highlight interaction is the default for all visuals on the canvas, you will need to edit the interaction so that the filter interaction is enabled; see Figure 18-5. When you do this, if you select data in a Power BI visual, the Charticulator chart will filter accordingly to show the subset of data.

Note   The exception to this is a Charticulator line chart that does not filter or highlight. However, you can build in your own filters and highlights by using DAX; see Chapter 19.

You will find the Edit Interactions button on the contextual Format tab of the Power BI screen.

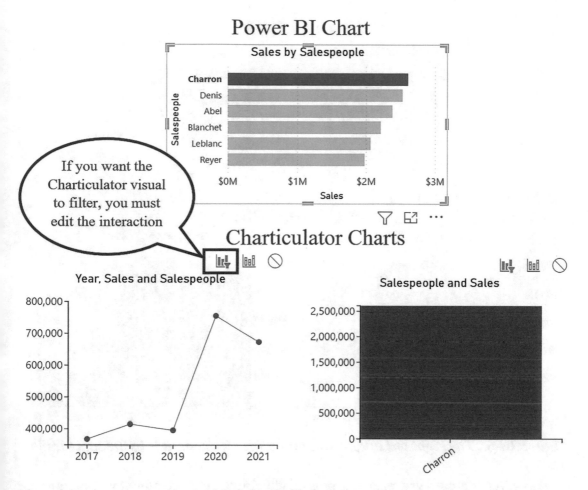

Figure 18-5. *Because the highlight is the default, the filtering interaction needs to be enabled*

In Figure 18-5, you can see that in the Power BI bar chart, we have clicked the bar for salesperson "Charron." The Charticulator line and column charts have responded accordingly and have been filtered to show just this salesperson's data.

Highlighting a Charticulator Visual

The highlight interaction on Charticulator visuals is a little more problematic. The highlight only works if the data you select in the Power BI visual is from the same table as the data in the Charticulator visual; see Figure 18-6.

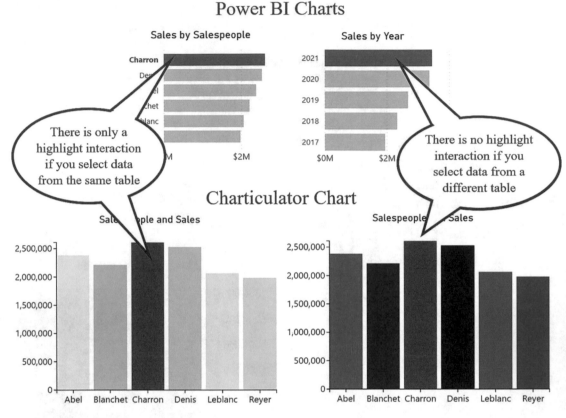

Figure 18-6. *The highlight interaction only works if the data is in the same table*

However, there is a way to enable cross-highlighting in Charticulator visuals, and that is to use the version of the numerical field in the Fields pane of Charticulator that is labeled "highlights." To turn on this feature, in Power BI on the Visualizations pane, under the format visual options, use the "Partial cross-highlight" card and turn on **Add highlight columns**; see Figure 18-7.

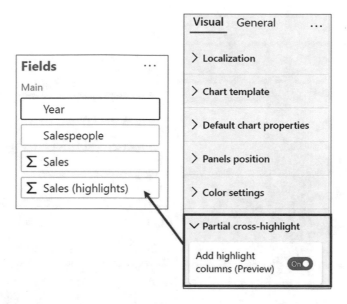

Figure 18-7. *Turning on the highlights feature*

The "highlights" numerical field responds to filters from other visuals on the canvas where the filter has been placed on fields that don't comprise the Charticulator chart. The idea is that you can use two separate marks in the glyph that respond to each numerical value, the normal field and the "highlights" field, and use different fill colors for each mark accordingly.

You can treat the "highlights" numerical field just as any numerical field you plot onto a Charticulator chart. We learned in Chapter 11 how to plot two numerical values onto the same glyph. You can either use two rectangle marks and bind each value to the Height attribute or use a data axis. In Figure 18-8, we've used a data axis to plot the "Sales" and "Sales (highlights)" numerical fields. Before you plot the "highlights" numerical value, don't forget to place a filter on your Charticulator visual; otherwise, the two numerical values will be identical, and it will be difficult to separate them on the data axis.

You can then decide how to format the highlighted and unhighlighted values. For instance, you could reduce the opacity of the fill color of the unhighlighted numerical field.

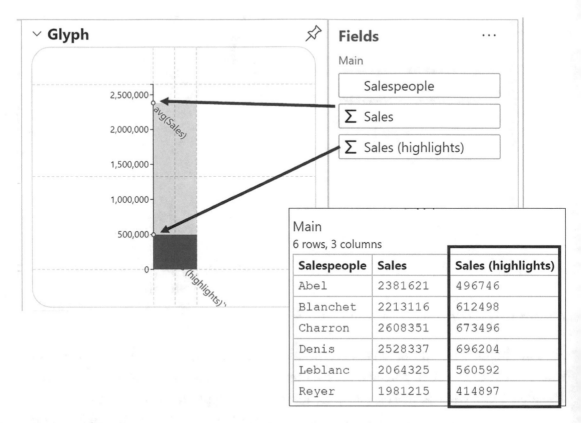

Figure 18-8. *Creating a glyph using the "highlights" numerical value*

In Figure 18-9, you can see the result of using the "Sales (highlights)" numerical field. Here, we have selected the year 2021 in the Power BI bar chart, and this data is now highlighted in the Charticulator chart. Note the use of the opacity to show the unhighlighted value which mimics the highlighting of Power BI.

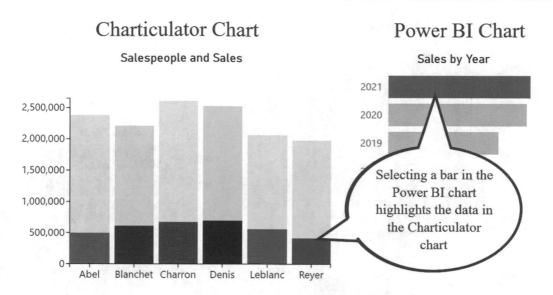

Figure 18-9. *Enabling cross-highlighting from Power BI visuals*

However, unlike Power BI charts, where there are no alternatives as to how you want the highlighting to show, in Charticulator you can make some interesting choices. In Figure 18-10, you can see that we have used a horizontal line to plot the "highlights" data, or you could use a smaller black rectangle mark.

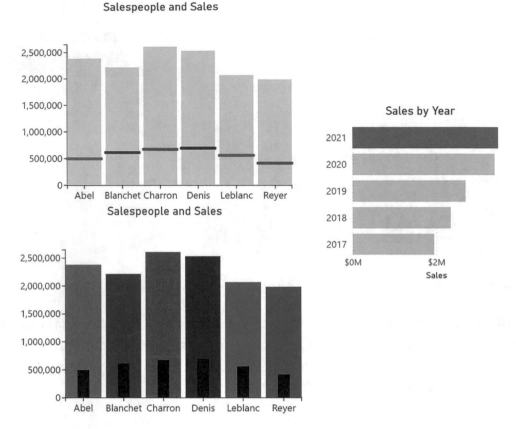

Figure 18-10. *You can have different responses in Charticulator charts to conventional highlighting*

You have learned in this chapter that all the visuals you build in Charticulator will respond correctly to user browsing, dynamically interacting with other visuals on the canvas, even if it requires a little extra work on your part for them to do so. You have seen also that when using highlighting, Charticulator yet again provides an alternative approach when identifying subsets of data. It seems that to get the best out of Charticulator, often you need to think laterally and to use the tools it provides in imaginative ways.

We are fast approaching the final chapter of this book, and you are now a fully qualified Charticulator user. Well done! You are now no longer limited in your level of knowledge; you are only limited by your level of creative skill. With this in mind, we are now ready to conclude our journey through Charticulator by exploring the potential of designing more challenging visuals and therefore taking Charticulator charts to the next level.

CHAPTER 19

Taking It to the Next Level

Let me first congratulate you on having come this far. You've worked through all the chapters in this book, so you're now an expert in generating visuals using Charticulator. It's always been an implicit understanding that the reason you've invested your time and attention in learning how to use Charticulator is so you can design visuals that tell the story of your data, uncompromisingly and unequivocally and that can truly inform and persuade. This has been the overriding objective through everything you have learned about this inspirational chart generating software.

In this chapter, it's time to prove that this objective has been achieved. It's time to look at designing more ambitious visualizations that will use the skills you have learned in this book. We look specifically at how you can use multiple plot segments and glyphs, sometimes layered one on top of the other, to achieve truly customized visuals. Using this technique, you can mix and match chart elements in almost limitless combinations. We also look at how we can make use of DAX measures to control the display of chart elements or the formatting of those elements. This again is a method that can be applied to many different charting scenarios.

In what follows, I'll be taking you through how to build the following visuals:

- Matrix and card combination

- Highlighted line chart

- Categorized line chart

- Jitter plot

- Arrow chart

Matrix and Card Combination Visual

In Figure 19-1, we have designed a visual that combines a matrix style table with a summary card and comprises the following analysis:

© Alison Box 2022
A. Box, *Introducing Charticulator for Power BI*, https://doi.org/10.1007/978-1-4842-8076-8_19

- Conditional formatting in the matrix to identify high and low sales values

- A bar chart on the right to show subtotals for each region

- A bar chart at the bottom to show subtotals for each year

- A card on the right that provides a summary of the data

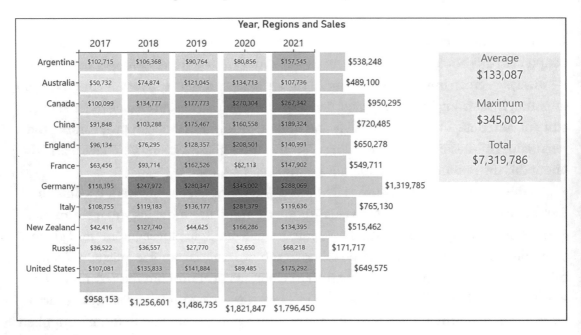

Figure 19-1. *A visual combining a table, bar charts, and a card*

This chart makes use of multiple plot segments, each with its own glyph. To generate the subtotals for each region and each year used by the bar charts and also the summary data in the card, we used Charticulator's "Group by..." option.

The problem you will meet, however, is that you can only group by categories that exist in the underlying data, in our case by year or by region. To group by all the data so that you can calculate the aggregations in the card, you will need to generate a value that puts every row into the same category. I used a DAX measure to do this and named the measure "All," populating it with a "Y"; see Figure 19-2.

Year	Regions	Sales	All
2017	Argentina	102715	Y
2017	Australia	50732	Y
2017	Canada	100099	Y
2017	China	91848	Y
2017	England	96134	Y
2017	France	63456	Y
2017	Germany	158395	Y
2017	Italy	108755	Y

Main
55 rows, 4 columns

1   All = "Y"

DAX measure to group all the data

Figure 19-2. *Create a DAX measure to group all the data*

We are now ready to build the combination visual. In Figure 19-3, the four plot segments used in the generation of this visual have been set out.

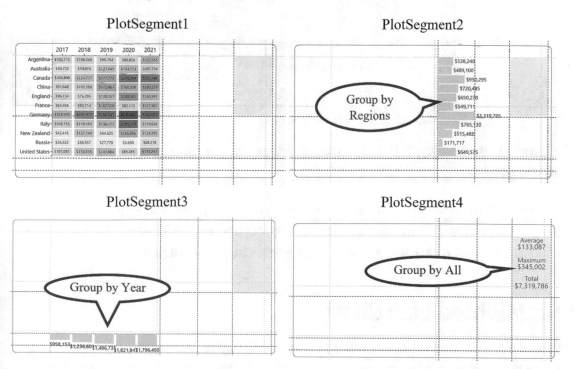

Figure 19-3. *The four plot segments used to generate the chart in Figure 19-1*

You can see the guides that were needed to anchor each plot segment in the correct place. PlotSegment1 comprises two categorical axes using the "Regions" and "Year" fields and a rectangle glyph where "Sales" has been bound to the Fill attribute, giving it the gradient color scale.

PlotSegment2 and PlotSegment3 are grouped as shown and use a rectangle glyph. The second plot segment has a Stack Y sub-layout, and in the third plot segment, the sub-layout is aligned at the top. Text marks were used to label the rectangles.

The card was designed in PlotSegment4 which was grouped by the "All" field. In the Glyph pane, I used text marks to show the aggregated data and changed the functions accordingly; see Figure 19-4.

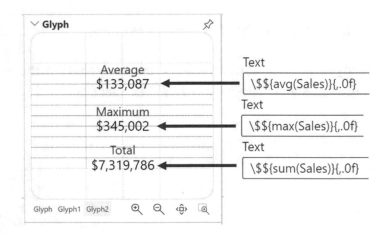

Figure 19-4. *The glyph in the fourth plot segment was grouped by "All" and text marks used to show the aggregated data*

To color the card, I used a rectangle shape, anchored to the plot segment, and gave it a generous opacity. I will also admit that aligning the text marks vertically was a little challenging, despite anchoring them to the guides in the Glyph pane.

Highlighted Line Chart

One of the frustrations in Power BI is that you can't highlight categories in a line chart according to slicer selections; you can only filter the lines. There is also no way that you can emphasize specific data points on the line to show values such as the maximum value. Consider the chart in Figure 19-5 which was produced using Charticulator. Here, we have selected two salespeople in the slicer, "Abel" and "Reyer," and their sales are highlighted in the line chart, identifying their maximum sales values.

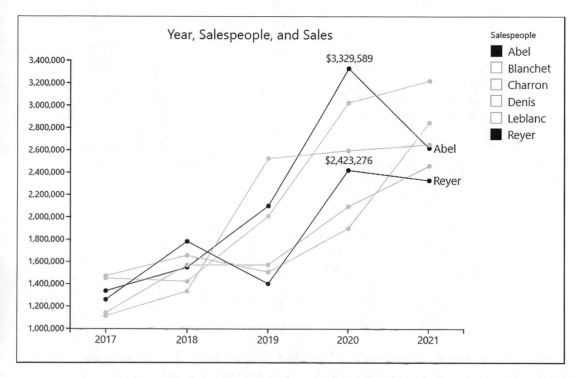

Figure 19-5. *A line chart that highlights the selected salespeople*

Before we explore how this chart was built, let's look first at the data that will be used by the Charticulator visual. We can do this best by using a Power BI table visual, alongside the slicer that will filter the data, and you can also see the tables in the data model from where the data comes; see Figure 19-6.

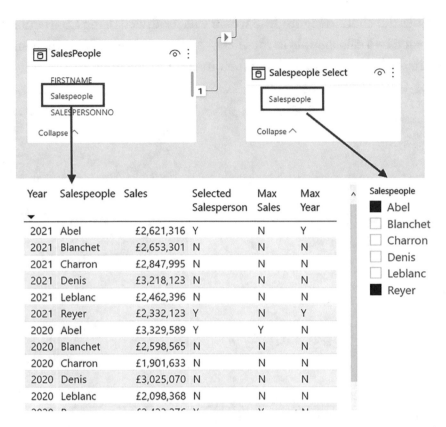

Figure 19-6. *The data used in the line chart visual. Note the salespeople's values for the slicer come from a different table from the values used in the visual*

The salespeople's names you can see in the slicer come from a column that resides in its own separate table, "Salespeople Select," not the table that will be used by the visual which is the "Salespeople" table. You can create the separate table that will hold the column for the slicer values using DAX or Power Query. Note that we only need a column containing the salespeople's names, and the table is unrelated to any other tables in the model.

Note also that there are three DAX measures in the data as follows:

1. Selected Salesperson

2. Max Sales

3. Max Year

These DAX measures all return either "Y" or "N," and these flags will be used by the Fill and Visibility attributes of the symbol and link line in the Charticulator chart. This will control the gray color of the line and data points and also control the visibility of the salespeople's names and maximum values when selections are made in the slicer.measures

This is the DAX code that we used for the measures (numbered for clarity):

```
1. Selected Salesperson =
--Returns "Y" if the sales are for the salespeople selected in the slicer
VAR SalespeopleSelect =
    VALUES ( 'Salespeople Select'[Salespeople] )
RETURN
    IF ( SELECTEDVALUE ( SalesPeople[Salespeople] ) IN
                            SalespeopleSelect,
                                "Y", "N" )
```

```
2. Max Sales =
--Returns "Y" if the sales are the maximum value for the selected
salespeople
VAR MaxforSP = maxx(all(DateTable[Year]),[Sales])
VAR SalespeopleSelect =
    VALUES ( 'Salespeople Select'[Salespeople] )
RETURN
    IF (
        [Sales]=MaxforSP
            && SELECTEDVALUE ( SalesPeople[Salespeople] ) IN
                                SalespeopleSelect,
                                    "Y", "N" )
```

```
3. Max Year =
--Returns "Y" if it's the last year for the selected salespeople
VAR maxyr =
    CALCULATE ( MAX ( DateTable[Year] ), ALLSELECTED (
                            DateTable[Year] ) )
VAR SalespeopleSelect =
    VALUES ( 'Salespeople Select'[Salespeople] )
```

```
RETURN
    IF (
        SELECTEDVALUE ( DateTable[Year] ) = maxyr
            && SELECTEDVALUE ( SalesPeople[Salespeople] ) IN
                                        SalespeopleSelect,
                                            "Y", "N" )
```

Let's now see how the line chart was created. The "Sales" field was bound to the y-axis and the "Year" field bound to the x-axis with a symbol in the Glyph pane. I then linked the Salespeople field using a line link.

The measures were used as follows:

"Selected Salesperson" was bound to the Fill attribute of the symbol and the Color attribute of the link line, assigning black to "Y" and light gray to "N."

The "Sales" field was bound to a text mark, anchored to the symbol. The "Max Sales" measure was bound to the Visibility attribute of the text mark and was set to "Y" (the text mark will only be visible if "Max Sales" returns "Y").

The "Salespeople" field was bound to a second text mark, anchored to the symbol. The "Max Yr" measure was bound to the Visibility attribute of this text mark and was again set to "Y" (the text mark will only be visible if "Max Year" returns "Y"); see Figure 19-7.

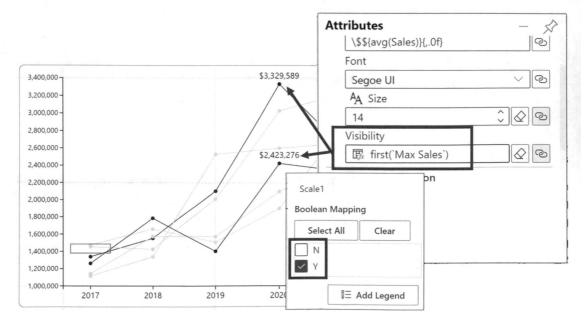

Figure 19-7. *Using the "Max Sales" measure in the Visibility attribute*

Now we can slice by Salespeople using the slicer, and in the line chart, the unselected salespeople's lines turn gray. The maximum sales value is shown for only the selected salespeople.

Categorized Line Chart

Let's look now at how we can design a visualization that will compare monthly sales across years. The data we are using is shown in Figure 19-8. Let me ask you this question; over the four-year period, which month's sales were best? Let's design a chart that will provide the answer to this question.

Month & Year	Month	Year	Sales	Month & Year	Month	Year	Sales
1 Jan 2017	Jan	2017	$40,795	4 Apr 2018	Apr	2018	$36,327
1 Jan 2018	Jan	2018	$28,384	4 Apr 2019	Apr	2019	$50,066
1 Jan 2019	Jan	2019	$34,500	4 Apr 2020	Apr	2020	$31,970
1 Jan 2020	Jan	2020	$20,111	4 Apr 2021	Apr	2021	$46,272
1 Jan 2021	Jan	2021	$24,689	5 May 2017	May	2017	$53,571
2 Feb 2017	Feb	2017	$11,803	5 May 2018	May	2018	$54,600
2 Feb 2018	Feb	2018	$20,203	5 May 2019	May	2019	$69,065
2 Feb 2019	Feb	2019	$20,467	5 May 2020	May	2020	$54,536
2 Feb 2020	Feb	2020	$10,665	5 May 2021	May	2021	$71,421
2 Feb 2021	Feb	2021	$29,822	6 June 2017	Jun	2017	$74,948
3 Mar 2017	Mar	2017	$44,540	6 June 2018	Jun	2018	$65,943
3 Mar 2018	Mar	2018	$33,225	6 June 2019	Jun	2019	$59,122
3 Mar 2019	Mar	2019	$31,069	6 June 2020	Jun	2020	$67,273
3 Mar 2021	Mar	2021	$49,316	6 June 2021	Jun	2021	$57,862

Figure 19-8. *Monthly sales, but which month's sales were good?*

Let's look more closely at the data in Figure 19-8. Note that we have used the "Month" and the "Year" fields from the date dimension but have added another field, "Month & Year" to the date dimension. The "Month" field will be used to categorize the sales accordingly, so, for instance, we can see all our sales for January across all four years. The "Month & Year" field, because this column holds unique values, will produce a data point for each row and therefore, we can plot sales for each year in each month. The "Year" field is only used in the Fill attribute to color the data points.

In Figure 19-9, I have designed a visual that shows unequivocally that June is our best month for sales, specifically June in 2017, and what was going on in February of 2020 when we had our worst month? Note in this chart, to add context to the data, I have added an average sales calculation (i.e., the field "Average") shown by the green horizontal line.

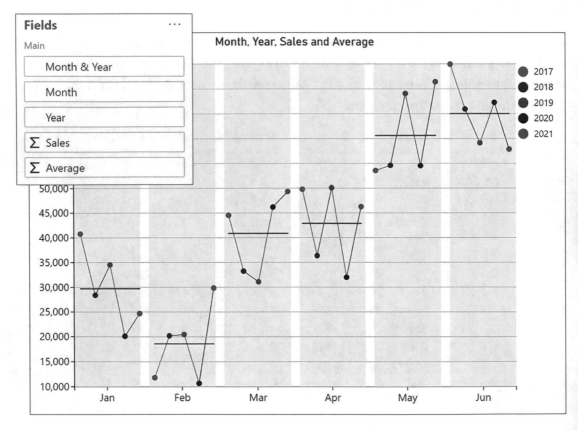

Figure 19-9. *The visual shows that June in 2017 was the best month*

The secret to designing the chart in Figure 19-9 is to layer three plot segments, one on top of the other, as shown in Figure 19-10.

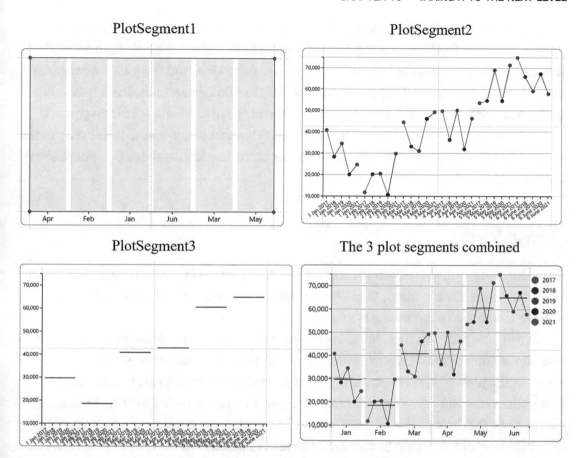

Figure 19-10. *The three plot segments used in Figure 19-9*

In PlotSegment1, we grouped the plot segment by the "Month" field and then bound "Month" to the x-axis, adding a rectangle glyph, colored light gray. It was then necessary to perform a custom sort on the month names on the x-axis.

Because another glyph is required for the data points that will plot sales for each year in each month, we added a new glyph and then added the second plot segment (PlotSegment2) that would plot this data, putting a symbol in the Glyph pane. The "Month & Year" field was bound to the x-axis and this axis was hidden as it's only used to plot the symbols correctly. The "Sales" field was then bound to the y-axis and the "Year" field bound to the Fill attribute of the symbol. Lastly, in this plot segment, the glyphs were linked by "Month."

PlotSegment3 was created in much the same way as PlotSegment2. The only difference is that the "Average" field was bound to the y-axis; therefore, the symbols in this plot segment are plotted according to the average value, and the y-axis was hidden. To tidy this plot segment, I hid the symbol so only the link line shows. I also needed to edit the numeric range of the y-axis to match the range of the y-axis of PlotSegment1.

You can see that you could easily repurpose this chart to show activity for days in the weeks of a year (i.e. days along the x-axis) or for hours in each weekday (i.e. hours along the x-axis).

Jitter Plot

As we have seen when we built the highlighted line chart in Figure 19-5, a technique we can often use in Charticulator is to identify the value or values that have been selected in a slicer, to focus on what interests us most.

In the jitter plot visual in Figure 19-11, we are analyzing the contestant's performance in a dance competition. The contestants for this year's competition are listed in the slicer. In the jitter plot, there is a data point for every contestant in all 19 years of the competition showing the scores for their dances. We are interested in "Dan Walker" and can see that he was one of the worst-performing contestants for the Foxtrot and Quickstep but didn't do too badly in the Jive and Viennese Waltz.

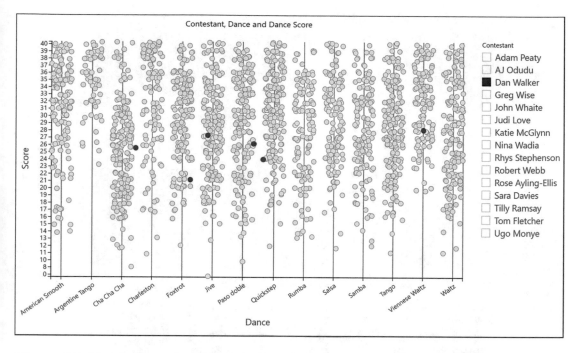

Figure 19-11. *A jitter plot showing the selected contestant's performance in each dance of the dance competition*

This is a great visual for browsing the contestants' performances, but how was it built? Just as in the line chart, I first generated a comparison table in Power BI to hold the column for the contestants' names used in the slicer.

In Figure 19-12, you can see the data that was used for the jitter plot visual and how the "Contestant" field for the slicer comes from a separate table, named "Just Contestants." The table containing the values for the slicer must not be related to any other table in the data model.

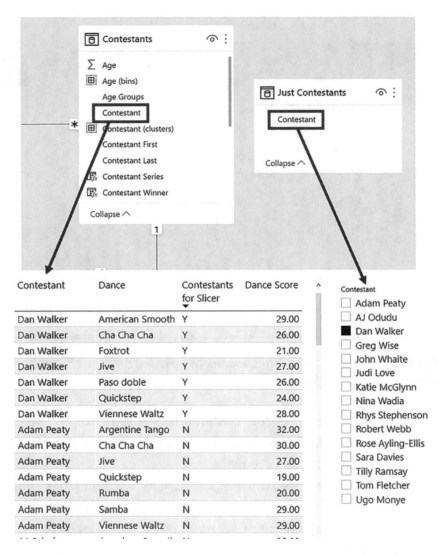

Figure 19-12. *The column for the slicer comes from a different table*

Next, I created a DAX measure, "Contestant for Slicer," to flag up the selected value in the slicer:

```
Contestants for Slicer =
--Returns "Y" of the contestant has been selected in the slicer
    IF (
        SELECTEDVALUE ( 'Just Contestants'[Contestant] )
            = SELECTEDVALUE ( Contestants[Contestant] ),
                                        "Y", "N")
```

I could then build the jitter plot visual which would require two plot segments, layered one on top of the other. The reason for the second plot segment is to show only the selected contestant's data points, colored bright pink, so they sit on top of the gray data points; otherwise, the pink data points would lurk behind the gray ones. In PlotSegment1 (Figure 19-13), the Jitter sub-layout was applied with the "Dance" field bound to the x-axis and "Dance Score" bound to the y-axis. Although "Dance Score" is a numerical field, I changed it to categorical and therefore generated a second categorical axis. This plot segment used a gray filled symbol, each symbol representing 1 of 264 contestants.

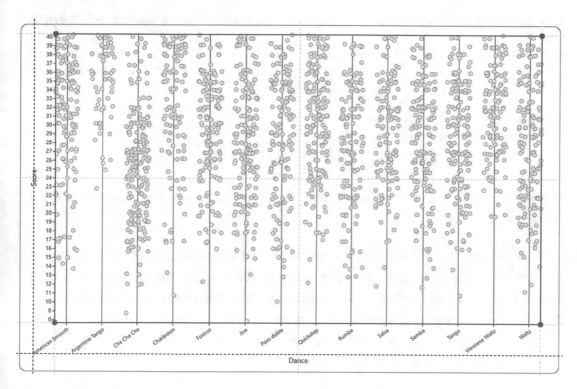

Figure 19-13. *The first plot segment used in the design of the jitter plot in Figure 19-11*

The second plot segment is only used to show the values for the contestant selected in the slicer. This plot segment is a duplication of the first plot segment with the difference that the symbol is colored bright pink and the x- and y-axes have been hidden. To control the visibility of the symbol to only show the selected contestant's data, I used the Visibility attribute of the symbol, binding the "Contestant for Slicer" measure and setting it to "Y"; see Figure 19-14.

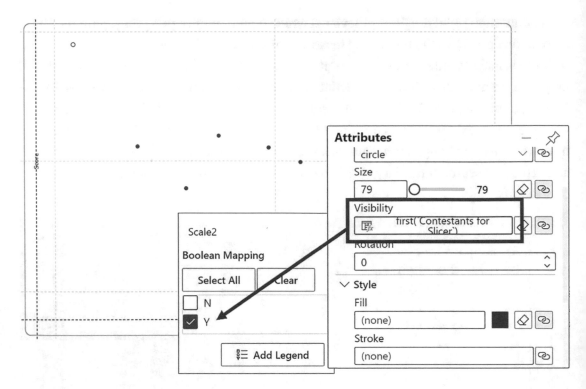

Figure 19-14. *The second plot segment shows the value for the contestant selected in the slicer*

To finish the visual, I added text marks anchored to guides to label the x- and y-axes.

The downside of using the jitter plot is that the data points are arranged randomly in line with the scores on the y-axis, and therefore it's difficult to see exactly where the clusters in the scores are gathered. An alternative way to visualize the contestants' performance might be to use the Packing sub-layout rather than Jitter, and you can see the alternative version of the chart in Figure 19-15.

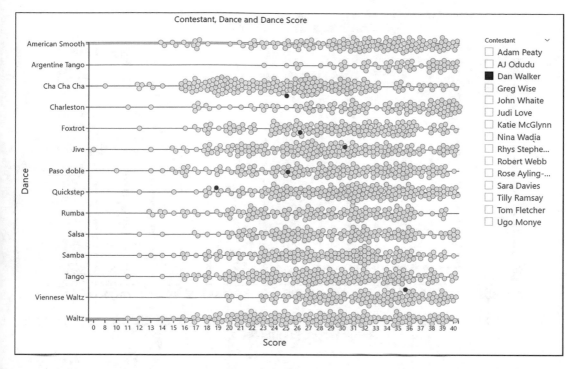

Figure 19-15. *The Packing sub-layout is an alternative to the Jitter sub-layout*

Which do you prefer? That's one of the great benefits of using Charticulator; it's so easy to render variations on a visual to get to the one that's exactly right.

Arrow Chart

Let's now consider a visualization that will make comparisons between two values selected in a slicer. In Figure 19-16, we are comparing salespeople's sales between two years. In the top chart, the years are between 2019 and 2020, and in the bottom chart, between 2018 and 2019, the years being selected in the slicer. You can see that when comparing 2019 and 2020, sales were greater for all the salespeople in 2020, but comparing 2018 and 2019, sales in 2019 were less for salespeople "Charron" and "Reyer," indicated by the reversed red arrow.

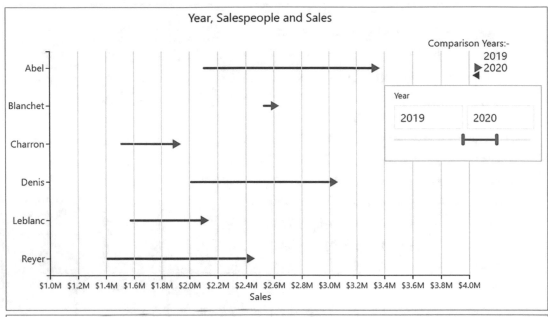

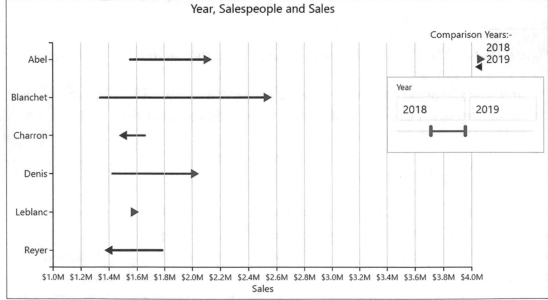

Figure 19-16. *Arrow chart comparing yearly sales*

The first consideration for this visual is to filter the sales so that only sales for the two years selected in the slicer show. For this, we used the following "Start or End" DAX measure:

```
Start or End =
VAR StartYr =
    MINX ( ALLSELECTED ( DateTable[Year] ), CALCULATE ( MIN (
                                    DateTable[Year] ) ) )
VAR EndYr =
    MAXX ( ALLSELECTED ( DateTable[Year] ), CALCULATE ( MAX (
                                    DateTable[Year] ) ) )
RETURN
    IF (
        SELECTEDVALUE ( DateTable[Year] ) = StartYr
            || SELECTEDVALUE ( DateTable[Year] ) = EndYr,
                                        "Y", "N" )
```

You can see in Figure 19-17 how the measure evaluates when placed in a table visual.

Year	Salespeople	Sales	Start or End
2018	Abel	£1,551,197	Y
2018	Blanchet	£1,337,054	Y
2018	Charron	£1,658,981	Y
2018	Denis	£1,424,910	Y
2018	Leblanc	£1,572,322	Y
2018	Reyer	£1,783,767	Y
2019	Abel	£2,103,324	N
2019	Blanchet	£2,527,798	N
2019	Charron	£1,509,771	N
2019	Denis	£2,011,394	N
2019	Leblanc	£1,574,804	N
2019	Reyer	£1,404,873	N
2020	Abel	£3,329,589	Y
2020	Blanchet	£2,598,565	Y
2020	Charron	£1,901,633	Y
2020	Denis	£3,025,070	Y
2020	Leblanc	£2,098,368	Y
2020	Reyer	£2,423,276	Y
Total		**£35,836,696**	N

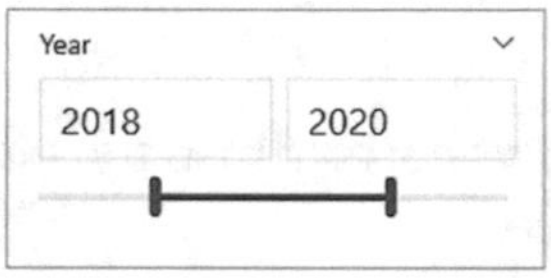

Figure 19-17. The "Start or End" measure will be used to filter sales for the years selected in the slicer

When we create our Charticulator visual, we can put this measure into the visual level filter bucket in Power BI to filter out rows where the value is "Y" (Figure 19-18) and so only use the data for the selected years.

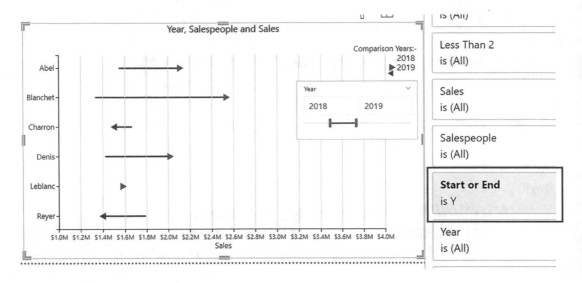

Figure 19-18. *Using the visual level filter to filter years according to the slicer selection*

To plot the arrows correctly on the chart according to the slicer selection, we can identify four rules:

1. Arrow symbols are only visible for the end year.

2. A blue arrow symbol is only visible when sales are greater in the end year.

3. A red arrow symbol is only visible when the sales are less in the end year.

4. The red arrow symbol must point in the opposite direction to the blue arrow symbol which will require two glyphs and therefore two plot segments.

This chart therefore makes extensive use of the Visibility attribute of the arrow symbol used in the Glyph pane to meet these rules, and we've used three DAX measures to provide the conditions whereby the arrow will be visible as follows (numbered for clarity):

```
1. Last Yr =
--Returns "Y" if the year is the end year.
IF (
    SELECTEDVALUE ( DateTable[Year] )
        = CALCULATE ( MAX ( DateTable[Year] ), ALLSELECTED (
                                    DateTable[year] ) ),
                                        "Y",  "N")
```

2. Less Than =
--Returns "Y" if sales in the end year are less than sales in the
start year.
VAR MinYr =
    CALCULATE (MIN (DateTable[Year]), ALLSELECTED (
                                        DateTable[year]))
VAR MinSales =
    CALCULATE ([Sales], DateTable[Year] = MinYr)
RETURN
    IF ([Sales] > MinSales || [Sales] = MinSales, "N", "Y")

3. Last and Not Less Than =
--Returns "Y" if sales are in the end year and sales are greater in the end
year than in the start year.
IF ([Last Yr] = "Y" && [Less Than] = "N", "Y", "N")

We can see the results of these measures when placed in a table visual in Figure 19-19.

Year	Salespeople	Sales	Last Yr	Less Than	Last and Not Less Than
2018	Abel	£1,551,197	N	N	N
2018	Blanchet	£1,337,054	N	N	N
2018	Charron	£1,658,981	N	N	N
2018	Denis	£1,424,910	N	N	N
2018	Leblanc	£1,572,322	N	N	N
2018	Reyer	£1,783,767	N	N	N
2019	Abel	£2,103,324	Y	N	Y
2019	Blanchet	£2,527,798	Y	N	Y
2019	Charron	£1,509,771	Y	Y	N
2019	Denis	£2,011,394	Y	N	Y
2019	Leblanc	£1,574,804	Y	N	Y
2019	Reyer	£1,404,873	Y	Y	N
Total		**£20,460,195**	**N**	**N**	**N**

Figure 19-19. The three measures used to show or hide the arrows depending on the slicer selection

It would be nice if this were now the end of the DAX measures required by the visual. Unfortunately, the problem is that when we link the glyphs for each salesperson, in effect creating the arrow shaft, there is no Visibility attribute associated with a Link; we can only control the color of the line. Also, because the link line is associated with the first instance of the glyph, that is, for the start year, we need to color the line red if the sales in the start year are greater than the sales in the end year. Here is the DAX measure that will find these sales:

```
Less Than 2 =
--Returns "Y" if sales in the start year are greater than sales in the
end year.
VAR MaxYr =
    CALCULATE ( MAX ( DateTable[Year] ), ALLSELECTED (
                                        DateTable[year] ) )
VAR MaxSales =
    CALCULATE ( [Sales], DateTable[Year] = MaxYr )
RETURN
    IF ( [Sales] < MaxSales || [Sales] = MaxSales, "N", "Y" )
```

You can see the evaluation of this measure when placed in a table visual in Figure 19-20.

Year	Salespeople	Sales	Less Than 2
2018	Abel	£1,551,197	N
2018	Blanchet	£1,337,054	N
2018	Charron	£1,658,981	Y
2018	Denis	£1,424,910	N
2018	Leblanc	£1,572,322	N
2018	Reyer	£1,783,767	Y
2019	Abel	£2,103,324	N
2019	Blanchet	£2,527,798	N
2019	Charron	£1,509,771	N
2019	Denis	£2,011,394	N
2019	Leblanc	£1,574,804	N
2019	Reyer	£1,404,873	N
Total		**£20,460,195**	**Y**

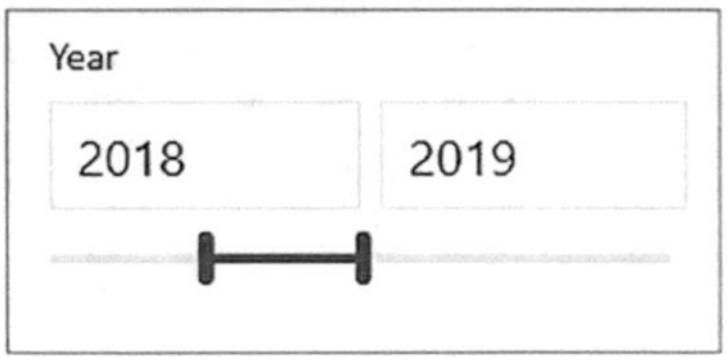

Year: 2018 — 2019

Figure 19-20. The "Less Than 2" measure that is required for the link line

Table 19-1 clarifies the conditions that return the "Y" flag using the DAX measures.

Table 19-1. *DAX measures and conditions that return "Y"*

Measure Name	Returns "Y" if sales for ...
Less Than	...End year < Start year
Last and Not Less Than	...End year > Start year
Less Than 2	...Start year > End year

At last, we are ready to build the arrow chart, and you can see the first plot segment required in Figure 19-21.

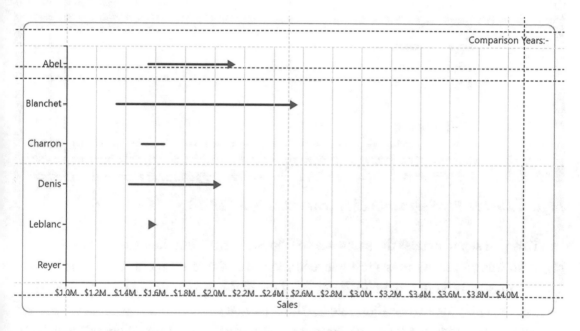

Figure 19-21. *PlotSegment1 of the chart in Figure 19-16*

You will see that "Sales" is bound to the x-axis, the Range attribute being edited to start at 1,000,000 and end at 4,000,000 (to account for values from any two years), and "Salespeople" bound to the y-axis. Gray gridlines have also been added.

A triangle symbol is used as the glyph, rotated to look like an arrowhead with a blue fill. The "Last and Not Less Than" measure has been bound to the Visibility attribute and set to "Y" (visible if sales in the end year are greater than sales in the start year).

The glyph is linked by Salespeople. The linking line takes its color from the start year, and so we need to bind the "Less Than 2" measure to the Link color and edit it so "Y" is red and "N" is blue (red if sales in the start year are greater than sales in the end year).

We are now ready to create the second plot segment that is required for the reverse pointing arrow; see Figure 19-22.

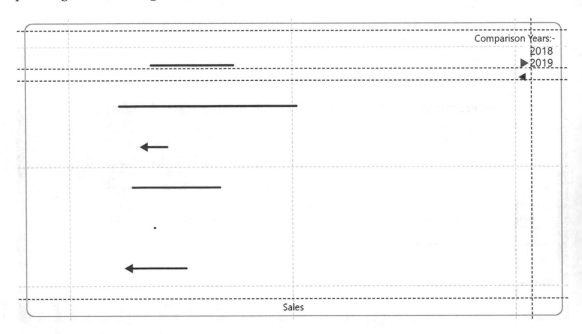

Figure 19-22. *PlotSegment2 of the chart in Figure 19-16*

This plot segment uses the same axes as PlotSegment1, but they are not visible. The glyph for this plot segment is a triangle, colored red and rotated accordingly. The "Less Than" measure is bound to the Visibility attribute of the arrow and set to "Y" (visible if sales in the end year are less than sales in the start year).

Finally, two additional plot segments were required to generate a "legend" which you can see in Figure 19-23.

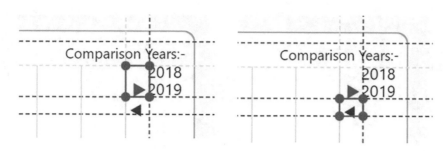

Figure 19-23. *PlotSegment3 and PlotSegment4 of the chart in Figure 19-16*

In PlotSegment3, to generate the blue triangle beside the selected end year, it was necessary to group the plot segment by the "Year" field and then bind "Year" to the y-axis and move it to the opposite side. The triangle is a glyph with a blue Fill, and the Visibility is set to "Last and Not Less Than" = "Y." To show a red triangle, a fourth plot segment was created in a similar way to PlotSegment3, but the triangle was given a red Fill, and the Visibility is set to "Last Yr" = "Y."

The techniques that we've used to build this visual and indeed the other visuals that we've explored in this chapter can be used in many creative ways, so all that remains is for you to try them out for yourself.

This now brings us to the end of our journey through Charticulator. I hope you have been inspired by the numerous charts and visuals that you have learned to create along the way to build informative, persuasive, and interactive visuals that would not be possible to generate in Power BI or indeed with any other custom visual that you may have considered importing into Power BI.

Happy Charticulating!

Index

A

Anchor elements
  canvas, 204
  chart/axis title, 202
  coordinators, 202, 203
  horizontal/vertical guide, 201
Arrow chart
  clarification, 385
  comparing data, 380
  DAX measures, 380, 382–384
  evaluation, 384
  link line, 384
  plot segment, 385–387
  rules, 382
  slicer selection, 382, 383
  table creation, 381
  visualization, 379, 383

B

Binding data
  attributes pane, 51, 52
  axes, 66–68
  categorical fields
    color scale, 58
    scales pane, 56
    stroke attribute, 57
  column chart, 55
  drives, 53, 54
  dropzones, 52, 53
  icon mark
    categories, 69

flag chart, 70
  image attribute, 71
learning process, 51
numerical fields, 54, 55, 59
  average function, 62
  gradient color scales, 64
  legend options, 65, 66
  non-numerical
    attributes, 62–64
  numerical attributes, 59–62

C

Categorical axes
  chart representation, 129, 130
  hide axis labels, 138
  layers pane, 138
  matrix style charts
    categories, 133
    chart representation, 135
    grid layout, 133
    plotting categories, 141
    spectral gradient color, 134
    stroke attribute, 136
    text mark, 136, 137
  methods, 131
  numerical values, 140
  packing sub-layout, 144
  Power BI charts, 132
  small multiples approach, 141–144
  toggle visibility buttons, 138, 139
  visibility attribute/filtering, 139–141

389

A. Box, *Introducing Charticulator for Power BI*, https://doi.org/10.1007/978-1-4842-8076-8

N, O

P, Q, R

Printed in the United States
by Baker & Taylor Publisher Services